Study Guide

for use with

Principles of
Macroeconomics

Third Edition

Robert H. Frank
Cornell University

Ben S. Bernanke
Princeton University (formerly)
Chairman of the President's Council of Economic Advisers

Prepared by
Jack Mogab
Texas State University – San Marcos

Louis Johnston
The College of Saint Benedict/Saint John's University

McGraw-Hill Irwin

Boston   Burr Ridge, IL   Dubuque, IA   Madison, WI   New York   San Francisco   St. Louis
Bangkok   Bogotá   Caracas   Kuala Lumpur   Lisbon   London   Madrid   Mexico City
Milan   Montreal   New Delhi   Santiago   Seoul   Singapore   Sydney   Taipei   Toronto

McGraw-Hill
Irwin

Study Guide for use with
PRINCIPLES OF MACROECONOMICS
Robert H. Frank, Ben S. Bernanke

Published by McGraw-Hill/Irwin, an imprint of The McGraw-Hill Companies, Inc., 1221 Avenue of the Americas, New York, NY 10020. Copyright © 2007 by The McGraw-Hill Companies, Inc. All rights reserved.

No part of this publication may be reproduced or distributed in any form or by any means, or stored in a database or retrieval system, without the prior written consent of The McGraw-Hill Companies, Inc., including, but not limited to, in any network or other electronic storage or transmission, or broadcast for distance learning.

1 2 3 4 5 6 7 8 9 0 QPD/QPD 0 9 8 7 6

ISBN-13: 978-0-07-321007-0
ISBN-10: 0-07-321007-2

www.mhhe.com

The McGraw-Hill Companies

To the Student

Welcome to the study of economics. We believe you will find the subject thoroughly intriguing. As you become an "economic naturalist" you will gain a clearer understanding of many important issues that currently may be perplexing to you. For example, what determines the cost of a car, or the salary you will earn when you graduate? Why does the economy experience booms and busts? How does the banking system create money? Why are federal deficits and surpluses so controversial?

These and many other topics are addressed in *Principles of Economics, Principles of Microeconomics,* and *Principles of Macroeconomics,* 3rd Editions by Robert H. Frank and Ben S. Bernanke, for which these Study Guides have been written. The Study Guide chapters parallel the chapters in the corresponding textbook, and each contains the following eight sections designed to assist your learning and to enhance your understanding of economics:

1. **Pretest.** This will test what you really know about the basic concepts and principles in the chapter and what you need to review before continuing on with more in-depth testing.
2. **Key Point Review.** The Learning Objectives for the chapter are listed to identify important concepts to master. The chapter's main ideas are summarized, and new terms are defined. **Hints** and **Notes** are provided to alert you to "tricks, clues and short-cuts".
3. **Self-Test: Key Terms**. All new terms are listed. Check your knowledge of key definitions by matching the term in the right-hand column with the appropriate definitions in the left-hand column.
4. **Self-Test: Multiple-Choice Questions.** Strengthen your grasp of the chapter material by choosing the correct answer from the alternatives for each question. Your ability to answer multiple-choice questions should serve as a good indicator of success on exams. You may wish to study for exams by reviewing these questions.
5. **Self-Test: Short Answer/Problems.** Here you will discover how the tools of economics can be applied to explore and clarify important issues. Problems are developed step by step. You are asked to analyze graphs and tables, to perform basic computations, and to select the best answers to a variety of fill-in statements.
6. **Economic Naturalist Applications.** Become an economic naturalist by applying the tools of economics to discuss these real-world issues with your classmates.
7. **Solutions**. Solutions, with explanations for the more complex and difficult items in the self-tests, are provided for the key-term, and multiple-choice questions, as well as for the short answer/problems.

The following suggestions will help make your study of economics successful:

Class Preparation or Must I Turn Off the TV?
It is essential that you prepare assignments BEFORE attending class so that you can understand the lecture and ask questions. Your instructor typically will not present all the materials in the text, but rather will concentrate on explaining the more complex ideas and applications. In preparing for class, first read the "Key Point Review" to identify the

learning objectives for the chapter. Next, go to the chapter in the text. Read the "Summary," "Core Principles," and the "Key Terms" at the **end** of the chapter. Then, read the introductory section that will provide an overview of the topics to be covered in the chapter. The number of topics will range from 4 to 7. Read and study one topic at a time, i.e., begin at the bold, upper-case red color heading and read until you get to the "Recap" box. Look for the paragraphs in the chapter that define and explain the concepts, principles, and laws related to that topic. These concepts, principles, and laws are listed at the end of each chapter as "Key Terms." As you read, mark these "terms" (as many as 3 to 5 per topic). You will notice that each topic can be presented in three modes--verbal, numerical (tables), and visual (graphs). This variety of presentation is important since economics is communicated through all three modes, and the test questions will reflect all three. After you have completed reading a topic, take a few minutes to read the Recap box. Verify that (1) you know (i.e. remember) the topic and important terms; (2) you understand (i.e. comprehend) that material; (3) you can relate the terms to one another when appropriate; and (4) you can relate the topic to the other topics in the chapter. Complete all the assigned topics in the above manner and write down any questions you have for the instructor.

Class Attendance or Why Not Go To the Rec Center?
Frankly, economics is such a demanding course that you will need all the help you can get. A great deal of that help comes from your instructor's lectures. The instructor's style and presentation will show you not only what the instructor considers to be important, but also how s/he approaches this subject. Getting notes from a friend will not give you this information. If you have followed the above suggestions in preparing for class, you will have some knowledge and understanding of the assigned topics. In class, the trick is to carefully combine four classroom skills - listening, taking notes, answering questions, and responding to questions. Listen with your mind. Be selective in what you write down. If you try to write everything that the instructor says, you will not have time to learn anything. For example, do not write a definition that has been given in the text. Listen for examples that differ from those in the text, special emphasis on a relationship between topics, and frequently repeated principles. Asking questions is the responsibility of the student. If you don't know enough to ask questions, you haven't done your job. If you have difficulty formulating questions during class, you should spend some time before class developing a list of questions you need to have answered. On the other side of the coin, you should also respond to the instructor's questions. You should not be shy about answering questions in class. An incorrect answer given in class is a free shot, while the same wrong answer on the test is very costly. The most effective way to use class time is to develop your ability to comprehend and apply economics concepts.

After Class or Do I Have To Do This Again?
Even if you have meticulously prepared for class and performed those four classroom behaviors, you still have a couple of things to do before you will be at the mastery level of the material. First, your class notes should be sketchy. You need to rewrite these notes in a more complete way before they get cold. Next, return to the Study Guide. Complete the three Self-Tests without referring to the text, and check your answers with the Solutions at the end of the Study Guide chapter. If your answers are correct, go onto the

Economic Naturalist section. If your answers to some of the questions are incorrect, go back and review the text and your class notes for those topics. Then return to the Study Guide Self-Tests to complete the questions you answered incorrectly (to further test your mastery of the material, go to the Electronic Learning Session in the Student Center at the Frank/Bernanke web site: http://www.mhhe.com/economics/frankbernanke3). If you still do not understand the answers to the questions, either ask questions in the next class or go see your instructor for help.

If You Want To Learn It, Teach It.
To further test your comprehension of a topic, try explaining it in your own words to a classmate. Illustrate the idea with an example. If you can explain it clearly and give a good example, you have mastered the concept and its time to move on to the next chapter.

A Final Word
If the strategy outlined above seems like a lot of work, it is. You cannot achieve success in economics without hard work. It is estimated that the average student should spend 2-3 hours of quality study time for every hour spent in class.

Acknowledgments
It is a pleasure to acknowledge the assistance and support of Irwin McGraw-Hill in the preparation of this Study Guide. Particular thanks go to our capable and patient editors Tom Thompson and Paul Shensa.

Contents

Chapter 1
Thinking Like An Economist

I. Pretest: What Do You Really Know?

Circle the letter that corresponds to the best answer. (Answers appear immediately after the final question).

1. When economists say there is no such thing as a free lunch, they mean that
    A. we must pay money for everything we get.
    B. it is against the law to accept goods or services without paying for them.
    C. the more lunch a person eats the more weight the person will gain.
    D. each day we decide to eat lunch is another day we must pay out money.
    E. every choice we make involves a tradeoff.

2. The concept of scarcity applies equally to Bill Gates and a homeless person because
    A. both have the same legal rights protected by the U.S. constitution.
    B. they have the same access to the markets for goods and services.
    C. there are only 24 hours in the day for both of them.
    D. the cost and benefit of picking up a $100 bill from the sidewalk would be the same to each of them.
    E. both must breathe air in order to live.

3. People who have well-defined goals and try to fulfill those goals as best they can are known as
    A. rational.
    B. macroeconomists.
    C. microeconomists.
    D. maximizers.
    E. opportunists.

4. When someone makes a choice, the value of the next best alternative not selected defines
    A. marginal costs.
    B. opportunity costs.
    C. opportunity benefits.
    D. average costs.
    E. economic surplus.

5. Which of the following is true of economic models and how they are used to study behavior?
   A. Economists believe people literally behave according to the model.
   B. Economic models capture every detail of a given situation not matter how small.
   C. Economists rely exclusively on verbal descriptions of their models.
   D. Economic models explain everyone's behavior.
   E. Economic models are simplifications of a given situation with the important details included.

6. Sunk costs are _____ when deciding between alternatives.
   A. irrelevant
   B. highly important
   C. important
   D. slightly important
   E. the only factor to consider

7. Which of the following is not a synonym for "marginal" in economics?
   A. Extra.
   B. Additional.
   C. One more.
   D. Change.
   E. Average.

8. Economics is conventionally divided into two subjects called
   A. marginal benefit and marginal cost.
   B. reservation price and opportunity cost.
   C. microeconomics and macroeconomics.
   D. rational economics and irrational economics.
   E. economic surplus and economic deficit.

9. In deciding the number of students to allow to enroll in the economics classes, the Chairperson of the Economics Department is making a(n) _____ decision.
   A. microeconomic
   B. macroeconomic
   C. economic surplus
   D. marginal choice
   E. imperfect

10. Which of the following topics is most likely to be studied in microeconomics?
    A. Tax policies.
    B. The rate of inflation.
    C. National output.
    D. The auto market.
    E. The unemployment rate.

Solutions and Feedback to Pretest
For each question you incorrectly answered, we strongly recommend taking the time to review the appropriate material before continuing. In the table below are listed for each question the pertinent Learning Objective from the following Key Point Review.

Correct Answer	Learning Objective
1. E	1
2. C	1
3. A	2
4. B	2
5. E	3
6. A	4
7. E	4
8. C	5
9. A	5
10. D	5

II. Key Point Review
The Forest

Chapter one presents the essence of economics as a field of study and as a way of thinking about the world around you. The central questions you need to be able to answer are:

- How does the Scarcity Principle affect the choices that people make?
- How do rational people resolve trade-offs?
- What is the role of models in economics?
- What are four decision pitfalls to avoid in making decisions?
- How can you become an economic naturalist?

The Trees

Learning Objective 1: Define the field of study known as economics. Explain the logical relationship between the Scarcity Principle and the Cost-Benefit Principle. Understand the universality of the two principles.
Economics is the study of how people make choices under conditions of scarcity and how the results of those choices affect society. The **Scarcity Principle** (aka the **No-Free-Lunch Principle**) indicates that all the resources available to the individual are finite, but the needs and wants of the individual are infinite. Satisfying all, or even most, of people's requirements and desires is impossible. Thus, people are forced to make choices because more of one item means less of some other item. The **Cost-Benefit Principle** of economics suggests people will choose to take an action, if and only if, the extra benefits from the action are greater than or equal to the extra cost of the action. Importantly, these two fundamental principles apply to all people, societies, countries, and to the entire history of mankind as well as the modern age.

Learning Objective 2: Discuss the meaning of a rational person in an economic context. How do the concepts of economic surplus and opportunity cost relate to rational behavior?
A **rational person** is one who has well-defined goals and endeavors to fulfill them as best they can. The Cost-Benefit Principle is one tool that assists individuals in making rational choices. The difference between the benefits of taking an action and the costs of the action defines **economic surplus**. Rational behavior, therefore, means taking the actions for which the economic surplus is positive and refusing those with negative economic surplus. The **opportunity cost** of a choice or decision yet to be made is the value of the next-best alternative that must be sacrificed. To practice rational behavior, the opportunity cost of the alternatives being considered must be recognized and counted, even if they do not involve explicit monetary payments.

Learning Objective 3: Explain economist's use of models to explain behavior.
Economists use abstract models to describe and predict behavior. The Cost-Benefit Principle is an example of a behavioral model: it indicates how an idealized rational person can maximize his economic surplus when choosing among alternatives. All fields of study that describe or predict behavior, from Physics to Sociology, use models. A model is a simplified version of reality. Superior models capture the most important elements of reality and ignore minor relationships and inconsequential details. A model that included every facet of a particular behavior wouldn't be a model; it would be reality. If reality could be understood, then a model would not have been needed initially. A frequent but misguided criticism directed at the field of economics indicts the use of models to describe and predict behavior. The critics point out that people do not explicitly calculate the net benefits of going to a movie or a basketball game when deciding how to spend a Friday night. Of course this is correct, but it misses the point. People behave *as if* they do the calculations using their experiences and trial and error to approximate the value of benefits and costs. Of course mistakes are made and people fail to choose rationally. But believing people are constantly using their calculators to assess whether to have Chinese take-out or pizza delivered is **not** necessary to use the Cost-Benefits Principle as a description of how people make choices.

> **Hint:** In order to understand economics and perform well on exams, you must think in terms of the ideas presented in the textbook and lectures. Do not give in to the temptation to create your own model. In a physics class it is unlikely you would question the existence or behavior of gravity. Even though you have made many economic decisions already, it does not mean you fully understand all the underlying concepts anymore than being held down to the planet means you fully understand the physicist's model of gravity.

Learning Objective 4: List and differentiate among the four decision-making pitfalls and relate the pitfalls to the Incentive Principle.
The usefulness of the Cost-Benefit Principle, at either an intuitive level or for an explicit calculation, depends on the proper assessment of the costs and benefits of the choices. While everyone may have a natural tendency to weigh costs and benefits, a natural tendency to accurately measure costs and benefits may not exist and certainly can be improved.

Measuring costs and benefits as proportions rather than absolute values defines the first decision-making pitfall. As the examples in the textbook emphasize, if it is worthwhile to take an action that saves you $10, then it is worthwhile when the list price of the item is $1,000 (a 1% savings) or $20 (a 50% savings). Net benefits (economic surplus) are measured in dollars, not percentages. The extent of the relative savings has no bearing on the decision to take the action, only the extent of the absolute savings should be considered.

Another common oversight is ignoring opportunity costs. Choosing a particular alternative means an infinite number of alternatives will not be chosen. To accurately gauge the net benefits of a decision, one must recognize the alternatives and value them honestly. If spending a beautiful, sunny Wednesday afternoon at the lake means you take an unpaid day off from work, then the forgone earnings must be included in the assessment of costs. The reason class attendance is nearly 100% on the day of an exam but noticeably less on lecture days stems from the difference in opportunity costs of not attending class.

Note: Frequently, to introduce the concept and importance of opportunity costs, economists use time and the resulting forgone earnings as example. Do not be misled by our tendencies. All choices have an opportunity cost. Buying a car means not buying a lot of other consumer goods, the most valuable of which measures the opportunity cost.

The third pitfall in evaluating the costs and benefits stems from including costs that are irrelevant. Costs that cannot be recovered define the concept of **sunk costs**. For example, suppose you purchased a nonrefundable, nontransferable front row ticket to see your favorite pop star. Suppose further your economics professor announces at the last minute a test on the day after the concert. Whether you go to the concert depends on your valuation of the costs and benefits. However, it is entirely incorrect to include the cost of your ticket in the decision. The ticket has been paid for and cannot be sold, given away, or refunded; it is a sunk cost. The temptation to count the ticket price is strong but it will lead to an inaccurate (overstated) estimate of the costs.

The fourth common pitfall in quantifying the consequence of choosing a particular alternative stems from a failure to distinguish between average and marginal measures. The change in the total costs of an activity resulting from a one unit change in the level of the activity defines **marginal costs**. The resulting change in total benefits of an activity when a one unit change in the level of activity occurs identifies the **marginal benefits**. The Cost-Benefit Principle indicates that as long as the marginal benefits are greater than the marginal costs, the level of the activity should be increased. The other type of measurement variables are the average measures. **Average benefits** are the total benefits of n units of the activity divided by n. The total costs of n units of the activity divided by n defines the **average costs**. Measuring average costs and benefits is much easier than measuring marginal costs and benefits, which contributes to the frequent reliance on averages to guide decision-making. The convenience of average measures, unfortunately, does not change the inappropriateness of using average measures to make marginal decisions. If the average benefits of a given level of activity exceed the average costs of the same level of activity, increasing the activity is not necessarily the maximizing choice. A comparison of the average benefit to the average cost offers no guidance on whether to lessen or expand the level of the activity to reach maximization.

> **Note:** The mathematically inclined reader may realize that comparing the marginal benefits to the marginal costs is an application of the first derivative test from calculus. Seeking to maximize the net benefits (total benefits minus total costs) of an activity results in choosing the level of activity where the marginal benefits equal the marginal costs

The four pitfalls listed above suggest that sometimes people make irrational choices. Most of the time, however, people make rational choices. Thus, economists focus on rational choices to offer useful advice, and to provide a basis for predicting and explaining human behavior. Rational choices can be summed up in the Incentive Principle. The Incentive Principle states that a person (or firm, or society) is more likely to take an action if its benefit rises, and less likely to take it if its cost rises.

Learning Objective 5: Distinguish between Normative and Positive Economics, and between Macroeconomics and Microeconomics.

Economic models are based upon the principles of rational choice. The models, therefore, do not always describe how people actually behave, but rather predict how people will behave. Thus, economists differentiate between normative economics and positive economics. A normative economic principle is a principle that says how people *should* behave, while a positive economic principle is a principle that *predicts* how people will behave.

Economics divides into two major sub-fields. **Microeconomics** concentrates on the choices individuals make under scarcity and the implications for prices and quantities in individual markets. The impact of a future war with Iraq on the price of gasoline would form a microeconomic topic. **Macroeconomics** studies the performance of economies at the national level and the effect of governmental policies on the national economy's output. The resulting change in gross domestic product from President Bush's tax reform proposal is a proper macroeconomic question.

Learning Objective 6: Recognize the abundance of opportunities to apply economic reasoning — to practice "Economic Naturalism."

Economic naturalism refers the to the application of the basic tenets of economics to understand and explain everyday behaviors. The textbook gives several examples of common phenomenon which can be easily understood by applying the Cost-Benefit Principle. Setting the specific examples aside, the main point is to encourage you to use what you are learning to understand behavior that has seemed perplexing or inconsistent. You may find actions or choices that once confused or baffled you can now be easily comprehended. Of particular importance, the behavior of the political process is more clearly grasped within the simple framework of the Cost-Benefit Principle.

Learning Objective 7 (Appendix): Understand how to translate a verbal statement into an equation. Clearly define the following: equation, variable, dependent variable, independent variable, constant (parameter).
Economic models are frequently expressed in mathematical terms. A mathematical model allows for a greater degree of precision than a model expressed in verbal terms. But, model development always begins with verbal statements before proceeding to a mathematical version of the statements. An **equation** is a mathematical expression of the relationship between two or more variables. **Variables** are items thought to be related and that can take on different numerical values. By convention, the variable (or variables) which is thought to determine the magnitude of some other variable is placed on the right-hand side of the equation; the variable being determined is placed on the left hand side. The right-hand side variables are called **independent variables** and the left-hand side variable is called the **dependent variable**. Often a **constant** (or **parameter**) is included on the right-hand side of the equation with a value that is fixed. The statement "I think my GPA will improve this semester because I got a laptop for Christmas" can be translated into an equation like GPA = f(new laptop). GPA is the dependent variable and the laptop is the independent variable. The laptop presumably improves your productivity in some fashion and, in turn, improves your test scores and your GPA. Obviously, GPA does not "cause" a laptop but a laptop may "cause" a higher GPA. Use the term cause with reservation; to say X "causes" Y is a difficult proposition to prove. More accurately, say X "strongly influences" or X has a "significant effect" on Y.

Learning Objective 8 (Appendix): Starting with an equation, illustrate the equation with a graph. Define the following: vertical intercept, slope, rise, run.
For an equation of the form $Y = a + b*X$, Y is the dependent variable and X is the independent variable. The **vertical intercept** is the value of Y when X is zero; it is the value of "a" in the equation above. The **slope** of the equation, signified by "b" in the equation above, is the ratio of the change in Y when some change in X occurs. The change in Y is termed **rise** and the change in X is called **run**. These terms come from the orientation of the graph: X is on the horizontal axis (hence run) while Y is placed on the vertical axis (hence rise). Slope is often defined as rise over run. To plot an equation, first determine the vertical intercept's value and put a point on the vertical axis at this value (remember X=0). Then calculate a value of Y when X is not equal to 0 (pick easy X values like 1 or 10). To accomplish this, take the value of X you picked, multiple it by "b" and then add "a" to arrive at the value of Y. For linear relationships (straight lines), two pairs of coordinates are enough to completely describe the equation. Thus, after marking the vertical intercept and calculated value of Y, you can run a line through the two points. You have now illustrated the equation in the form of a graph.

Learning Objective 9 (Appendix): Starting with a graph, determine the underlying equation.
If this were a repair manual for a car, it would say installation is the reverse of disassembly. Look at the graph and note where the curve crosses or intersects the vertical axis. This is the vertical intercept "a." Now calculate the slope. Depending on the scale (the units X and Y are measured in) of the graph, pick two X values and note the resulting Y values in the graph. Say the values of X are 10 and 15 and the corresponding values for Y are 30 and 20. Slope is calculated as $(20-30)/(15-10) = (-10)/(5) = -2$. The rise of the graph is -10 when the run is 5. A negative relationship exists between X and Y, i.e., as X gets larger, Y gets smaller. Now simply

take your results for "a" and "b" and write it out in equation form (as in the preceding learning objective).

Learning Objective 10 (Appendix): Demonstrate how a change in 1) the vertical intercept and 2) the slope affect the graph of the equation.
Continuing with the $Y = a + b*X$ example, a change in the vertical intercept means a change in how large Y is when $X = 0$. When "a" changes, the position of the line in the graph changes. The change in position can be called a "shift" in the curve. It shifts up if the value of "a" gets larger and it shifts down if the value of "a" decreases. Note that the slope of the equation is the same as before and therefore the new line *must* be parallel to the original line. When the slope changes, the shape of the line in the graph changes. The line pivots through the unchanging vertical intercept. The new line will be steeper if the absolute value of the slope is greater than it was before; the line will be flatter if the absolute value of the slope is smaller than it was before. Recall that the flattest line is a horizontal line with a slope of zero and the steepest line is a vertical line with a slope of infinity.

Learning Objective 11 (Appendix): Beginning with a table of data, know how to construct a graph and how to determine the underlying equation.
When working with tabular data, first figure out which variable is the dependent variable and which is the independent variable. Next, write the name of the dependent variable on the vertical axis of your graph and the independent variable on the horizontal axis. Plot some of the data points by locating the value of the dependent variable and the associated value of the independent variable. Now use the techniques outlined above to either graph the function or determine the underlying equation.

III. Self-Test

Key Terms
Match the term in the right-hand column with the appropriate definition in the left-hand column by placing the letter of the term in the blank in front of its definition. (Answers are given at the end of the chapter.)

1. ____ The study of how individuals make choices under conditions of scarcity and the resulting effects.   a. average benefit
2. ____ A person with well-defined goals and tries to achieve them.   b. average cost
3. ____ The subfield of economics that concentrates on the performance of the national economy and the effects of governmental policies.   c. economics
4. ____ The value of the next best alternative not selected.   d. economic surplus
5. ____ The difference between the benefits of taking an action and the costs of taking the action.   e. macroeconomics
6. ____ The extra benefit experienced as a result of a one unit increase in the amount of activity chosen.   f. marginal benefit
7. ____ The total cost of *n* units of activity divided by *n*.   g. marginal cost
8. ____ The subfield of economics that concentrates on the behavior of individual markets.   h. microeconomics

9. ____ The extra costs experienced as a result of a one unit increase in the amount of activity chosen.

10. ___ Costs that cannot be recovered regardless of the alternative chosen.

11. ___ The total benefits of *n* units of activity divided by *n*.

12. ___ A principle that predicts how people will behave.

13. ___ A principle that says how people should behave.

i. normative economic principle

j. opportunity cost

k. positive economic principle

l. rational person

m. sunk cost

Appendix

14. ___ A value in an equation that is fixed.

15. ___ The variable or variables that cause or determine the relationship in an equation.

16. ___ In a straight line, the ratio of the vertical distance to the corresponding horizontal distance between any two points.

17. ___The variable that is caused by or is being determined in an equation.

18. ___A mathematical statement of the relationship between two or more variables.

19. ___Items thought to be related which can take on different numerical values.

20. ___ When calculating slope, the vertical distance a straight line travels between any two points.

21. ___The value of the dependent variable when the value of the independent variable is zero.

22. ___ When calculating slope, the horizontal distance a straight line travels between any two points .

Appendix

n. Constant (or parameter)

o. dependent variable

p. equation

q. independent variable

r. rise

s. run

t. slope

u. variables

v. vertical intercept

Multiple-Choice Questions
Circle the letter that corresponds to the best answer. (Answers are given at the end of the chapter.)

1. The scarcity principle indicates that
   A. no matter how much one has, it is never enough.
   B. compared to 100 years ago, individuals have less time today.
   C. with limited resources, having more of "this" means having less of "that."
   D. because tradeoffs must be made, resources are therefore scarce.
   E. the wealthier a person is, the fewer the number of tradeoffs he must make.

2. Benny has one hour before bedtime and he can either watch TV or listen to his new Korn CD. He chooses to listen to the CD. The scarcity principle's influence on Benny is seen in
   A. the decision to listen to music.
   B. the decision not to watch TV.
   C. the fixed amount of time before bed.
   D. the decision to choose between TV and music.
   E. Benny's taste in music.

3. Choosing to study for an exam until the extra benefit (improved score) equals the extra cost (mental fatigue) is
    A. not rational.
    B. an application of the cost-benefit principle.
    C. an application of the scarcity principle.
    D. the relevant opportunity cost.
    E. less desirable than studying for the entire evening.

4. The scarcity principle indicates that _____ and the cost-benefit principle indicates _____.
    A. choices must be made; how to make the choices
    B. how to make the choices; choices must be made
    C. choices must be made; just one of many possible ways to make the choices
    D. choices must be made; the choices will be poor
    E. choices must be made; the costs can never outweigh the benefits of the choices

5. Amy is thinking about going to the movies tonight to see Star Wars III: Revenge of the Siths. A ticket costs $7 and she will have to cancel her dog-sitting job that pays $30. The cost of seeing the movie is
    A. $7.
    B. $30.
    C. $37.
    D. $37 minus the benefit of seeing the movie.
    E. indeterminate.

6. The use of economic models, such as the cost-benefit principle, means economists believe that
    A. this is how people explicitly chose between alternatives.
    B. this is a reasonable abstraction of how people chose between alternatives.
    C. those who explicitly make decisions this way are smarter.
    D. with enough education, all people will start to explicitly make decisions this way.
    E. this is the way the world ought to explicitly make decisions.

7. Tony notes that an electronics store is offering a flat $20 off of all prices in the store. Tony reasons that if he wants to buy something with a price of $50 that it is a good offer but if he wants to buy something with a price of $500 it is not a good offer. This is an example of
    A. inconsistent reasoning; saving $20 is saving $20.
    B. the proper application of the cost-benefit principle.
    C. rational choice because in the first case he saves $40% and in the second case he saves 4%.
    D. marginal cost equals marginal benefit thinking.
    E. opportunity costs.

8. That individuals make inconsistent choices and the inconsistencies have a strong pattern is, in the view of the textbook,
    A. evidence of the severe limitations of economic models.

B. an indication of widespread irrationality.
C. support for the study of economics to improve decision making.
D. of limited importance.
E. a well-kept secret that should remain that way.

9. Sunk cost are different from other concepts of cost in that they
   A. can be either variable or fixed.
   B. cannot be lessened by choosing any particular course of action.
   C. influence the decision of which activity to do or not do.
   D. rise as the level of the activity rises.
   E. must be included for an accurate cost-benefit analysis.

10. Which of the following questions would not be part of microeconomics?
    A. What college major to select.
    B. How to make the largest profit.
    C. Whether to study or watch TV tonight.
    D. How will an early freeze in California affect the price of fruit.
    E. Should the federal budget always be balanced.

11. When making a decision, the important costs to identify and consider are the _____ costs and the _____ costs.
    A. opportunity; marginal
    B. opportunity; fixed
    C. sunk; marginal
    D. marginal; average
    E. marginal; fixed

12. Janie can either mow the lawn or wash clothes, earning her a benefit of $30 or $45, respectively. Janie will therefore choose to _____ because the economic surplus is _____.
    A. mow; greater
    B. wash; greater
    C. mow; smaller
    D. wash; smaller
    E. mow; the same as for washing

13. Anytime one purchases a ticket in advance of an event, if the ticket is non-refundable and non-transferable then on the day of the event, then the ticket is
    A. part of the cost of going.
    B. a variable cost.
    C. part of the cost of going if it was expensive.
    D. a sunk cost and should play no role in the decision to go or not.
    E. a fixed cost but not a sunk cost.

14. The average cost of 20 units of an activity is the
    A. total cost of 20 units of the activity divided by 20.
    B. 20 divided by the total cost of 20 units of the activity.
    C. extra cost of 20 units of the activity divided by 20.
    D. reciprocal of the total cost of 20 units of the activity.
    E. change in total cost of the activity.

15. Class attendance on exam days is nearly 100% but on lecture days it is less. The likely
    explanation for this would be
    A. the opportunity cost of not attending on exam day is much higher than usual.
    B. random chance.
    C. the episode of Jerry Springer was a rerun.
    D. students thought today's class was a review.
    E. the opportunity cost of attending on exam day is much higher than usual.

16. To avoid the mistake of ignoring opportunity costs, the textbook recommends framing
    questions in the form of
    A. should I do A?
    B. should I do B?
    C. why should I do A?
    D. should I do A or B?
    E. should I do A or B or C or... Z?

17. On the first day of the semester, David finds he has one hour of time in the evening to
    allocate. He can do one of two things. He can watch TV for one hour or he can open his
    economics textbook and read for an hour. The benefit of watching TV is 30; the benefit or
    reading about economics is 20. The cost of watching TV is _____ and the cost of
    reading his economics textbook is _____.
    A. 20; 30
    B. 0; 0
    C. 30; 20
    D. 20; 0
    E. indeterminate; indeterminate

18. Continuing with the information in question 17, if David applies the cost-benefit principle
    accurately, he will
    A. read his economics textbook.
    B. watch TV.
    C. watch TV but fret that he should be reading.
    D. read his economics textbook but resent missing TV.
    E. flip a coin because the net benefits are the same.

19. Continuing with the information in question 17, suppose that instead of the first day of the
    semester, it is the night before David's first exam in economics. One could reasonably predict
    that
    A. the benefit of watching TV will rise.

B. the benefit of reading about economics will fall.
C. the cost of watching TV will rise.
D. the cost of reading economics will rise.
E. he will continue to make the same choice.

20. In general, to make optimal decisions, one needs information on the
  A. average benefits and marginal costs.
  B. marginal benefits and marginal costs.
  C. marginal benefits and average costs.
  D. average benefits and average costs.
  E. benefits and costs, which can be either average or marginal.

Short Answer Problems
(Answers and solutions are given at the end of the chapter.)

1. Enid has 2 exams tomorrow: one in economics and one in marketing. She has a total of 4 hours available for studying. The table below shows the test scores she will make with different amounts of studying time. For example, if she spends one hour studying economics, she makes a 77 on the economics test and makes a 79 on the marketing test, having spent 3 hours (4-1) studying for it.

	Hours Spent Studying Economics				
	0	1	2	3	4
Economics Score	65	77	86	89	91
Marketing Score	80	79	77	70	50

  A. The scarce resource Enid is allocating is (time/intelligence) _____. The opportunity cost of an extra hour studying economics is the (improvement in economics score/reduction in marketing score) _____.

  B. Calculate the marginal benefit of spending 1, 2, 3, and 4 hours studying economics: the 1st hour ____; the 2nd _____; the 3rd ____; and the 4th ____.

  C. Calculate the marginal cost of spending 1, 2, 3, and 4 hours studying economics: the 1st hour ____; the 2nd _____; the 3rd ____; and the 4th ____.

  D. If Enid is rational, she should spend _____ hours studying economics and _____ hours studying marketing.

  E. Calculate the total points from both tests when 0 to 4 hours are spent studying economics: 0 hours ____; 1 hour ____; 2 hours _____; 3 hours _____; and 4 hours _____. Does the answer to "D" agree with the answer here (yes/no) _____.

2. Ontel engineers proposed developing a 5 Gigahertz microprocessor in early 2003 at a cost of $50 million for a working prototype. By mid 2004, the $50 million had been spent with no prototype. The engineers request an additional $10 million to finish the project. For

convenience, assume 1) the marginal cost of producing the chip once it is developed is zero and 2) with the additional funding, the probability of a prototype is 1.

A. In January, 2003 the sunk costs of this project was _____ and in July 2004, the sunk costs of the project are _____.

B. Assume Ontel estimates it will earn revenues of $40 million on a 5 Gigahertz chip. If the extra funding is not approved, then Ontel will lose ($50 million/$10 million) _____. If the extra $10 million is granted, Ontel will lose ($60 million/$20 million) _____. Therefore, the extra $10 million (should/should not) _____ be granted.

3. The following table contains information about the costs and benefits of engaging in different amounts of an activity. Assume that cost data reflects both monetary and opportunity costs.

Units of Activity	Costs	Benefits	Average Costs	Average Benefits	Marginal Costs	Marginal Benefits
0	$0	$0	$0	$0	n/a	n/a
1	30	100				
2	35	150				
3	50	180				
4	70	200				
5	120	205				

A. Calculate the average costs and benefits for the different levels of activity. Likewise, calculate the marginal costs and benefits.

B. The level of activity consistent with the Cost-Benefit Principle occurs at (4/5) _____ units. The (4/5) _____ units would represent excess activity because the (marginal costs/average costs) _____ are greater than the (marginal benefits/average benefits) _____.

C. The difference between the benefits and the costs is the same for units (3 and 4/2 and 3) _____. Why then is there only one maximum point? Explain. _____ _____.

IV. Economic Naturalist Application

A frequent complaint of the wealthy is that, while they can purchase virtually any item they want, the one item they can't purchase more of is time. How are the wealthy identical to the lower classes with respect to time? Is their a difference in their opportunity cost of time compared with the lower classes? Suppose some wealthy person decides to retire. Will he still lament his lack of time? Why?

V. Self-Test Solutions

Key Terms

1. c
2. l
3. e
4. j
5. d
6. f
7. b
8. h
9. g
10. m
11. a
12. k
13. i
Appendix
14. n
15. q
16. t
17. o
18. p
19. u
20. r
21. v
22. s

Multiple-Choice Questions

1. C
2. C
3. B
4. A
5. C
6. B
7. A
8. C
9. B
10. E
11. A
12. B
13. D
14. A
15. A
16. D

17. A
18. B
19. C
20. B

Short Answer Problems

1.
A. time; reduction in marketing score
B. 12; 9; 3; 2.
C. 1; 2; 7; 20.
D. 2; 2.
E. 145; 156; 163; 159; 141. yes.

2.
A. 0; $50 million.
B. $50 million. $20 million. should.

3.

Units of Activity	Costs	Benefits	Average Costs	Average Benefits	Marginal Costs	Marginal Benefits
0	$0	$0	$0	$0	n/a	n/a
1	30	100	30.0	100	$30	$100
2	35	150	17.5	75	5	50
3	50	180	16.7	60	15	30
4	70	200	17.5	50	20	20
5	120	205	24.0	41	50	5

A. See table.
B. 4. 5; marginal costs; marginal benefits.
C. 3 and 4. The difference is *maximized* at 4 units; if one stops at 3 units, the maximum net
   benefits will not be realized.

Chapter 2
Comparative Advantage:
The Basis for Exchange

I. Pretest: What Do You Really Know?
Circle the letter that corresponds to the best answer. (Answers appear immediately after the final question).

1. Bill can write one computer program in an hour while Larry can write two computer programs in one hour. In this case,
   A. Larry has a comparative advantage in writing simple computer programs.
   B. Bill has a comparative advantage in writing simple computer programs.
   C. Larry has an absolute advantage in writing simple computer programs.
   D. Bill has an absolute advantage in writing simple computer programs.
   E. neither person has an absolute advantage.

2. The Principle of Comparative Advantage implies that
   A. each person should specialize in those tasks in which he or she does not have a comparative advantage.
   B. each person should specialize in those tasks in which he or she has a comparative advantage.
   C. each person should be self-sufficient.
   D. each person will be poorer if they trade with others.
   E. each person should specialize in those tasks in which they have an absolute advantage.

3. The production possibilities curve shows
   A. the minimum combinations of two goods that can be produced by a country.
   B. the only combinations of two goods that can be produced by a country.
   C. the maximum combinations of two goods that can be produced by a country.
   D. the minimum combinations of two resources that a country needs to produce a good.
   E. the maximum combinations of two resources that a country needs to produce a good.

4. A production possibilities curve slopes downward because
   A. in order to produce more of one good you must produce less of another good.
   B. in order to produce more of one good you must produce more of another good.

C. in order to produce less of one good you must produce less of another good.
D. it just has to, that's all.
E. resources are unlimited.

5. All points on the production possibilities curve are
   A. unattainable points.
   B. efficient points.
   C. inefficient points.
   D. attainable points.
   E. both efficient and attainable points.

6. The Principle of Increasing Opportunity Cost states that
   A. wherever you go, there you are.
   B. to increase the production of a good, a country must produce less of another good.
   C. to increase the production of a good, a country should first employ those resources with the highest opportunity cost and then turn to resources with lower opportunity costs.
   D. to increase the production of a good, a country should first employ those resources with the lowest opportunity cost and then turn to resources with higher opportunity costs.
   E. to increase the production of a good, a country must improve its technology.

7. A production possibilities curve that reflects The Principle of Increasing Opportunity Cost will
   A. slope downward.
   B. be bowed outward.
   C. be bowed inward.
   D. be a straight line.
   E. slope upward.

8. Which of the following will *not* cause a production possibilities curve to shift outward?
   A. An increase in a country's productivity.
   B. An increase in a country's resources.
   C. An improvement in a country's technology.
   D. Specialization in the production of one good.
   E. All of the above will cause a production possibilities curve to shift outward.

9. Bill can write one computer program or one speech in an hour. Larry can write one computer program or two speeches in an hour. In this case,
   A. Larry should write computer programs and Bill should write speeches because these are the tasks in which each has a comparative advantage.
   B. Larry should write speeches and Bill should write computer programs because these are the tasks in which each has a comparative advantage.
   C. They should each write computer programs and speeches and not specialize.
   D. Bill has an absolute advantage in speeches and should therefore write speeches.
   E. Larry has an absolute advantage in speeches and should therefore write speeches.

10. Which of the following is a benefit of specialization and trade on the basis of comparative advantage?
   A. Two countries can produce more of two goods with no change in their resources or productivities.
   B. Both countries' production possibilities curves will shift outward.
   C. The opportunity costs of both goods will increase for both countries.
   D. The opportunity cost of one good will rise in both countries.
   E. Both countries production possibilities curves will shift inward.

Solutions and Feedback to Pretest
The answers to the pretest are provided below along with the relevant Learning Objective from the Key Point Review. We strongly recommend that you take the time to review the appropriate material for each question you answered incorrectly.

Correct Answer	Learning Objective
1. C	1
2. B	2
3. C	3
4. A	3
5. E	4
6. D	5
7. B	5
8. D	6
9. B	7
10. A	8

II. Key Point Review
The Forest

This chapter focuses on the concepts of specialization and trade. You will apply these ideas throughout your work in economics. In particular, the study of international trade is built with these tools. It is therefore very important to master these concepts <u>now</u>.

The central questions you need to be able to answer are as follows:
- What is absolute advantage?
- What is comparative advantage?
- How is opportunity cost related to comparative advantage?
- How does comparative advantage determine specialization?
- What is the production possibilities curve?
- How is the production possibilities curve used to determine comparative advantage, specialization and trade patterns?

The Trees

Learning Objective 1: define and contrast these terms: absolute advantage, comparative advantage.

A person has an **absolute advantage** over another person if she can complete a task using fewer resources than the other person. A person has a **comparative advantage** over another person if she has a lower opportunity cost of completing a task than the other person.

For example: many professors have teaching assistants (TAs) to help them grade student work. Suppose that in a ten minute period, a professor can either grade one exam or enter 30 scores into a spreadsheet. In the same amount of time, a TA can either grade one-half of an exam or enter 20 scores.

- The professor has an absolute advantage in both tasks: she can grade an exam in ten minutes while it will take the TA twenty minutes, and she can enter 30 scores in 10 minutes while the TA can only enter 20.
- The professor has a comparative advantage in grading exams: her opportunity cost of grading an exam is 30 scores while the TA's opportunity cost is 40. The TA, however, has a comparative advantage in entering scores since his opportunity cost is 1/40 of an exam per score versus 1/30 of an exam for the professor.

Learning Objective 2: Define and explain the importance of The Principle of Comparative Advantage. Briefly identify some of the sources of comparative advantage for individuals and countries.

The Principle of Comparative Advantage states that everyone does best when each person or country concentrates on the activities for which his or her opportunity cost is lowest.

For example, since the TA has a comparative advantage in entering scores and the professor has a comparative advantage in grading exams, the best thing to do is to have the professor grade the exams and then have the TA enter the scores in a spreadsheet.

> Note: This might not fit your intuition; you might think that since the professor has absolute advantage she should do both tasks. This is an important example of why it is important to learn how to think like an economist: economic concepts often lead to conclusions that are correct but are not intuitively obvious.

The sources of comparative advantage for individuals include education and training, life experience, and innate abilities. Climate, natural resources, and historical circumstances are three among many sources of comparative advantage for nations and regions.

Learning Objective 3: Define the production possibilities curve and explain how the slope of the production possibilities curve is related to The Scarcity Principle.

You must learn how to apply production possibilities curves in two ways: to individuals and to countries. The definition of the production possibilities curve is the same for both: it shows the maximum amount of two goods that can be produced given the person or country's productivity and resources.

The Scarcity Principle states that having more of one good thing usually means having less of another. The production possibilities curve obeys this principle: the negative slope of the production possibilities curve is caused by the fact that in order to produce more of one good, a person or country must produce less of another good.

Note: The absolute value of the slope of the production possibilities curve is equal to the opportunity cost of the good plotted on the horizontal axis.

Hint: The slope of a line is discussed in both the textbook (appendix to Chapter 1) and this study guide (Chapter 1).

Learning Objective 4: For a given production possibilities curve, explain the differences among attainable points, unattainable points, efficient points, and inefficient points.

Attainable points are points that are inside or on the production possibilities curve. **Unattainable points** lie outside the production possibilities curve. Points on the production possibilities curve are **efficient points** while those that are inside the production possibilities curve are **inefficient points**. Thus, all efficient points are attainable but all attainable points are not efficient. This is important since much of economics consists of distinguishing efficient economic outcomes from attainable, but inefficient, ones.

Learning Objective 5: Define and explain The Principle of Increasing Opportunity Cost (also called the "Low-Hanging-Fruit Principle").
The Principle of Increasing Opportunity Cost states that to expand the production of any good, a person or country should first employ those resources with the lowest opportunity cost, and only afterward turn to resources with higher opportunity costs.

For example: suppose that a professor is grading exams and has only two red pens, one that works well and one that does not. The Principle of Increasing Costs implies that the professor should use the pen that works well first and use the other pen only after the better one runs out of ink.

Learning Objective 6: Identify and discuss the reasons why a production possibilities curve might shift.

There are two reasons why a production possibilities curve might shift. The first is that a person or country acquires more resources such as human capital, physical capital or natural capital. The second is that the person or country increases its productivity holding its resources fixed. This can happen through improvements in technology and advancements in knowledge.

Note: A shift in the production possibilities curve can turn a point that was previously considered to be unattainable into an attainable point. Indeed, this is the central story of the past 200 years of world economic history!

Learning Objective 7: Identify and explain the relationships among these concepts: comparative advantage, specialization, and trade.

Comparative advantage determines **specialization**: each person or country should specialize in the task in which they have a comparative advantage. (This is the Principle of Comparative Advantage.) The people or countries should then **trade** with one another for those tasks in which they do not have a comparative advantage.

For example: we discussed the professor and the TA in Learning Objectives 1 and 2 and found that the professor has a comparative advantage in grading and the TA in entering scores. This implies that the professor should specialize in grading, the TA in entering scores and then they should trade (i.e. work together) to complete the grading and the entering of scores for the class.

Learning Objective 8: Discuss the benefits and costs of specialization and trade. Do this for both individuals and countries.

There are two important benefits of specialization and trade. The first is that it allows two people or two countries to produce and consume more goods and services than they could produce or consume if they worked independently. This provides both with higher living standards. Second, specialization allows people or countries to get better at what they do, what economists call "learning-by-doing." Of course, excessive specialization can impose costs as well as benefits. For example, a country may have a comparative advantage in producing oil. This means that it will not be able to take advantage of learning-by-doing in other areas and may be stuck producing oil rather than manufacturing other goods. Further, specialization can lead to mind-numbing, repetitive work if it is carried too far.

III. Self-Test

Key Terms
Match the term in the right-hand column with the appropriate definition in the left-hand column by placing the letter of the term in the blank in front of its definition. (Answers are given at the end of the chapter.)

1. ____ A combination of goods that cannot be produced using a person's current resources and productivity.

    a. absolute advantage

2. ____ A person can perform a task with fewer resources (for example, in less time) than another person.

    b. attainable point

3. ____ A combination of goods that can be produced using a person's current resources and productivity.

    c. comparative advantage

4. ____ A graph that shows the maximum combinations of goods that can be produced by a person given their current resources and productivity.

    d. efficient point

5. ____ A person can perform a task at a lower opportunity cost than another person.

    e. inefficient point

6. ____ A combination of goods in which the production of one good can be increased without reducing the production of another good.

    f. production possibilities curve

7. ____ A combination of goods in which the production of one good cannot be increased without reducing the production of another good.

    g. unattainable point

Multiple-Choice Questions
Circle the letter that corresponds to the best answer. (Answers are given at the end of the chapter.)

1. If Kirby can perform a task using fewer resources than Frank, we say that Kirby
   A. has a comparative advantage in this task.
   B. has an absolute advantage in this task.
   C. has increasing opportunity costs in this task
   D. has a comparative disadvantage relative in this task.
   E. has an absolute disadvantage in this task.

2. If Kirby can perform a task at a lower opportunity cost than Frank, we say that Kirby
   A. has a comparative advantage in this task.
   B. has an absolute advantage in this task.
   C. has increasing opportunity costs in this task
   D. has a comparative disadvantage relative in this task.
   E. has an absolute disadvantage in this task.

Use the following information for problems 3 and 4: Bob can do 7 loads of laundry or make 3 complete meals per day. Carol can do 10 loads of laundry or make 2 complete meals per day.

3. Given the information above, Carol has
   A. no absolute advantage in either task but a comparative advantage making meals.
   B. an absolute advantage doing laundry and a comparative advantage doing laundry.
   C. an absolute advantage making meals and a comparative advantage making meals.
   D. an absolute advantage in doing laundry but no comparative advantage in either task.

4. According to the Principle of Comparative Advantage and given the information above,
   A. Bob should do the laundry and Carol should make the meals.
   B. Carol should do the laundry and Bob should make the meals.
   C. they should alternate tasks depending on the day of the week since neither of them has an absolute or comparative advantage in either task.
   D. Bob should make 2 meals and do 3 loads of laundry and Carol should make 1 meal and 7 loads of laundry.
   E. we cannot tell which person should do which task since not enough information is provided.

5. Production possibilities curves
   A. always slope downward.
   B. slope downward only if the Principle of Increasing Cost applies.
   C. bow inward if the Principle of Increasing Cost applies.
   D. always slope upward.
   E. slope downward only if the Principle of Comparative Advantage applies.

6. Which of the following will cause a production possibilities curve to bow outward?
   A. Scarcity.
   B. The Principle of Comparative Advantage.
   C. The Principle of Increasing Cost.
   D. Absolute advantage.
   E. None of the above will cause the production possibilities curve to bow outward.

Use the following information for problems 7, 8, and 9: Jan can crochet two headbands or 4 purses in one day. Marcia can crochet 5 headbands or one purse in one day.

7. If we plot each woman's production possibilities curve with headbands on the vertical axis and purses on the horizontal axis,
   A. the absolute value of the slope of Jan's production possibilities curve will be ½ and Marcia's will be 1/5.
   B. the absolute value of the slope of Jan's production possibilities curve will be ½ and Marcia's will be 2/5.
   C. the absolute value of the slope of Jan's production possibilities curve will be 2 and Marcia's will be 1/5.
   D. the absolute value of the slope of Jan's production possibilities curve will be ½ and Marcia's will be 5.
   E. the absolute value of the slope of Jan's production possibilities curve will be 2 and Marcia's will be 5.

8. Given the information above, Marcia has
   A. an absolute advantage crocheting headbands and a comparative advantage crocheting purses.
   B. no absolute advantage in either task but a comparative advantage crocheting purses.
   C. an absolute advantage crocheting headbands and a comparative advantage crocheting headbands.
   D. an absolute advantage crocheting purses and a comparative advantage crocheting purses.
   E. an absolute advantage in crocheting purses but no comparative advantage in either task.

9. According to the Principle of Comparative Advantage and given the information above, Jan should
   A. yell, "Marcia, Marcia, Marcia!"
   B. only crochet purses and trade them for any headbands she wants.
   C. only crochet headbands and trade them for any purses she wants.
   D. crochet both headbands and purses and not engage in trade.
   E. produce nothing since she does not have an absolute advantage in either headbands or purses.

10. Billie can compose two songs in one day or sing and record 4 songs in one day. Given this information, a combination of composing one song and singing and recording 4 songs all in one day is an
    A. efficient and attainable point.
    B. efficient point but is also an unattainable point.
    C. inefficient point but is also an attainable point.
    D. inefficient and unattainable point.
    E. unattainable point.

11. A point on a production possibilities curve is
    A. an efficient point.
    B. an inefficient point.
    C. an efficient but unattainable point.
    D. an inefficient but attainable point.
    E. an unattainable point.

12. An increase in a country's resources will
    A. cause that country's production possibilities curve to bow outward.
    B. cause that country's production possibilities curve to bow inward.
    C. shift that country's production possibilities curve outward.
    D. have no effect on that country's production possibilities curve.
    E. shift that country's production possibilities curve inward.

13. A worker learns a new skill that is applicable in his or her job. This will cause the worker's production possibilities curve to
    A. bow inward.
    B. bow outward.

C. shift inward.
D. shift outward.
E. remain unchanged.

Use the following information for problems 14, 15, and 16: Mr. Jones can photocopy 10 pages from a book or type 2 pages of handwritten text in 10 minutes. Mr. Smith can photocopy 40 pages from a book or type 3 pages of handwritten text in 10 minutes.

14. Given the information above, Mr. Jones has
    A. an absolute advantage in photocopying and a comparative advantage in photocopying.
    B. an absolute advantage in typing and a comparative advantage in typing.
    C. no absolute advantage in either task but a comparative advantage in photocopying.
    D. no absolute advantage in either task but a comparative advantage in typing.
    E. absolute advantage in neither task nor a comparative advantage in either task.

15. Given the information above, if Mr. Smith and Mr. Jones follow the Principle of Comparative Advantage
    A. Mr. Smith will do all of the typing and Mr. Jones will do all of the photocopying.
    B. Mr. Smith will do all of the photocopying and Mr. Jones will do all of the typing.
    C. Mr. Jones will photocopy 5 pages and type one page, and Mr. Smith will photocopy 20 pages and type 2 pages.
    D. Mr. Smith will photocopy 5 pages and type one page, and Mr. Jones will photocopy 20 pages and type 2 pages.
    E. they will not know what to do since not enough information is provided.

16. Given the information above, if Mr. Jones takes a course and learns how to type 3 pages in 10 minutes and can still photocopy 10 pages in 10 minutes, then
    A. Mr. Smith will do all of the typing and Mr. Jones will do all of the photocopying.
    B. Mr. Smith will do all of the photocopying and Mr. Jones will do all of the typing.
    C. Mr. Jones will photocopy 5 pages and type one page, and Mr. Smith will photocopy 20 pages and type 2 pages.
    D. Mr. Smith will photocopy 5 pages and type one page, and Mr. Jones will photocopy 20 pages and type 2 pages.
    E. they will not know what to do since not enough information is provided.

17. Which of the following statements reflects the correct relationship among absolute advantage, comparative advantage, specialization and trade?
    A. People should specialize in those tasks in which they have an absolute advantage and have someone else perform those tasks in which they do not have an absolute advantage.
    B. People should specialize in those tasks in which they have a comparative advantage and have someone else perform those tasks in which they do not have a comparative advantage.
    C. People should specialize in those tasks in which they have comparative advantage but only have others perform those tasks in which they do not have an absolute advantage.
    D. People should specialize in those tasks in which they have an absolute advantage but only have others perform those tasks in which they do not have a comparative advantage.

E. People should only specialize in those tasks in which they have both comparative and absolute advantage and have others perform those tasks in which they have neither comparative nor absolute advantage.

18. A benefit of specialization and trade between two people is that
   A. each can consume more than before they traded with no increase in resources or productivity.
   B. each can consume the same amount as before they traded with fewer resources and no change in productivity.
   C. each can consume the same amount as before they traded with the same resources and lower levels of productivity.
   D. None of the above are correct.
   E. Answers A, B and C are all correct.

19. If a production possibilities curve obeys The Principle of Increasing Opportunity Cost, then the absolute value of the slope this production possibilities curve will
   A. be constant.
   B. rise.
   C. fall.
   D. rise then fall.
   E. not be affected.

20. Paula has absolute advantage in two tasks compared to Olivia. Paula has a comparative advantage in one task while Olivia has a comparative advantage in the other. This implies that
   A. Olivia will gain from trading with Paula but Paula will not gain from trading with Olivia
   B. Paula will gain from trading with Olivia but Olivia will not gain from trading with Paula.
   C. both Olivia and Paula will gain from trading with each other.
   D. neither Olivia nor Paula will gain from trading with each other.
   E. there is not enough information to know whether or not either or both will gain from trade.

Short Answer Problems
(Answers and solutions are given at the end of the chapter.)

1. **A production possibilities curve for an economy**
    The table below presents data on the country of Johnnyland, an economy that produces two goods: potato chips and computer chips:

Potato chips (millions of bags)	0	2	4	6	8
Computer chips (millions of chips)	30	27	21	12	0

A. Draw the production possibilities curve on the graph below.

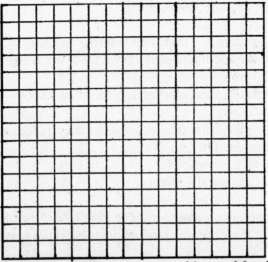

A. If Johnnyland is producing 21 million computer chips and 2 million bags of potato chips this is a(n) _____ point.

B. Suppose Johnnyland is producing 30 million computer chips and no potato chips. If this country decides to start producing potato chips, the opportunity cost of the first 2 million bags of potato chips will be _____ computer chips.

C. Suppose Johnnyland is producing 27 million computer chips and 2 million bags of potato chips. If this country decides to produce 2 million more bags of potato chips, the opportunity cost will be _____ computer chips.

D. Suppose Johnnyland is producing 21 million computer chips and 4 million bags of potato chips. If this country decides to produce 2 million more bags of potato chips, the opportunity cost will be _____ computer chips.

E. Given your answers to parts (C), (D) and (E), does this production possibilities curve obey The Principle of Increasing Opportunity Cost? _____. Why? _____

_____

F. Does the shape of the production possibilities curve you drew in part (A) support your answer to part (F)? _____ Explain why or why not: _____

_____

2. **Production Possibilities and Comparative Advantages for Two People**

Let's return to Susan and Tom, the people discussed in Chapter 2 of the text who gather nuts and pick coffee. Susan can gather 2 pounds of nuts or pick 4 pounds of coffee per hour while Tom can gather 4 pounds of nuts or pick 2 pounds of coffee per hour. Suppose that they each work 6 hours per day.

A. Draw the production possibilities curve for both Tom and Susan on the graph below.

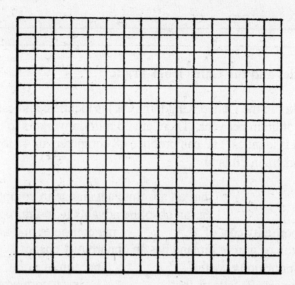

B. Susan has a comparative advantage in _____ and Tom has a comparative advantage in _____ . We can see this on the graph because the slope of Susan's production possibilities frontier is (steeper/flatter) _____ than Tom's.

C. Suppose that Susan and Tom decide to work together so that they can maximize their production of nuts and coffee. If both Susan and Tom only gather nuts, they will gather _____ pounds of nuts in 6 hours. If both Susan and Tom only pick coffee, they will pick _____ pounds of coffee in 6 hours. If Susan and Tom specialize according to their comparative advantages they will pick _____ pounds of coffee and _____ pounds of nuts in 6 hours.

D. Use the information from part (C) to draw the production possibilities curve for Susan and Tom working together.

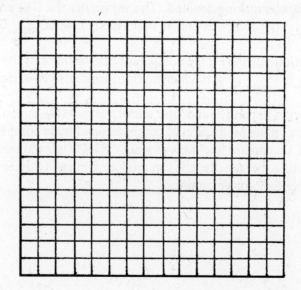

E. Compare the graphs you drew in parts (A) and (D) and explain how they are related to one another:

_____

_____

3. Production Possibilities and the Gains from Trade

Suppose that each worker in the United Kingdom (UK) is identical and can produce 72 computers or 180 tons of grain per year. There are 30 million workers in the UK. Suppose that each worker in Finland is identical and can produce 48 computers or 48 tons of grain per year. There are 3 million workers in Finland.

A. (The UK/Finland) _____ has an absolute advantage in computer production and (the UK/Finland) _____ has an absolute advantage in grain production.

B. The UK has an opportunity cost of _____ per computer and an opportunity cost of _____ per ton of grain. Finland has an opportunity cost of _____ per computer and an opportunity cost of _____ per ton of grain.

C. The information in part (B) tells us that _____ has a comparative advantage in grain production and _____ has a comparative advantage in computer production. This is because _____.

D. Suppose that Finland offered to specialize in the production of computers and trade computers to the UK for grain at the rate of 1 computer for 2 tons of grain. The UK should (accept/reject) _____ this offer because the UK produces computers at a (lower/higher) opportunity cost than 1 computer for 2 tons of grain.

E. Suppose that Finland offered to specialize in the production of computers and trade computers to the UK at the rate of 1 computer for 3 tons of grain. The UK should (accept/reject) _____ this offer because the UK can produce grain at a (lower/higher) opportunity cost than 1 computer for $\frac{1}{2}$ ton of grain.

F. Suppose that the ability of UK workers to produce computers improved so that their productivity in computer making doubled. This means that the UK now has an opportunity cost of _____ per computer and an opportunity cost of _____ per ton of grain.

G. Given the information in part (F), the comparative advantages of the UK and Finland (have/have not) _____ been changed from your answer in part (C). This is because _____.

H. Given the information in part (F) and your answer to part (G), suppose that Finland offered to specialize in the production of computers and trade computers to the UK for grain at the rate of 1 computer for 2 tons of grain. The UK should (accept/reject) _____ this offer because the UK can produce grain at a (lower/higher) opportunity cost than 1 computer for 2 tons of grain.

IV. Becoming an Economic Naturalist: Case Study

Farmers in Minnesota and South Dakota grow sunflower seeds and soybeans. The table below provides data on yields per acre for both crops in 2004:

State	Soybeans (bushels per acre)	Sunflower seeds (pounds per acre)
Minnesota	33	1068
South Dakota	34	1462

The table below contains data on the number of acres planted in all crops, in soybeans and in sunflower seeds for each state (in 1000s of acres):

State	All crops	Soybeans	Sunflower seeds
Minnesota	19,481	7,050	415
South Dakota	17,146	4,120	530

Source: U.S. Department of Agriculture website (www.usda.gov)

Using these data, identify which state has a comparative advantage in each crop. Do you think that The Principle of Comparative Advantage explains the planting behavior of farmers in Minnesota and South Dakota? Why or why not?
Answer:

V. Self-Test Solutions
Key Terms
1. g
2. a
3. b
4. f
5. c
6. e
7. d

Multiple-Choice Questions
1. B
2. A
3. B; Carol can do more laundry in a day than Bob (absolute advantage). Her opportunity cost of a load of laundry is 2/10 of a meal, which is lower than Bob's opportunity cost of a load of laundry (3/7 of a meal).
4. B
5. A; this is because of The Scarcity Principle.

6. C
7. D
8. C; Marcia's opportunity cost of headbands is 1/5 of a purse while Jan's is 2 purses.
9. B
10. E
11. A
12. C; the opportunity costs are not affected but the country can now produce more of both goods.
13. D
14. C
15. A
16. A; Mr. Jones still has a lower opportunity cost of typing. Neither Mr. Jones nor Mr. Smith now has an absolute advantage in typing.
17. B
18. E
19. B
20. C

Short Answer Problems

1. A. See graph at right.

   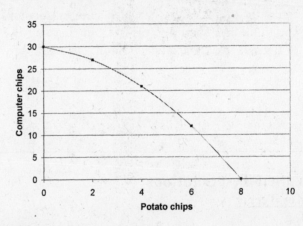

   B. inefficient point. They could produce 4 million bags of potato chips but do not.
   C. 3 million.
   D. 4 million.
   E. 9 million
   F. Yes. The opportunity cost of producing 2 million bags of potato chips rises from 3 million computer chips to 4 million computer chips to 9 million computer chips.
   G. Yes. The production possibilities curve is bowed out, implying that the absolute value of the slope is increasing. The absolute value of the slope is equal to the opportunity cost of potato chips, and thus the graph shows that opportunity cost of potato chips is indeed increasing.

2. A. See graph below:

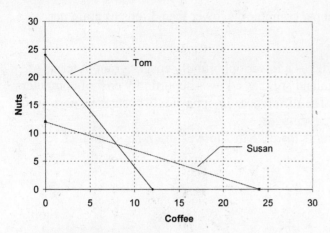

B. Coffee; nuts; flatter.
C. 36; 36; 24; 24.
D. See graph below

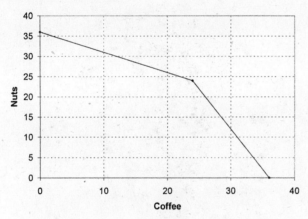

E. The upper segment of the graph is Susan's production possibilities curve shifted up by 36
    units, 24 of which consist of Tom only gathering nuts and Susan gradually shifting from
    gathering nuts to picking coffee. When Susan is picking 24 pounds of coffee, she is
    using all of her resources and in order for the two of them to produce more coffee Tom
    must move from gathering nuts to picking coffee. This segment of the graph is thus
    Tom's production possibilities curve shifted to the right by 24 units. Notice: Susan shifts
    out of nuts first! She has the comparative advantage in coffee and so they will gain more
    coffee if Susan gathers it instead of Tom. This is an illustration of the The Principle of
    Increasing Opportunity Cost.

3. A. UK, UK
    B. 2.5 tons of grain, 0.4 computers; 1 ton of grain, 1 computer.
    C. the UK; Finland. This is because the UK has a lower opportunity cost of grain in terms
        of computers than does Finland, and Finland has a lower opportunity cost of computers in
        terms of grain than does the UK.
    D. accept; higher. Note: 2.5 tons of grain per computer is higher than 2 tons of grain per
        computer.

E. reject; lower. Note: 2.5 tons of grain per computer is lower than 3 tons of grain per computer.

F. 1.25 tons of grain; 0.8 computers.

G. have not. This is because the UK still has a lower opportunity cost of grain in terms of computers than does Finland, and Finland still has a lower opportunity cost of computers in terms of grain than does the UK. The differences in opportunity costs have narrowed but still yield the same comparative advantages.

H. reject; 1.25 tons of grain per computer is lower than 2 tons of grain per computer.

Chapter 3
Supply and Demand:
An Introduction

I. Pretest: What Do You Really Know?

Circle the letter that corresponds to the best answer. (Answers appear immediately after the final question).

1. Which of the following is not one of the basic economic questions that every society must answer?
   A. What goods will be produced?
   B. Where will goods be produced?
   C. How will goods be produced?
   D. How will goods be distributed to members of society?
   E. None of the above is a basic economic question.

2. The demand for milk slopes downward because
   A. a lower price of milk allows a buyer to purchase more milk.
   B. a lower price of milk allows a buyer to substitute milk for other beverages.
   C. a lower price of milk causes sellers to produce less milk.
   D. both (A) and (B) are correct.
   E. of gravity.

3. An increase in the price of beef will probably cause
   A. the demand for chicken to decrease.
   B. the demand for beef to increase.
   C. the demand for chicken to increase.
   D. the quantity demanded of beef to increase.
   E. the demand for beef to decrease.

4. As the price of milk increases, suppliers will
   A. increase the supply of milk.
   B. increase the quantity supplied of milk.
   C. decrease the supply of milk.
   D. decrease the quantity supplied of milk.
   E. be unaffected and not change their behavior at all.

5. An increase in the price of chicken feed will
   A. cause the supply of chicken to fall.
   B. cause the demand for chicken to fall.
   C. cause the demand for chicken to rise.
   D. cause the supply of chicken to rise.
   E. cause the quantity supplied of chicken to rise.

6. If a market is in equilibrium, then
   A. the quantity demanded equals the quantity supplied.
   B. the buyer's reservation price equals the seller's reservation price.
   C. there is no excess demand or excess supply.
   D. (A), (B) and (C) are all true.
   E. none of the above answers are true.

7. The price of milk is currently above the equilibrium price in the milk market. This means
   that
   A. there will be excess supply at this price.
   B. there will be excess demand at this price.
   C. there will be a decrease in demand.
   D. there will be a decrease in supply.
   E. the equilibrium price of milk will rise.

8. If the price of tea falls, then the price of coffee will
   A. rise because the demand for coffee will rise.
   B. fall because the demand for coffee will fall.
   C. rise because the supply of coffee will rise.
   D. fall because the supply of coffee will fall.
   E. be unaffected because the price of tea only affects the market for tea.

9. If the price of gasoline is $2.50 per gallon and the buyer's reservation price is $3.00 per
   gallon, then
   A. the buyer's surplus is $0.50 per gallon.
   B. the seller's surplus is $0.50 per gallon.
   C. the market is in equilibrium.
   D. the demand for gasoline will fall.
   E. the demand for gasoline will rise.

10. Economic efficiency means that
    A. all machines in the economy are running at their full capacity.
    B. there is "cash on the table."
    C. the socially optimal amount of the good is being bought and sold.
    D. the buyer's reservation price is greater than the seller's reservation price.
    E. the seller's reservation price is greater than the buyer's reservation price

Solutions and Feedback to Pretest
The answers to the pretest are provided below along with the relevant Learning Objective from the Key Point Review. We strongly recommend that you take the time to review the appropriate material for each question you answered incorrectly.

Correct Answer	Learning Objective
1. B	1
2. D	2
3. C	2
4. B	3
5. A	3
6. D	4
7. A	5
8. B	6
9. A	7
10. C	8

II. Key Point Review
The Forest

This chapter focuses on the most important tool in economics: supply and demand analysis. If you want to succeed in economics, you <u>must</u> learn to work with this tool and be able to apply it both to problems in the text and to situations in the real world.

The central questions you need to be able to answer are:
- What is a market?
- What is a demand curve?
- What is a supply curve?
- What is market equilibrium?
- What causes a market equilibrium to change?
- What is economic efficiency?

The Trees

Learning Objective 1: Understand the three basic economic questions posed at the beginning of the chapter and describe how the use of markets addresses these questions.
The first question, **What to produce**, refers to the fact that if we produce something we cannot produce something else. **How to produce** indicates that there are always multiple ways of producing goods and services and that we must choose a particular technique before we can actually produce something. Finally, **for whom** means that societies must always face the fact that what is produced, no matter how it is produced, must be distributed among the members of society. **Markets** address these questions by providing a mechanism for people to decide for themselves how much should be produced, how it should be produced and how the resulting

production should be distributed. Specifically, markets allow buyers and sellers of goods to interact using prices as their means of communication.

> Note: "What to produce" is another way of phrasing the Scarcity Principle.

Learning Objective 2: Understand the demand curve. Specifically,
- define a demand curve and explain the two effects that determine its shape;
- explain the difference between a change in quantity demanded and a change in demand;
- list the variables that cause a demand curve to shift and explain why they do this.
- explain the concept of the buyers' reservation price and how the demand curve can be interpreted in two ways.

A **demand curve** shows the quantity of a good that buyers wish to buy and are able to buy (the quantity demanded) at each possible price holding everything other than price constant. The **substitution effect** causes the demand curve to slope downward because an increase in the price of a good will cause people to decrease their purchases of the good and purchase a substitute. The **income effect** also makes the demand curve slope downward; an increase in the price of that good means the buyer cannot afford to buy as large a quantity at the higher price than they could at the lower price.

A **change in quantity demanded** is movement along a demand curve; this is *only* caused by a change in the price of a good. A **change in demand** is a shift of the entire demand curve and can be caused by the following:
1. A change in the number of buyers. An increase in the number of buyers will shift the demand curve to the right while a decrease in the number of buyers will shift the demand curve to the left.
2. A change in the price of another good. Suppose that the price of another good increases; there are two possible effects:
   a. the demand curve shifts to the right. This means that the two goods are **substitutes**.
   b. The demand curve shifts to the left. This means that the two goods are **complements**.
3. A change in buyers' income. Suppose that buyers' income increases; there are two possible effects:
   a. The demand curve shifts to the right. This means that the good is a **normal good**.
   b. The demand curve shifts to the left. This means that the good is an **inferior good**.

> Note: Don't get too attached to the literal meaning of the words substitute, complement, normal and inferior. For example, there are goods that are perfectly normal, like hamburger, that actually are inferior goods in the sense we are using the phrase. Similarly, there are goods that are not literally substitutes for one another but when the price of one good rises the demand for the other increases.

4. A change in buyers' preferences. This can cause the demand curve to shift either to the right or the left. Suppose, for example, that buyers' find out that a good will prevent

cancer; they will want to buy more of the good regardless of even if the prices of other goods stay the same and their incomes remain constant. This will cause the demand curve to shift to the right.

5. A change in buyers' expectations. This can also cause the demand curve to shift either to the right or the left. For example, if people believe that a good will not be available next week, they will increase their demand for the good this week.

The **buyers' reservation price** is the highest price that buyers are willing to pay for a given quantity of a good. This gives us a second way to define a demand curve: a **demand curve** shows the buyers' reservation price for every possible quantity of the good.

Learning Objective 3: Understand the supply curve. Specifically,
- **define a supply curve;**
- **explain the difference between a change in quantity supplied and a change in demand;**
- **list the variables that cause a supply curve to shift and explain why they do this.**
- **explain the concept of the sellers' reservation price and how the supply curve can be interpreted in two ways.**

A **supply curve** shows the quantity of a good that sellers are able to sell and wish to sell (the quantity supplied) at each possible price holding everything other than price constant. A **change in quantity supplied** is movement along a supply curve; this is *only* caused by a change in the price of a good. A **change in supply** is a shift of the entire supply curve and can be caused by the following:

1. A change in the number of sellers. An increase in the number of sellers will shift the supply curve to the right while a decrease in the number of sellers will shift the supply curve to the left.
2. A change in the price of resources used to produce the good. An increase in resource prices will cause the supply curve to shift to the left while a decline in resource prices will shift the supply curve to the right.
3. A change in the technology used to produce the good. An improvement in technology will shift the supply curve to the right; a technological decline will shift the supply curve to the left.
4. A change in sellers' expectations. This can also cause the supply curve to shift either to the right or the left. For example, if sellers believe that buyers will need the good next week, they may decrease their supply of the good this week.

The **sellers' reservation price** is the lowest price that sellers are willing to receive for a given quantity of a good. This gives us a second way to define a supply curve: a **supply curve** shows the sellers' reservation price for every possible quantity of the good.

Hint: Much of the language we used to describe the supply curve is parallel to the words we employed to describe the demand curve. This is something to look for whenever you are working with supply and demand: if a concept is important for one curve there is probably a parallel concept that is important for the other curve.

Learning Objective 4: Define the following terms: equilibrium, equilibrium price, equilibrium quantity and market equilibrium.
Equilibrium is a condition where nothing will change unless an outside force acts on the situation. Think of throwing a ball: if the ball lands on the ground it will not move unless something else happens (e.g. someone picks it up and throws it.) The ball is thus in equilibrium.

We apply the same idea to markets; we just need to be careful about what we mean by a situation where nothing will change. This means we must focus on the two key variables of the supply and demand model: prices and quantities. An **equilibrium price** is a price at which the quantity demanded equals the quantity supplied. An **equilibrium quantity** is the quantity that buyers and sellers agree to at the equilibrium price. **Market equilibrium** is a situation where an equilibrium price has established an equilibrium quantity.

Learning Objective 5: Define excess supply and excess demand and explain how they differ from market equilibrium.
Excess supply exists when the quantity supplied of a good exceeds the quantity demanded of a good at a given price. **Excess demand** exists when the quantity demanded of a good exceeds the quantity supplied of a good at a given price. Both of these are situations where a market is not in equilibrium.

Note: You cannot talk about excess supply or excess demand without reference to a price. For example, the phrase "there is excess demand for gasoline" does not make sense since a high enough price for gasoline will eliminate the excess demand. The phrase "there is excess demand for gasoline at $1.50 per gallon" is a correct way to describe the situation.

Learning Objective 6: Use shifts in supply and/or demand to analyze and explain changes in market equilibria.
This is the culmination of ALL THE PREVIOUS LEARNING OBJECTIVES. You have learned about how all of the individual parts of the supply and demand model work and now you have to apply them. There is a simple, 3-step rubric for applying the model:

1. Draw a pair of supply and demand curves at an initial equilibrium of P_0 and Q_0:

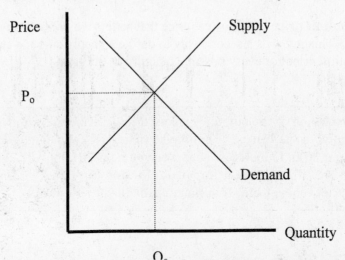

2. Use Learning Objectives 2 and 3 to identify whether the supply curve shifts and in what direction, the demand curve shifts and in what direction or both curves shift and what directions. For example: suppose that the number of buyers in a particular market increases. This will cause the demand curve to the right and will have no effect on the supply curve. Draw this out:

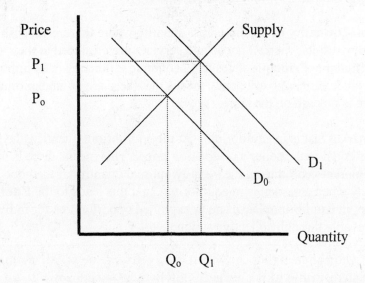

3. Find the new market equilibrium and compare it to the initial market equilibrium. For example: since the demand curve shifted to the right, the graph shows that the new market equilibrium, P_1 and Q_1 will be at both a higher equilibrium price and a higher equilibrium quantity.

Hint: Figures 3.17, 3.18, and 3.19 in the text illustrate all of the possible outcomes of shifts in supply and demand. IT DOES NOT PAY TO MEMORIZE THIS INFORMATION! Rather, use the rubric above and let the graph do the work.

Learning Objective 7: Define the following terms: buyer's surplus, seller's surplus and total surplus. Explain how these terms are related to the concept of "cash on the table." **Buyer's surplus** is the difference between the buyers' reservation price and the market price for a given quantity of a good. Similarly, the **seller's surplus** is the difference between the market price and the sellers' reservation price for a given quantity of a good. The **total surplus** is the difference between the buyers' reservation price and the sellers' reservation price for a given quantity of a good.

When total surplus for a given quantity of a good is positive, that means that the buyer and the seller can both gain by agreeing to a price that is between their reservation prices. The buyer will gain because he pays less than his reservation price and the seller will gain since she receives a price that is higher than her reservation price. **Cash on the table** is the name economists give to a situation when the buyer and seller cannot take advantage of this difference in their reservation prices, either because they cannot come to an agreement or something else prevents them from doing so (e.g. a law or regulation).

Learning Objective 8: Explain the relationship between the socially optimal quantity of a good and economic efficiency. Use this relationship to explain the relationship between the Efficiency Principle and the Equilibrium Principle.

The **socially optimal quantity of a good** is that quantity where there is no cash on the table. **Economic efficiency** results when all goods and services are produced at their socially optimal quantities. The **Efficiency Principle** states that economic efficiency is an important goal for society to achieve since economic efficiency means that there are no unexploited gains from exchange, i.e. there is no cash on the table.

Now, consider a market that is in equilibrium. At the equilibrium quantity, the buyer's reservation price is equal to the seller's reservation price. This means there is no cash on the table and thus the market is producing the socially optimal quantity of the good. Thus, we have economic efficiency when a market is in equilibrium, and this leads to the **Equilibrium Principle**: a market in equilibrium leaves no unexploited opportunities for individuals, but there may be gains achievable through collective action.

> **Note: Collective action can mean either private or public action. For example, a group of people getting together on their own to do something is private, while the same group of people acting through their city government would constitute a public action. The equilibrium principle says nothing about which type of collective action will allow a group to reap the unexploited gains, only that some type of collective action will do this.**

Learning Objective 9 (Appendix): Solve for the equilibrium price and equilibrium quantity for a market using equations for the supply and demand curves.

Supply and demand curves can be expressed as linear equations and then solved to find the equilibrium price and equilibrium quantity. This is an application of the "two equations, two unknowns" types of problems you did in high school algebra. In this case, the two equations are the supply curve and the demand curve and the two unknowns are the equilibrium price and the equilibrium quantity.

III. Self-Test
Key Terms
Match the term in the right-hand column with the appropriate definition in the left-hand column by placing the letter of the term in the blank in front of its definition. (Answers are given at the end of the chapter.)

1. ____ A graph that shows the quantity of a good that buyers wish   a. buyer's reservation price
to buy and are able to buy at each possible price holding
everything other than price constant.

2. ____ A type of good where the amount buyers are willing and   b. buyer's surplus
able to purchase at every price rises when buyers' income rises.

3. ____ Movement along a supply curve.

4. ____ A price at which the quantity of a good that buyers wish to buy and are able to buy equals the quantity of a good that sellers wish to sell and are able to sell.

5. ____ A situation where the quantity demanded exceeds the quantity supplied at a given price.

6. ____ The difference between the market price and the sellers' reservation price.

7. ____ The result of there being a difference between the buyers' reservation price and the sellers' reservation price.

8. ____ A pair of goods in which an increase in the price of one good will cause an increase in the demand for the other good.

9. ____ The highest price that a buyer is willing to pay for a given quantity of a good.

10. ____ the difference between the buyers' reservation price and the market price.

12. ____ A state of affairs where nothing will change unless it is disturbed by an outside force.

13. ____ A maximum price at which buyers and sellers can make exchanges legally.

14. ____ A situation where the quantity supplied exceeds the quantity demanded at a given price.

15. ____ The lowest price that a seller is willing to receive for a given quantity of a good.

16. ____ The condition of a market when the quantity of a good buyers wish to buy and are able to buy equals the quantity of a good that sellers wish to sell and are able to sell.

17. ____ A pair of goods in which an increase in the price of one good will cause a decrease in the demand for the other good.

18. ____ A decrease in the price of a good allows buyers to purchase a larger quantity of that good with the same income.

19. ____ The name of the quantity at which the quantity of a good that buyers wish to buy and are able to buy equals the quantity of a good that sellers wish to sell and are able to sell.

20. ____ A change in the amount sellers are willing and able to offer for sale at every price.

21. ____ A group of buyers and sellers of a single good who interact through prices.

22. ____ The response of buyers to a change in the price of a good.

23. ____ The concept of all markets producing the socially optimal quantity of a good.

24. ____ the difference between the buyers' reservation price and the sellers' reservation price.

25. ____ A type of good where the amount buyers are willing and able to purchase at every price falls when buyers' income rises.

26. ____ A decrease in the price of a good causes people to increase

c. cash on the table

d. change in demand

e. change in quantity demanded

f. change in quantity supplied

g. change in supply

h. complements

i. demand curve

j. economic efficiency

k. equilibrium

l. equilibrium price

m. equilibrium quantity

n. excess demand

o. excess supply

p. income effect

q. inferior good

r. market

s. market equilibrium

t. normal good

u. price ceiling

v. seller's reservation price

w. seller's surplus

x. socially optimal quantity

y. substitutes

their purchases of the good and buy less of another good.

27. ____A change in the amount buyers are willing and able to   z. substitution effect
purchase at every price.

28. ___ A quantity at which there is no difference between buyers'   aa. supply curve
reservation price and sellers' reservation price.

29. ___A graph that shows the quantity of a good that sellers wish   bb. total surplus
to sell and are able to sell at each possible price holding everything
other than price constant.

Multiple-Choice Questions
Circle the letter that corresponds to the best answer. (Answers are given at the end of the chapter.)

1. A market
   A. allows buyers and sellers of a good to communicate through prices.
   B. is a way society answers the three basic economic questions.
   C. consists of supply and demand when drawn in a graph.
   D. (A), (B) and (C) all are true of a market
   E. None of the above is true of a market.

2. The last time that you went to the store milk was $2.50 per gallon. You go to the store with $5 and intend to buy two gallons of milk but find that the price has risen to $3.00 per gallon. Since you can only buy one gallon of milk, you have experienced
   A. the substitution effect.
   B. the income effect.
   C. a price ceiling.
   D. excess supply.
   E. excess demand

3. You usually buy a particular brand of bottled water. If you purchase a different beverage when the price of bottled water rises, you have experienced
   A. the substitution effect.
   B. the income effect.
   C. a price ceiling.
   D. excess supply.
   E. excess demand

4. If buyers' reservation price falls,
   A. There will be an increase in the quantity demanded of a good.
   B. There will be an increase in the demanded for a good.
   C. There will be no effect on the quantity supplied or the quantity demanded.
   D. There will be an increase in the quantity supplied of a good.
   E. There will be an increase in the supply of a good.

5. If sellers' reservation price rises,
   A. There will be an increase in the quantity demanded of a good.

B. There will be an increase in the demanded for a good.

C. There will be no effect on the quantity supplied or the quantity demanded.

D. There will be an increase in the quantity supplied of a good.

E. There will be an increase in the supply of a good.

6. Suppose that bread and butter are complements. If the price of bread rises, then
    A. the supply of butter will increase.
    B. the demand for butter will increase.
    C. the demand for butter will decrease.
    D. the demand for bread will increase.
    E. the quantity demanded of butter will increase.

7. If orange juice and pineapple juice are substitutes,
    A. an increase in the price of orange juice will cause the demand for pineapple juice to fall.
    B. an increase in the price of orange juice will cause the demand for pineapple juice to rise.
    C. an increase in the demand for orange juice will cause a decrease in the demand for pineapple juice.
    D. an increase in the demand for orange juice will cause an increase in the demand for pineapple juice.
    E. a decrease in the price of orange juice will cause the demand for pineapple juice to rise.

8. Which of the following would *not* cause an increase in the US supply of gasoline?
    A. A decrease in the price of crude oil.
    B. A technological improvement in gasoline refining.
    C. An increase in the fuel efficiency of cars.
    D. An increase in the number of refineries in the US.
    E. None of the above would cause an increase in the US supply of gasoline.

9. Suppose that shoe producers think that flip-flops will go out of fashion next year. This will
    A. cause the supply of flip-flops to decrease next year.
    B. cause the supply of flip-flops to increase next year.
    C. cause an increase in the quantity of flip-flops supplied next year.
    D. cause a decrease in the quantity of flip-flops supplied next year.
    E. cause the demand for flip-slops to increase next year.

10. If a market is *not* in equilibrium at a given price, then
    A. there is excess demand.
    B. there is excess supply.
    C. the equilibrium price is not equal to the current price.
    D. (A), (B) and (C) all are possible for market that is not in equilibrium.
    E. None of the above is true of a market that is not in equilibrium.

11. A new medical study is published showing that eating oatmeal reduces the risk of colon cancer. We should observe that
    A. the price of oatmeal falls.
    B. the price of oatmeal rises.

C. the equilibrium quantity of oatmeal falls.
D. the supply of oatmeal falls.
E. the demand for oatmeal falls.

12. An increase in the price of gasoline will most likely cause
    A. the supply of low gas mileage cars to increase and the price of low gas mileage cars to rise.
    B. the supply of low gas mileage cars to decrease and the price of low gas mileage cars to fall.
    C. excess supply in the market for low gas mileage cars.
    D. the demand for low gas mileage cars to increase and the price of low gas mileage cars to rise.
    E. the demand for low gas mileage cars to decrease and the price of low gas mileage cars to fall.

Use the graph below for problems 13, 14 and 15; it represents the market for songs downloaded from the internet:

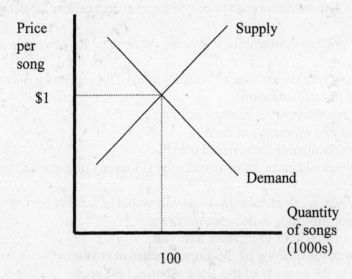

13. An increase in the demand for music downloads would
    A. not affect the equilibrium price or equilibrium quantity.
    B. cause an increase in the equilibrium price and a decrease in the equilibrium quantity.
    C. cause a decrease in the equilibrium price and an increase in the equilibrium quantity.
    D. cause an increase in the equilibrium price and an increase in the equilibrium quantity.
    E. cause a decrease in the equilibrium price and a decrease in the equilibrium quantity.

14. An improvement in the technology used to place downloads on the internet would
    A. not affect the equilibrium price or equilibrium quantity.
    B. cause an increase in the equilibrium price and a decrease in the equilibrium quantity.
    C. cause a decrease in the equilibrium price and an increase in the equilibrium quantity.
    D. cause an increase in the equilibrium price and an increase in the equilibrium quantity.
    E. cause a decrease in the equilibrium price and a decrease in the equilibrium quantity.

15. If a price ceiling of $0.50 per song was placed on music downloads,
    A. not affect the equilibrium price or equilibrium quantity.
    B. this would create excess demand.
    C. this would create excess supply.
    D. this would cause a decrease in demand and an increase in supply.
    E. this would cause an increase in demand and a decrease in supply.

16. An increase in consumer income will
    A. cause the equilibrium price of a normal good to fall if supply remains constant.
    B. cause the equilibrium price of a normal good to rise if supply remains constant.
    C. not affect the equilibrium price of a good.
    D. cause the equilibrium price of an inferior good to rise if supply remains constant.
    E. cause the supply of a good to fall.

Use the graph below for problems 17 and 18:

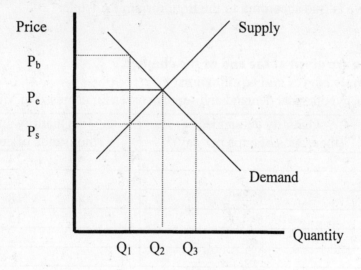

17. If P_e is the equilibrium price, a price ceiling at P_s will
    A. create a situation where there is "cash on the table."
    B. generate excess demand.
    C. create a greater amount of buyers' surplus at Q_1 than when the market is in equilibrium.
    D. cause (A), (B) and (C) to all happen.
    E. have none of the effects given in (A), (B) or (C).

18. If P_e is the equilibrium price, a price ceiling at P_b will
    A. create a situation where there is "cash on the table."
    B. generate excess demand.
    C. create a greater amount of buyers' surplus at Q_1 than when the market is in equilibrium.
    D. cause (A), (B) and (C) to all happen.
    E. have none of the effects given in (A), (B) or (C).

19. The socially optimal quantity of a good
    A. cannot be produced in a market.
    B. is that quantity where there are no unexploited opportunities for gain.
    C. is that quantity where there are unexploited opportunities for gain.
    D. is a situation where quantity supplied exceeds quantity demand.
    E. is a situation where quantity demanded exceeds quantity supplied.

20. According to the Equilibrium Principle,
    A. there is no "cash on the table" for individuals but there may be "cash on the table" for society as a whole.
    B. there is no "cash on the table" for society as a whole but there may be "cash on the table" for individuals.
    C. every market is always in equilibrium.
    D. no market is ever in equilibrium.
    E. None of the above is true according to the Equilibrium Principle.

Short Answer Problems
(Answers and solutions are given at the end of the chapter.)
1. Demand curves, supply curves and equilibrium
The table below provides hypothetical demand and supply curves for espresso in Minneapolis:

Price per cup	Quantity demanded (thousands of cups per day)	Quantity supplied (thousands of cups per day)
$4.00	0	24
$3.50	3	21
$3.00	6	18
$2.50	9	15
$2.00	12	12
$1.50	15	9
$1.00	18	6
$0.50	21	3

A. Graph the supply and demand curves on the axes below.

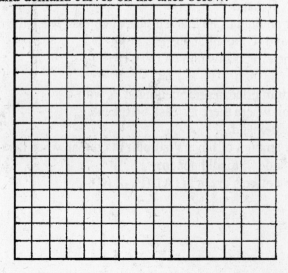

B. Label the equilibrium price and the equilibrium quantity on the graph.
C. Suppose that a price ceiling is imposed at $1.50 per cup. What is the quantity demanded?
    _____ What is the quantity supplied? _____ This information implies that at
    $1.50 per cup there is (excess demand / excess supply / equilibrium in the market)
    _____.

D. Suppose that a price ceiling is imposed at $3.50 per cup. What is the quantity demanded?
    _____ What is the quantity supplied? _____ This information implies that at
    $3.50 per cup there is (excess demand / excess supply / equilibrium in the market)
    _____.

2. Working with supply and demand shifts

Suppose that the market for ice cream cones in St. Cloud, Minnesota, is represented by the demand
and supply curves below:

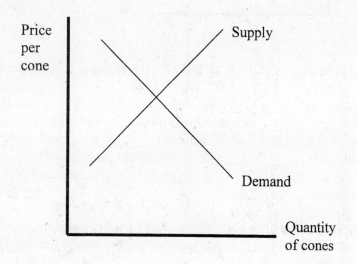

A. Label the equilibrium price and equilibrium quantity on the graph above.
B. A heat wave will (increase/decrease) _____ the demand for ice cream cones.
    Draw this on the graph above.
C. As a result of part (A), the equilibrium price will (rise/fall) _____ and the
    equilibrium quantity will (rise/fall) _____. Label the new equilibrium price and
    new equilibrium quantity on your graph.
D. Suppose that the heat wave also encourages new sellers to offer ice cream cones. This
    will (increase/decrease) _____ the (demand/supply) _____. Draw this on
    the graph above.
E. Compared to the original equilibrium, the action you analyzed in part (D) will cause the
    equilibrium price to (rise/fall/either rise or fall depending on the size of the change)
    _____ and the equilibrium quantity to (rise/fall/either rise or fall depending on the
    size of the change) _____.

3. **Understanding why equilibrium prices and quantities change.** Consider the graph below:

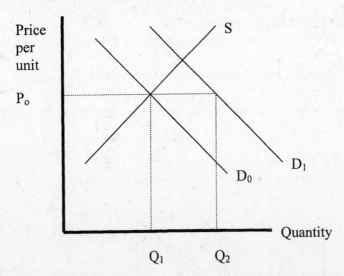

A. When the demand curve shifts from D_0 to D_1 then there is (excess demand/excess supply) _____ at P_0.
B. There (are/are not) _____ buyers willing to pay higher prices than P_0. There (are/are not) _____ sellers willing to sell the good at prices higher than P_0.
C. An increase in price above P_0 (will/will not) _____ increase the quantity supplied and (will/will not) _____ reduce the quantity demanded.
D. The market price (will/will not) _____ rise until the quantity demanded equals the quantity supplied.

4. **(Appendix problem) Working with the algebra of supply and demand**
Suppose that hypothetical demand and supply curves for espresso in Minneapolis/St. Paul are given by the following equations:

$$\text{Demand:} \quad P = 4 - \frac{1}{6}Q \quad ; \qquad \text{Supply:} \quad P = \frac{1}{6}Q$$

A. Solve for the equilibrium price and equilibrium quantity in this market:

B. Compare your answers in part (A) to your answers in question 1, part (B) above. Are they the same? _____. Explain why or why not _____
_____
_____

IV. Becoming an Economic Naturalist: Case Study

A story in the March 15, 2005 issue of the *Minneapolis Star-Tribune* reported that

- the price of coffee beans more than tripled between 2001 and 2005. The quantity of coffee purchased over this period
- "Americans are drinking more coffee than they have in a decade;"

Explain how these two facts can both be true using supply and demand analysis. In particular, consider whether the either the demand for coffee changed or the supply of coffee changed or both; and take into account the size of the changes in supply and/or demand in your analysis.

Answer:

V. Self-Test Solutions

Key Terms

1. i	6. w	11. k	16. h	21. e	26. d
2. t	7. c	12. u	17. p	22. j	27. x
3. f	8. y	13. o	18. m	23. bb	28. aa
4. l	9. a.	14. v	19. g	24. q	
5. n	10. b	15. s	20. r	25. z	

Multiple-Choice Questions

1. D	6. D	11. B	16. B
2. C	7. B	12. E	17. D
3. B	8. C	13. D	18. E
4. C	9. A	14. C	19. B
5. A	10. D	15. B	20. A

Short Answer Problems

1. A and B:

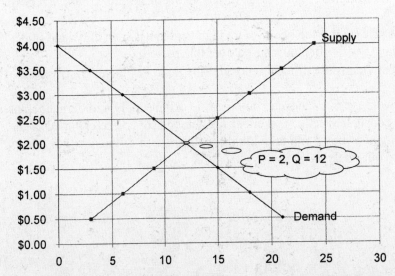

C. quantity demanded = 15, quantity supplied = 9; there is excess demand.
D. quantity demanded and quantity supplied both are 12. There is equilibrium in this market because the price ceiling is placed above the equilibrium price.

2. Graph for all sections:

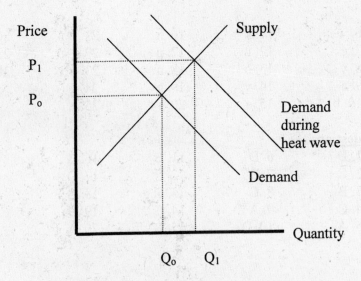

B. increase. See graph above for demand shift.
C. Rise, rise. In the graph, equilibrium price rises from P_0 to P_1 and equilibrium quantity rises from Q_0 to Q_1.
D. Increase, supply. The supply curve will shift to the right (not drawn on graph above.)

E. Either rise or fall depending on the size of the change, rise. Since both supply and demand are shifting to the right the equilibrium quantity will definitely rise. However, depending on the size of the shifts in demand and supply the equilibrium price could rise, fall or stay the same relative to the original market equilibrium.

3. A. excess demand

B. are, are.

C. will, will

D. will. This problem illustrates the way that markets respond to shifts in demand and supply: excess demand or excess supply is created and prices either rise or fall to establish a new equilibrium.

4. A. In equilibrium the price to the buyer and to the seller must be the same. Thus,

$$4 - (1/6)\, Q = (1/6)Q$$

This implies

$$4 = (1/3)\, Q$$

And hence

$$Q = 12$$

The equilibrium price is found by substituting $Q = 12$ into either the demand or supply curve:

$$\text{Demand: } P = 4 - (1/6)(12) = 4 - 2 = 2$$
$$\text{Supply: } P = (1/6)(12) = 2$$

B. The answers are the same. This is because the equations used in this problem generate the same supply and demand curves as does the table in question 1.

Chapter 4

Macroeconomics: The Bird's-Eye

View of the Economy

I. Pretest: What Do You Really Know?

Circle the letter that corresponds to the best answer. (Answers appear immediately after the final question).

1. Macroeconomic policies are government policies designed to affect
   A. the legal system of the whole country.
   B. the performance of the economy as a whole.
   C. particular sectors of the economy.
   D. the environmental impact of all industries.
   E. the economic activity of the government.

2. Average labor productivity equals
   A. average production per year.
   B. total output.
   C. output per person.
   D. output per employed worker.
   E. production per person.

3. The value of output was $400 billion in Northland and $500 billion in Southland. The population of Northland was 80 million and the population of Southland was 90 million. There were 40 million employed workers in Northland and 80 million employed workers in Southland. Average labor productivity was higher in _____ and the standard of living was _____.

A. Northland; the same in both countries
B. Northland; higher in Southland
C. Southland; higher in Northland
D. Southland; higher in Southland
E. Southland; the same in both countries

4. When jobs are hard to find, profits are low, few wage increases are given, and many companies go out of business, the economy is most likely in a(n)
    A. expansion.
    B. boom.
    C. recession.
    D. surplus.
    E. shortage.

5. The unemployment rate is the
    A. number of workers unemployed.
    B. number of workers in the labor force.
    C. number of workers minus those without a job.
    D. percentage of the labor force that is out of work.
    E. percentage of the population that is out of work.

6. The rate at which prices in general are increasing is called
    A. the inflation rate.
    B. the unemployment rate.
    C. average labor productivity.
    D. the standard of living.
    E. the trade balance.

7. A trade deficit occurs when
    A. government spending exceeds government revenue.
    B. government revenue exceeds government spending.
    C. exports equal imports.
    D. exports exceed imports.
    E. exports are less than imports.

8. Monetary policy refers to
    A. decisions to determine the government's budget.
    B. policy directed toward increasing exports and reducing imports.
    C. the determination of the nation's money supply.
    D. policies to reduce the power of unions and monopolies.
    E. government policies aimed at changing the underlying structure or institutions of the economy.

9. _____ analysis addresses the question of whether a policy should be used, while _____ analysis addresses the economic consequences of a particular policy.
   A. Normative; positive
   B. Positive; normative
   C. Structural; monetary
   D. Monetary; fiscal
   E. Fiscal; monetary

10. Which of the following statements is an example of positive analysis?
   A. If the Federal Reserve increases the money supply, interest rates decrease.
   B. Large budget deficits should be avoided.
   C. Higher taxes are needed to support education.
   D. A tax cut that benefits low-income households is acceptable.
   E. The Federal Reserve should increase interest rates to slow down the economy.

Solutions and Feedback to Pretest
For each question you incorrectly answered, we strongly recommend taking the time to review the appropriate material before continuing. In the table below is listed for each question the pertinent Learning Objective from the following Key Point Review.

Correct Answer	Learning Objective
1. B	7
2. D	2
3. B	1
4. C	3
5. D	4
6. A	5
7. E	6
8. C	7
9. A	8
10. A	8

II. Key Point Review
The Forest
This chapter focuses on introducing the subject matter of macroeconomics and the issues that are central to macroeconomics, as well as the basic tools of macroeconomics.
Macroeconomics is the study of the performance of national economies and the policies governments use to try to improve that performance. The central questions you need to be able to answer are as follows:
   • What are the central issues of macroeconomics?
   • What are the three types of macroeconomic policy?
   • How does normative macroeconomic analysis differ from positive macroeconomic analysis?
   • What are the strengths and weaknesses of aggregation?

The Trees

Learning Objective 1: Explain economic growth and standard of living

Among the issues macroeconomists study are the sources of long-run economic growth and living standards. By standard of living, economists mean the degree to which people have access to goods and services that make their lives easier, healthier, safer, and more enjoyable. People with a higher standard of living have more goods to consume, but even the wealthiest people are subject to the principle of scarcity. Standard of living is inextricably linked to economic growth because the more we produce, the more we can consume. The high standard of living that contemporary Americans enjoy, for example, is the result of several centuries of economic growth in the U.S. Economic growth is a process of increasing the quantity and quality of goods and services that an economy can produce. Two questions economists try to answer are, What causes economic growth to fluctuate over time? and Why does economic growth and the standard of living vary among countries?

Learning Objective 2: Calculate output per person and average labor productivity

One factor related to economic growth is the growth in population and hence the number of workers available to produce the goods and services. Increases in population allow the total output of goods and services to increase, but because the goods and services must be shared among a larger population it does not necessarily equate with a higher standard of living. Because of changes in population over time, output per person (output divided by the number of people in an economy) is a much better indicator of living standards than total output. Macroeconomists also study the relationship between average labor productivity, or output divided by the number of employed workers, and living standards. Because of the connection between production and consumption, average labor productivity is closely related to output per person and living standards.

Learning Objective 3: Define recession, depression, expansion and boom

Economies do not, however, always grow steadily; they go through periods of strength and weakness. Periods of rapid economic growth are called expansions, and when an expansion is particularly strong it is called a boom. Slowdowns in economic growth are called recessions, and particularly severe slowdowns (for example, during the 1930s) are referred to as depressions.

Note: There is no consensus among economists as to specific rates of economic growth that demarcate when an expansion should be called a boom, nor when a recession should be considered a depression. The difference between expansion and boom, and recession and depression is more qualitative than quantitative.

Learning Objective 4: Define unemployment rate and explain its relationship to recessions and expansions.

These fluctuations in the rate of economic growth cause changes in the unemployment rate, the fraction of people who would like to be employed but can't find work. Unemployment tends to rise during recessions and fall during expansions. But even during the "good times" some people are unemployed. Questions that macroeconomists try to answer include: Why does unemployment rise during periods of recession; why are there always unemployed people, even when the economy is booming; and why do unemployment rates sometimes differ markedly from country to country.

Learning Objective 5: Define inflation and explain why macroeconomists study inflation.

Inflation is another important macroeconomic variable. Inflation is the rate at which prices in general are increasing over time. Inflation imposes a variety of costs on the economy and, as such, macroeconomists are interested in understanding its causes. Two questions that macroeconomists grapple with are why the rate of inflation varies from one period to another, and what causes the rate of inflation to differ markedly from country to country. Inflation and unemployment are often linked in policy discussions because it is often argued that unemployment can only be reduced if the inflation rate is allowed to rise. Macroeconomists have studied this issue to provide a better understanding of this policy debate.

Note: Inflation does **not** imply that all prices are rising. The prices of some goods will be rising, but the prices of other goods may be falling, while the prices of a third group of goods may be constant. You can think of inflation as essentially an increase in the average price of goods and services. The average may rise even though all prices are not rising.

Learning Objective 6: Define trade deficit and trade surplus.

While macroeconomics focuses on national economies, macroeconomists recognize that national economies do not exist in isolation. They are increasingly interdependent. The international flows of goods and services are both an economic issue and a political issue. Trade imbalances, which occur when the quantity of goods and services that a country sells abroad (its exports) differ significantly from the quantity of goods and services its citizens buy from abroad (its imports), often cause economic and political problems. When a nation exports more than it imports, it runs a trade surplus, while the reverse results in a trade deficit. Macroeconomists try to determine the causes of trade surpluses and deficits, and determine whether they are harmful or helpful.

Note: Because one country's exports are another country's imports, a trade surplus for one country implies a trade deficit for at least one other country.

Learning Objective 7: Identify the three types of macroeconomics policy: monetary, fiscal and structural policy.
In addition to analyzing the factors that affect the performance of the national economies, macroeconomists also study macroeconomic policy. Understanding the effects of various policies and helping government officials develop better policies are important objectives of macroeconomics. There are three major types of macroeconomic policy: monetary policy, fiscal policy, and structural policy. Monetary policy refers to the determination of the nation's money supply. In virtually all countries monetary policy is controlled by the central bank. Fiscal policy refers to decisions that determine the government's budget, including the amount and composition of government expenditures and government revenues. When government expenditures are greater than government revenues, the government runs a deficit, and when government revenues are greater than government expenditures, the government runs a surplus. The term structural policy includes government policies aimed at changing the underlying structure, or institutions, of the nation's economy.

Learning Objective 8: Explain the importance of normative and positive analyses.
Macroeconomists are often called upon to analyze the effects of a proposed policy. An objective analysis aimed at determining only the economic consequences of a particular policy is called positive analysis, while a normative analysis includes recommendations on whether a particular policy should be implemented. Positive analysis is objective and scientific, but normative analysis involves the values of the person or organization doing the analysis. Economists generally agree on issues related to positive analysis, but often disagree on normative analysis.

Learning Objective 9: Define aggregation and identify the strengths and weaknesses of aggregation.
Although macroeconomics take a "bird's eye" view of the economy and microeconomics work at the ground level, the basic tools of analysis are much the same. They apply the same core principles in their efforts to understand and predict economic behavior. Because the national economy is much bigger, however, macroeconomists use aggregation to link individual behavior to national economic performance. **Aggregation** is the adding up of individual economic variables to obtain economy-wide totals.

Note: While macroeconomists and microeconomists employ the same basic tools of analysis, it does not always follow that the conclusions of macroeconomic analyses are the same as those of microeconomic analyses. An analogy: if an individual stands up during a football game, s/he can see better. If all spectators stand up, not everyone can see better.

III. Self-Test

Key Terms
Match the term in the right-hand column with the appropriate definition in the left-hand column by placing the letter of the term in the blank in front of its' definition. (Answers are given at the end of the chapter.)

1. ____ Decisions that determine the government's budget, including the amount and composition of government expenditures and government revenues

a. aggregation

2. ____ Output per employed worker

b. average labor productivity

3. ____ Addresses the consequences of a particular event or policy, not whether those consequences are desirable

c. fiscal policy

4. ____ The adding up of individual economic variables to obtain economy-wide totals

d. macroeconomic policies

5. ____ Determines the nation's money supply

e. monetary policy

6. ____ Addresses the question of whether a policy should be used; involves the values of the person doing the analysis

f. normative analysis

7. ____ Government actions designed to affect the performance of the economy as a whole

g. positive analysis

8. ____ Government policies aimed at changing the underlying structure, or institutions, of the nation's economy

h. structural policy

Multiple-Choice Questions
Circle the letter that corresponds to the best answer. (Answers are given at the end of the chapter.)

1. Economic growth is defined as a process of
   A. steady increase in the price of goods and services produced in the economy.
   B. steady increase in the quantity and quality of goods and services the economy can produce.
   C. constant increase in the quantity and quality of goods and services the economy can produce.
   D. constant increase in the price and quality of goods and services the economy can produce.
   E. constant increase in the number of jobs needed to produce the goods and service in the economy.

2. Our standard of living is directly tied to economic growth because
   A. everyone in society shares equally in the fruits of economic growth.
   B. the two terms are synonymous.
   C. in most cases economic growth brings an improvement in the average person's standard of living.

62

   D. the government can only improve people's standard of living if the economy is
       growing.
   E. a higher standard of living causes an increase in economic growth.

3. Microland has a population of 50 people and 40 of them worked last year with a total
   output of $200,000. The average labor productivity of Microland equaled
   A. $200,000.
   B. $200.
   C. $4,000.
   D. $40,000.
   E. $5,000.

4. During the 1930s, economies around the world were in a(n)
   A. recession.
   B. depression.
   C. expansion.
   D. boom.
   E. aggregation.

5. The unemployment rate is the
   A. percentage of people who would like to be employed but can't find work.
   B. number of people who would like to be employed but can't find work.
   C. fraction of people who are not working.
   D. number of people who are not working.
   E. the number of unemployed people.

6. The unemployment rate increases during
   A. expansions and booms.
   B. expansions and recessions.
   C. booms and recessions.
   D. recessions and depressions.
   E. booms and depressions.

7. The inflation rate
   A. was higher in the 1990s than during the 1970s.
   B. increases the standard of living for people on fixed incomes.
   C. is the rate at which prices in general are increasing over time.
   D. is roughly equal in most countries.
   E. rises during recessions along with the unemployment rate.

8. If a country imports more than it exports, it has a
   A. trade balance.
   B. trade deficit.
   C. trade surplus.
   D. budget deficit.
   E. inflation.

9. Government policies that affect the performance of the economy as a whole are called
    A. positive analysis.
    B. normative analysis.
    C. aggregation.
    D. microeconomic policy.
    E. macroeconomic policy.

10. Monetary policy
    A. refers to decisions that determine the government's budget.
    B. is controlled by a government institution called the Congressional Budget Office.
    C. is aimed at changing the underlying structure, or institutions, of the nation's economy.
    D. refers to the determination of the nation's money supply.
    E. can result in a budget deficit or budget surplus.

11. The amount and composition of government expenditures and government revenues is determined by
    A. fiscal policy.
    B. monetary policy.
    C. structural policy.
    D. normative analysis.
    E. positive analysis.

12. When a government collects more in taxes than it spends, it runs a
    A. trade deficit.
    B. trade surplus.
    C. budget deficit.
    D. budget surplus.
    E. trade imbalance.

13. Supporters of structural policy argue that economic growth can be stimulated and living standards improved if
    A. the money supply is controlled by the central bank.
    B. the underlying structure, or institutions, of a nation's economy are changed.
    C. positive analysis is used to determine macroeconomic policy.
    D. normative analysis is used to determine macroeconomic policy.
    E. the federal budget is balanced.

14. Normative analysis differs from positive analysis in that
    A. normative analysis is limited to determining the consequences of a particular policy, while positive analysis includes recommendations on the desirability of the policy.
    B. positive analysis is limited to determining the consequences of a particular policy, while normative analysis includes recommendations on the desirability of the policy.

C. normative analysis is supposed to be objective and scientific, while positive analysis involves values of the person or organization doing the analysis.
D. economists typically agree on normative analysis, but often disagree on positive analysis.
E. liberal economists use positive analysis, while conservative economists use normative analysis.

15. When macroeconomists add together the purchases of houses, cars, food, clothing, entertainment, and other goods and services by households in an economy, they are using
A. normative analysis.
B. positive analysis.
C. aggregation.
D. macroeconomic policy.
E. fiscal policy.

16. The strength of aggregation is that it helps to reveal the "big picture," but its weakness is that it
A. adds together "apples and oranges."
B. involves the values of the person doing the analysis.
C. gives excessive importance to the details.
D. adds together data on different individuals.
E. may obscure important details.

17. Microland has a population of 50 people and 40 of them worked last year with a total output of $200,000. The output per person of Microland equaled
A. $200,000.
B. $200.
C. $4,000.
D. $40,000.
E. $5,000.

18. If Macroland sells more goods to foreign buyers than it purchases from them, it will have a
A. trade balance.
B. trade deficit.
C. trade surplus.
D. budget deficit.
E. budget surplus.

19. When a government's expenditures are greater than its revenues, it has a
A. budget deficit.
B. budget surplus.
C. trade deficit.
D. trade surplus.
E. trade imbalance.

20. In debating a government program for agriculture, Senator Agus from Kansas stated that the spending should be increased because many farmers have suffered crop losses in the last year. Senator Scrimp from New York replied that his analysis indicates that an increase in spending for the program will increase the budget deficit. Senator Agus' statement is based on
   A. aggregation, while Senator Scrimp's statement is based on disaggregation.
   B. disaggregation, while Senator Scrimp's statement is based on aggregation.
   C. positive analysis, while Senator Scrimp's statement is based on normative analysis.
   D. normative analysis, while Senator Scrimp's statement is based on positive analysis.
   E. positive analysis, as is the statement of Senator Scrimp.

Short Answer Problems
(Answers and solutions are given at the end of the chapter.)

1. Economic Growth and Standard of Living
Use the data in the following table on output, employment, and population in the United States and Canada during 2003 to answer the questions below.

Economic variable	United States	Canada
Output (GDP)	$10,948,546,920,448	$856,522,817,536
Population	290,809,984	31,630,000
Employed persons	140,178,802	29,178,765

A. Output per person in the United States during 2003 equaled _____ and in Canada equaled _____ .
B. The average labor productivity in the United States during 2003 equaled _____ and in Canada equaled _____ .
C. Based on the data in the table above, which country had the highest standard of living during 2003? _____

2. Normative and Positive Analysis
In the blank following each statement, write an N if the statement is based on normative analysis, or a P if the statement is based on positive analysis.

A. The U.S. Energy Department stated that "increased production of oil in April and May 2000 will result in lower gasoline prices in the summer of 2000." _____
B. Alan Greenspan, Chairman of the Board of Governors of the Federal Reserve System, stated in March 2000 that "the stock prices should rise no faster than household income." _____
C. In April 2000, William Sullivan, chief economist at Morgan Stanley Dean Witter, stated, "the retrenchment in equity [stock] prices will undoubtedly affect the economy later in the year." _____
D. On April 4, 2000 in an article published in *The Wall Street Journal*, Brian Blackstone and Jonathan Nicholson wrote, "The National Association of Purchasing Management

monthly index, a broad measure of the health of the manufacturing sector, slipped a bit to 55.8 in March from 56.9 in February. That corresponds to a 4.8% annualized growth in gross domestic product." _____

E. In an article published on the Dismal Science web site, entitled, "Krugman vs. Republican Gas Tax Relief," Michael Boldin analyzed a tax policy proposed by the Republican Party congressional leaders. He states, "the Republican plan to immediately repeal the 4.3 cents per gallon federal surcharge that was added in 1993 and suspend the larger 18.4 cents per gallon federal tax if gasoline hits $2 per gallon is both untimely and unwise as a basic policy. For one it would hurt the highway fund that is a direct beneficiary of the tax. Worse yet, it would encourage gas consumption at a time when OPEC is keeping to a tight supply schedule and domestic inventories are dwindling." _____

F. In response to the question, what is the best Fed monetary policy course at this time (March 2000), Kevin Hassett, Resident Scholar at the American Enterprise Institute, responded, "The best Fed move right now would be no move, but it is a close call." _____

G. In an article published on the Dismal Science web site, entitled, "The New Economy's Dark Side," Mark Zandi states, "Families in the top 20% of the wealth distribution own well over 80% of the nation's wealth, while the top 5% of families own 60% of the wealth." _____

3. Aggregation
Use the data in the following table on production in Macrolandia to answer the questions below.

Product	Price per unit	Units produced in 2005	Units produced in 2006
Clothing	$5	1000	600
Food	$2	5000	4000
Houses	$100	25	80

A. The total value of Macrolandia's output in 2005 equaled _____ and in 2006 equaled _____

B. Based on your answer to Question 3A, in 2006 Macrolandia produced (more/less) _____ output than in 2005.

C. The change in output from 2005 to 2006 would suggest the Macrolandia economy experienced _____ and, thus, one could deduce that the Macrolandian standard of living had (improved/worsened) _____ .

D. The workers of Macrolandia are equally divided into three groups who each specialize in producing a single good (i.e., clothing, food, or houses). Calculate the output produced by each group in 2005 and 2006. The clothing workers produced _____ output in 2005 and _____ in 2006, the food workers produced _____ output in 2005 and _____ in 2006, and the housing workers produced _____ output in 2005 and _____ in 2006.

E. Thus, the output and standard of living of the (clothing/food/housing) _____ workers of Macrolandia's increased, while the output and standard of living of (clothing/food/housing) _____ and (clothing/food/housing) _____ workers of Macrolandia's decreased .

F. Thus, the aggregation in Question 3A obscures the fact that a majority of Macrolandia workers output and standard of living (decreased/increased) _____ in 2006 compared to 2005.

IV. Economic Naturalist Application
{No Economic Naturalist examples in text}

V. Self-Test Solutions

Key Terms
1. c
2. b
3. g
4. a
5. e
6. f
7. d
8. h

Multiple-Choice Questions
1. B
2. C
3. E Average labor productivity = output/number of employed workers, (i.e., $200,000/40 = $5,000)
4. B
5. A
6. D
7. C
8. B
9. E
10. D
11. A
12. D
13. B
14. B
15. C
16. E
17. C Output per person = output/number of people in the economy, (i.e., $200,000/50 = $4,000)
18. C
19. A

20. D Senator Agus' statement refers to the desirability of the policy, while Senator Shrimps' statement only refers to the effect of the policy on the government's budget.

Short Answer Problems

1.
A. Output per person = Output divided by population $37,648.46; $27,079.44
B. Average labor productivity = Output divided by the number of employed persons $78,104.16; $54,979.32
C. The United States has the highest standard of living because both output per person and average labor productivity are higher than in Canada.

2.
A. P because the analysis is a prediction based on an application of the supply and demand model.
B. N because the analysis is based on his values (key word is "should")
C. P because the analysis is a statement of the effect of the change in stock market prices on the economy
D. P because it only indicates the statistical analysis
E. N because it is a statement of the desirability of the policy based on his values
F. N because it is a statement of the desirability of the policy based on his values
G. P because it only indicates the statistical findings of the economic analysis

3.
A. (1,000 x$5) + (5,000 x $2) + (25 x $100) = $17,500; (600 x $5) + (4,000 x $2) + (80 x $100) = $19,000
B. more
C. economic growth; improved
D. 1,000 x $5 = $5,000; 600 x $5 = $3,000; 5,000 x $2 = $10,000; 4,000 x $2 = $8,000; 25 x $100 = $2,500; 80 x $100 = $8,000
E. housing; clothing; food
F. decreased

Chapter 5

Measuring Economic Activity:
GDP and Unemployment

I. Pretest: What Do You Really Know?
Circle the letter that corresponds to the best answer. (Answers appear immediately after the final question).

1. Gross domestic product (GDP) equals the _____ of final _____ produced within a country during a given period of time.
   A. market value; goods
   B. market value; services
   C. market value; goods and services
   D. quantity; goods
   E. quantity; goods and services

2. Three equivalent ways to measure GDP are total _____, total _____, and total _____.
   A. profits; production; saving.
   B. expenditure; income; profits
   C. investment; consumption; saving
   D. production; income; expenditure
   E. revenue; profits; production

3. If Bountiful Orchard grows $200,000 worth of peaches, sells $50,000 worth of peaches to consumers and uses to rest to make jam that is sold to consumers for $200,000, Bountiful Orchard's contribution to GDP is:
   A. $50,000.
   B. $100,000.
   C. $200,000.
   D. $250,000.
   E. $450,000.

4. Goods and services that are used up in the production of other goods and services are called _____ goods and services.
   A. intermediate
   B. final
   C. value added
   D. nominal

E. real

5. Capital goods are treated as _____ goods and, therefore, _____ GDP.
    A. final; included in
    B. final; excluded from
    C. intermediate; included in
    D. intermediate; excluded from
    E. non-market; excluded from

6. Suppose a jar of DeLux popcorn, which is ultimately sold to a customer at Friendly
    Groceries, is produced by the following production process:

Name of Company	Revenues	Cost of Purchased Inputs
Fulton Family Farm	$1.00	0
DeLux Popcorn Co.	$2.50	$1.00
Friendly Groceries	$5.00	$2.50

    What is the value added of Friendly Groceries?
    A. $1.00
    B. $2.50
    C. $5.00
    D. $7.50
    E. $8.50

7. Given the following data for an economy, compute the value of GDP.

Consumption expenditures	1,500
Imports	500
Government purchases of goods and services	800
Construction of new homes and apartments	600
Sales of existing homes and apartments	500
Exports	400
Government payments to retirees	300
Household purchases of durable goods	400
Beginning-of-year inventory	600
End-of-year inventory	700
Business fixed investment	400

    A. 2,800
    B. 2,900
    C. 3,300
    D. 3,400
    E. 6,700

8. Consumption spending includes spending on:
    A. durables, nondurables, and services.
    B. stocks, bonds, and other financial instruments.
    C. capital goods, residential housing, and changes in inventories.
    D. goods and services by federal, state, and local governments.
    E. goods and services sold abroad minus goods and services produced abroad.

9. Which of the following would increase the investment component of U.S. GDP?
    A. You purchase a vacation at Disney World in Florida.
    B. You purchase shares of Disney stock.
    C. Disney World purchases tires for the monorail from a firm in Ohio.
    D. A French man purchases a vacation at a Disney theme park in France.
    E. A French child purchases mouse ears made in California at a Disney theme park in France.

10. Which of the following would increase the government purchases component of U.S. GDP?
    A. The U.S. federal government pays $3 billion in pensions to government workers.
    B. The U.S. federal government pays $3 billion in interest on the national debt.
    C. The U.S. federal government pays $3 billion in salaries to soldiers in the military.
    D. The U.S. federal government pays $3 billion in interest to foreign holders of U.S.
       government bonds.
    E. The U.S. federal government pays $3 billion to social security recipients.

Solutions and Feedback to Pretest
For each question you incorrectly answered, we strongly recommend taking the time to review
the appropriate material before continuing. In the table below are listed for each question the
pertinent Learning Objective from the following Key Point Review.

Correct Answer	Learning Objective
1. C	1
2. D	2
3. D	2
4. A	2
5. A	2
6. B	2
7. B	2
8. A	2
9. C	2
10. C	2

II. Key Point Review
The Forest

This chapter focuses on how economists measure two basic macroeconomic variables, gross
domestic product (GDP) and the rate of unemployment. It also discusses how the measures are
used, and provides some insight into the debates on the accuracy of the measurements. The
central questions you need to be able to answer are
*   How do economists define and measure an economy's output?
*   What is the relationship between real GDP and economic well-being?
*   How do economists define and measure the unemployment rate?
*   What are the costs of unemployment and criticisms of the official unemployment rate?

The Trees

The **gross domestic product (GDP)** is the market value of the final goods and services produced in a country during a given period. To calculate GDP, economists aggregate, or add up, the market values of the different goods and services the economy produces. Economists, however, do not include the value of all goods and services in the calculation. Only the market values of **final goods and services**, the goods or services consumed by the ultimate user, are counted as part of GDP. The market values of **intermediate goods and services**, those used up in the production of final goods and services, are not included when calculating GDP because they are already included in the market value of the final goods and services.

> **Note**: The distinction between final and intermediate goods is difficult to determine for some goods, e.g., capital goods. **Capital goods** are long-lived goods that are used to produce other goods and, thus, are not exactly final goods but neither are they intermediate goods. To overcome this difficulty, economists have conventionally classified newly-produced capital goods as final goods for the purposes of calculating GDP.

Because GDP is a measure of domestic production, only goods and services produced within a nation's borders are included in its calculation. Similarly, because GDP is measured for a given period, only goods and services produced during the current year (or the portion of the value produced during the current year) are counted as part of the current year's GDP.

Learning Objective 2: Calculate GDP using the value-added, expenditure, or income methods

There are three methods for measuring GDP: (1) by aggregating the value added by each firm in the production process, (2) by adding up the total amount spent on final goods and services and subtracting the amount spent on imported goods and services, and (3) by adding labor income and capital income. The **value added** by any firm equals the market value of its product or service minus the cost of inputs purchased from other firms. The value added by each firm represents the portion of the value of the final good or service that the firm creates in its stage of the production process. Summing the value added by all firms in the economy yields the total value of final goods and service, or GDP. An advantage of the value-added method is that it eliminates the problem of dividing the value of a final good or service between two periods.

To calculate GDP using the expenditure method, economic statisticians add together consumption expenditures, investment, government purchases, and net exports. **Consumption expenditure (C)** is spending by households on goods and services. Consumption spending can be divided into three subcategories; (1) consumer durables, long-lived consumer goods such as cars and furniture; (2) consumer nondurables, shorter-lived goods like food and clothing; and (3) services, including everything from haircuts to taxi rides to legal, financial and educational services. **Investment (I)** is spending by firms on final goods and services, primarily capital goods and housing. Investment is also divided into three subcategories: (1) business fixed investment, the purchase of new capital goods such as machinery, factories and office buildings;

(2) residential investment, the construction of new homes and apartment buildings; and (3) inventory investment, the addition of unsold goods to company inventories. **Government purchases (G)** are purchases of final goods by federal, state, and local governments. Government purchases do not include transfer payments (payments made by the government in which no current goods or services are received), or interest paid on the government debt. In the foreign sector, **net exports (NX)** equal exports minus imports. Exports are domestically produced final goods and services that are sold abroad. Imports are purchases by domestic buyers of goods and services that were produced abroad. Using symbols for each of the components, the algebraic equation for calculating GDP (Y) is written: $Y = C + I + G + NX$.

Hint: When calculating GDP using the expenditure method, be careful to not include in the calculation an expenditure component and one or more of the subcategories. For example, if a dollar value is give for consumption expenditures and for consumer durables, only include the value of the consumption expenditures in your calculation. On the other hand, if no dollar value is given for consumption expenditures, then add together the value of consumer durables, consumer nondurables and services to calculate the consumption expenditures component of GDP.

The third method of calculating GDP is to sum total labor and capital incomes. Labor income, before taxes includes wages, salaries, and the income of the self-employed. It represents about 75% of GDP. Capital income is made up of payments to the owners of physical capital (factories, machines, and office buildings) and intangible capital (such as copyrights and patents), and it represents about 25% of GDP. The components of capital income include such items as pre-tax profits earned by business owners, the rents paid to owners of land or buildings, interest received by bondholders, and the royalties received by holders of copyrights or patents.

Learning Objective 3: Define nominal GDP and real GDP

As a measure of the total production of an economy during a given period, GDP is useful in comparisons of economic activity in different places, but cannot be used to make comparisons over time. To make comparisons of production in an economy over time, GDP must be adjusted for inflation. To adjust for inflation economists differentiate between nominal GDP and real GDP. **Nominal GDP** measures the current dollar value of production, in which the quantities of final goods and services produced are valued at current-year prices. **Real GDP** measures the actual physical volume of production, in which the quantities of final goods and services produced are valued at the prices in a base year.

Hint: Nominal GDP for different years is essentially calculated in two different units of measures (e.g., 2002 prices for 2002 GDP and 2003 prices for 2003 GDP). Because they are two different units of measure they are not comparable. Deriving conclusions about the state of the economy by comparing nominal GDP for two different periods is the equivalent of weighing yourself on two different scales to determine whether you had lost or gained weight.

Learning Objective 4: Explain the relationship between GDP and economic well-being
While economists and policymakers often assume that a higher GDP is better, real GDP is not the same as economic well-being. With the major exception of government-produced goods and services, real GDP captures only those goods and services that are priced and sold in markets. There are many factors that contribute to people's economic well-being that are not priced and sold in markets. Thus, at best, it is an imperfect measure of economic well-being. Some important factors that are excluded from real GDP are leisure time; environmental quality; resource depletion; nonmarket activities such as volunteer services, home-grown foods, homemaker services, and underground economic activities from informal babysitting to organized crime; "quality of life" issues such as crime, traffic congestion, civic organization, and open space; and income inequality. Nevertheless, real GDP per person does tend to be positively associated with many things people value, including a high material standard of living, better health and life expectancies, and better education.

Note: In evaluating the effects of a proposed economic policy, considering only the likely effects on GDP is not sufficient. The correct way is to apply the cost-benefit principle.

Learning Objective 5: Explain how the Bureau of Labor Statistics calculates unemployment
A second macroeconomic measure that receives a great deal of attention from economists and policymakers, as well as the general public, is the rate of unemployment. In the United States, the Bureau of Labor Statistics (BLS) conducts a monthly survey of approximately 60,000 households in order to calculate the official unemployment rate. Each person in those households who is 16 years or older is placed in one of three categories: employed, unemployed, or out of the labor force. A person is employed if he or she worked full time or part time during the week preceding the survey, or is on vacation or sick leave from a regular job. A person is unemployed if he or she did not work during the week preceding the survey, but made some effort to find work during the previous four weeks. All other persons are considered out of the labor force. In assessing the impact of unemployment on jobless people, economists estimate how long individual workers have been without work. The BLS asks respondents how long they have been continuously unemployed to determine the **unemployment spell**. The length of an unemployment spell is called its **duration**. The duration of unemployment rises during recessions and falls during expansions.

Learning Objective 6: Calculate the unemployment rate and participation rate
To calculate the unemployment rate, the BLS first adds the total number of employed and unemployed people in the economy to determine the size of the **labor force**. The **unemployment rate** is then calculated as the number of unemployed people divided by the labor force and expressed as a percentage. Another useful statistic calculated by the BLS is the **participation rate**, or the percentage of working-age population that is in the labor force.

Learning Objective 7: Discuss the costs of unemployment
Unemployment imposes economic, psychological, and social costs on a nation. The main
economic cost, borne by both the unemployed individuals and society, is the output that is lost
because the work force is not fully utilized. The psychological costs of unemployment are felt
primarily by the unemployed workers and their families, and include a loss of self-esteem,
feelings of loss of control over one's life, depression, and suicidal behavior. The social costs,
borne by both the unemployed individuals and society, include increases in crime, domestic
violence, drug abuse, and other social problems.

Learning Objective 8: Discuss the criticisms of the official unemployment rate
There are some criticisms of the techniques used by the BLS to measure the rate of unemployment.
One criticism is that the official unemployment rate understates the true extent of unemployment
because of so-called discouraged workers and involuntary part-time workers. **Discouraged workers**
are people who say they would like to have a job, but have not made an effort to find one in the past
four weeks. Some observers have suggested that treating discouraged workers as unemployed would
provide a more accurate picture of the labor market. Involuntary part-time workers are people who
say they would like to work full time but are able to find only part-time work.

III. Self-Test

Key Terms
**Match the term in the right-hand column with the appropriate definition in the left-hand
column by placing the letter of the term in the blank in front of its' definition. (Answers
are given at the end of the chapter.)**

1. ____Purchases by federal, state, and local governments of final goods and services — a. capital good

2. ____ The percentage of the working-age population in the labor force — b. consumption expenditure

3. ____ Exports minus imports — c. discouraged workers

4. ____ A measure of GDP in which the quantities produced are valued at the prices in a base year rather than at current prices — d. duration (of an unemployment spell)

5. ____ The length of an unemployment spell — e. final goods and services

6. ____ Goods or services consumed by the ultimate user — f. government purchases

7. ____ The total number of employed and unemployed people in the economy — g. gross domestic product (GDP)

8. ____ The market value of any firm's product or service minus the cost of inputs purchased from other firms — h. intermediate goods and services

9. ____ People who say they would like to have a job but have not made an effort to find one in the past 4 weeks — i. investment

10.____ A measure of GDP in which the quantities produced are valued at current-year prices — j. labor force

11.____ Spending by firms on final goods and services, primarily capital goods and housing — k. net exports

12.____ A period during which an individual is continuously unemployed — l. nominal GDP

13.____ Spending by households on goods and services, such as   m. participation rate
food, clothing, and entertainment
14.____ A long-lived good, which is itself produced and used to   n. real GDP
produce other goods and services
15.____The market value of the final goods and services produced   o. unemployment rate
in a country during a given period
16.____ The number of unemployed people divided by the labor   p. unemployment spell
force
17.____ Goods or services used up in the production of final goods   q. value added
and services and therefore not counted as part of GDP

Multiple-Choice Questions
Circle the letter that corresponds to the best answer. (Answers are given at the end of the chapter.)

1. Which of the following would be included in the calculation of GDP for 2006?
    A. the price of a home built in 2001 and sold in 2006
    B. the price of 100 shares of Exxon stock purchased in 2006
    C. the price of a classic 1960 Thunderbird purchased in 2006
    D. the price of a new punch press built and purchased in 2006 to replace a worn out machine
    E. the price of a used bicycle purchased at a garage sale in 2006

2. Which of the following is an intermediate good and, therefore, would be excluded from the calculation of GDP?
    A. a new set of tires sold to a car owner
    B. a new set of tires purchased by Ford to install on a new Explorer
    C. 100 shares of stock in Microsoft
    D. a new home
    E. a pre-owned automobile

3. The value-added method eliminates the problem of
    A. differentiating between final and intermediate goods and services.
    B. inflation when comparing GDP over time.
    C. determining whether capital is a final good or intermediate good.
    D. dividing the value of a final good or service between two periods.
    E. aggregation.

4. Consumption expenditure is subdivided into three categories, including
    A. consumer durables, consumer nondurables, and new homes.
    B. consumer services, consumer durables and new homes.
    C. consumer durables, consumer nondurables, and services.
    D. exports, imports, and services.
    E. consumer durables, consumer nondurables, and net exports.

5. Which of the following is included when using the expenditure method to measure GDP?
   A. corporate profits
   B. gross private domestic investment
   C. capital income
   D. net interest on the government debt
   E. labor income

6. Which of the following is included when using the labor and capital income method to measure GDP?
   A. government purchases of goods and services
   B. net exports of goods and services
   C. household consumption expenditures
   D. gross private domestic investment
   E. business profits

7. If the value of imports is greater than the value of exports, then
   A. net exports are negative.
   B. net exports are positive.
   C. net exports are zero.
   D. net exports are not, under such circumstances, included in the calculation of GDP.
   E. net exports cannot be determined from the information provided.

8. To calculate nominal GDP, the quantities of goods and services are valued at prices in the
   _____ year, but to calculate real GDP they are valued at _____-year prices.
   A. current, base
   B. base; current
   C. current; current
   D. base; base
   E. current; last

9. Real GDP is GDP adjusted for
   A. changes in the quality of goods and services.
   B. value added during a previous year.
   C. inflation.
   D. imports.
   E. changes in the cost of intermediate goods and services.

10. One shortcoming of GDP as an indicator of economic well-being is that it fails to measure the
    A. growth in productivity.
    B. increase in the quantity of goods.
    C. nonmarket production.
    D. change in the price level.
    E. increase in the number of imported goods.

11. GDP would be a better measure of economic well-being if it included
    A. the costs of education.
    B. the total value of intermediate goods.
    C. the market value of final goods.
    D. the sales of corporate stock.
    E. leisure.

12. Despite some problems with equating GDP with economic well-being, real GDP per person
    does imply greater economic well-being because it tends to be positively associated with
    A. crime, pollution, and economic inequality.
    B. better education, health, and life expectancy.
    C. poverty, depletion of nonrenewable resources, and congestion.
    D. unemployment, availability of goods and services, and better education.
    E. the total quantity of goods and services available.

13. The official unemployment rate is calculated as
    A. the number of working-age people 16 years or older who are employed divided by the
       number of people in the labor force.
    B. all people 18 years of age or older who are employed, plus all those unemployed who are
       actively seeking work.
    C. the percentage of the working-age population 16 years or older who are not working but are
       actively seeking work.
    D. the number of people 16 years or older who are not employed and are actively seeking work
       divided by the number of people in the labor force.
    E. all people 16 years of age or older who are employed, plus all those unemployed who are
       actively seeking work, divided by the number of people in the labor force.

14. In the monthly survey conducted by the Bureau of Labor Statistics, a person who was not
    working during the previous week and was not actively seeking work during the last four weeks
    is classified as
    A. employed.
    B. unemployed.
    C. underemployed.
    D. part-time employed.
    E. not a member of the labor force.

15. From an economic perspective, the main cost of unemployment is
    A. increased crime, domestic violence, alcoholism, and drug abuse.
    B. a loss of output and income because the labor force is not fully employed.
    C. increased stress, loss of self-esteem and deterioration in the workers skills from lack of use.
    D. workers' loss of income and control over their lives.
    E. the increase in the cost of social programs to combat increased crime, alcoholism, drug
       abuse, and other social problems.

16. The cost of unemployment that is almost exclusively borne by workers and their families is the
    _____ cost.
    A. economic
    B. social
    C. psychological
    D. historical
    E. total

17. An unemployment spell begins when a worker
    A. losses his/her job and ends when he/she finds a new job.
    B. losses his/her job and ends when he/she finds a new job or leaves the labor force.
    C. starts to actively look for employment and ends when he/she finds a new job.
    D. is not working and starts to actively look for employment and ends when he/she finds a new
       job or leaves the labor force.
    E. becomes discouraged and stops seeking employment and ends when he/she begins to actively
       look for employment.

18. The duration of unemployment
    A. rises during recessions.
    B. falls during recessions.
    C. is a period during which an individual is continuously unemployed.
    D. is shorter for the chronically unemployed than it is for the long-term unemployed.
    E. is of less importance to macroeconomics than the costs of unemployment.

19. The accuracy of the official unemployment rate is criticized because
    A. unemployed homemakers and students who are not actively seeking employment are not
       included in the number of unemployed people.
    B. people who would like to work but have given up trying to find work are not included in the
       number of unemployed people.
    C. it fails to indicate how many people work at more than one job.
    D. people less than 16 years of age and over 70 years of age are excluded from the data.
    E. the BLS survey does not include all the households in the United States.

20. In recent years, the Bureau of Labor Statistics has released special unemployment rates that
    include estimates of the number of discouraged and part-time workers that indicate the number
    of
    A. discouraged workers is insignificant, but the number of part-time workers is significant.
    B. part-time workers is insignificant, but the number of discouraged workers is significant.
    C. part-time workers and discouraged workers is insignificant.
    D. discouraged workers and part-time workers is fairly significant.
    E. discouraged workers and part-time workers is decreasing

Short Answer Problems
(Answers and solutions are given at the end of the chapter.)

1. The Expenditure Approach to GDP

This problem will give you practice calculating GDP using the expenditure method. Use the data in following table to answer the questions below.

Expenditure Components	1st Quarter, 2005 ($ Bil.)
Business fixed investment	1,305.9
Durable Goods	1,023.6
Exports	1,244.5
Federal government purchases	842.0
Imports	1,938.1
Inventory investment	69.4
Nondurable goods	2,490.0
Residential investment	709.3
Services	5,029.2
State and local government purchases	1,415.9

Source: U.S. Department of Commerce, Bureau of Economic Analysis. BEA News Release (Gross Domestic Product and Related Measures, Table 3), May 26, 2005.

A. Total consumption spending in the U.S. economy during the third quarter of 2002 equaled
    $_____ billion.
B. Total investment spending in the U.S. economy during the third quarter of 2002 equaled
    $_____ billion.
C. Net export spending in the U.S. economy during the third quarter of 2002 equaled
    $_____ billion.
D. Total government purchases in the U.S. economy during the third quarter of 2002 equaled
    $_____ billion.
E. The expenditure method of calculating indicates that gross domestic product for the U.S.
    economy during the third quarter of 2002 equaled $ _____ billion.

2. The Income Approach to GDP

This problem will give you practice calculating GDP using the labor and capital income method. Use the data in following table to answer the questions below.

Income Components	3rd Quarter, 2002 ($ Bil.)
Compensation of employees	6967.0
Corporate profits	2,243.5
Net interest	557.4
Proprietor's income	962.0
Rental income	153.7

Source: U.S. Department of Commerce, Bureau of Economic Analysis. BEA News Release (Relation of GDP, GNP and NI, Table 9), May 26, 2005.

A. Total incomes received by the owners of capital during the third quarter of 2002 equaled $_____ billion.
B. Total incomes received by labor during the third quarter of 2002 equaled $ _____ billion.
C. The income method of calculating indicates that gross domestic product for the U.S. economy during the third quarter of 2002 equaled $ _____ billion.

3. Nominal and Real GDP

This problem will give you practice calculating GDP using the value-added method and adjusting nominal GDP to calculate real GDP.

A. Mr. Jones harvested logs (with no inputs from other companies) from his property in Northern California that he sold to a Nevada Mill for $1,500. The Nevada Mill cut and planed the logs into lumber and sold it for $4,000 to the Mesa Company, to be used to build tables. The Mesa Company used the lumber in producing 100 tables that they sold to customers for $70 each. Complete the table below to calculate the value added by each firm.

Company	Revenues	Cost of purchased inputs	Value added
Mr. Jones			
Nevada Mill			
Mesa Company			

B. The total value added in the production of the tables equals $_____ . This is equal to the _____ of the 100 tables.
C. If Mr. Jones had harvested the logs in October of 2000 but did not sell them to the Nevada Mill until January 2001, which then sold the lumber to Mesa Company that produced the tables in June 2001, the contribution to GDP in 2000 would equal $ _____ and in 2001 would equal $ _____ .
D. The nation of Mandar specializes in the production of vehicles. The table below provides data on the prices and quantities of the vehicles produced in 2001 and in 2005. Assume that 2001 is the base year. In 2001, nominal GDP equals $_____ and in 2005 it equals $_____ . In 2001, real GDP equals $_____ and in 2005 it equals $_____ .

| | Bicycles | | Automobiles | | Trucks | |
Year	Quantity	Price	Quantity	Price	Quantity	Price
2001	1,000	$50	100	$10,000	400	$15,000
2005	1,500	$60	50	$12,500	500	$15,000

4. Measures of Employment

This problem will give you practice in calculating employment measures. Use the data in following table to answer the questions below.

Year	Employed	Unemployed	Not in Labor Force	Working Age Population	Labor Force	Unemployment rate (%)	Participation rate (%)
2000	136,891	5,692	69,994				
2001	136,933	6,801	71,359				
2002	136,485	8,378	72,707				

2003	137,736	8,774	74,658				
2004	139,252	8,149	75,956				

Source: 2005 *Economic Report of the President,* February 2005, Table B-35.--Civilian population and labor force, 1929-2004

A. Calculate the working age population for 2000 through 2004 to complete column 5 of the table.
B. Calculate the size of the labor force for 2000 through 2004 to complete column 6 of the table.
C. Calculate the official unemployment rate for 2000 through 2004 to complete column 7 of the table.
   (Round your answers to the nearest tenth of a percent.)
Calculate the participation rate for 2000 through 2004 to complete column 8 of the table. (Round your answers to the nearest tenth of a percent.)

IV. Becoming an Economic Naturalist: Case Study

The Economic Naturalist 5.5 states that opportunity cost of sending children to school is higher in low-income agrarian societies the than in high-income non-agricultural countries. The following data from the United Nations Department of Economic and Social Indicators give the per capita income in 2003 (in the equivalent of U.S. dollars) and expected number of years of formal schooling, respectively: Canada $27,097, 16; Denmark $34,497, 17; Ethiopia $91, 5; Greece $15,690, 15; Lesotho $594, 11. Is the Economic Naturalist statement supported by the data? Explain your answer.
Answer

V. Self -Test Solutions

Key Terms
1. f
2. m
3. k
4. n
5. d
6. e
7. j
8. q
9. c
10. l
11. i
12. p
13. b
14. a
15. g
16. o
17. h

Multiple-Choice Questions
1. D The punch press is newly produced capital.
2. B The set of tires is an intermediate good and, therefore, is not included in GDP.
3. D
4. C
5. B
6. E Profit is a component of capital income.
7. A
8. A
9. C
10. C
11. E
12. B
13. D
14. E
15. B
16. C
17. D An unemployment spell begins when a person becomes unemployed (i.e., is not working and is actively seeking paid employment) and ends when s/he either becomes employed or leaves the labor force (ceases to actively seek paid employment).
18. A
19. B
20. C

Short Answer Problems
1.
A. $1,023.6 + $2,490.0 + $5,029.2 = $8,542.8 billion
B. $1,305.9 + $709.3 + 69.4 = $2.084.6 billion
C. $1,244.5 – $1,938.1 = $-693.6 billion
D. $842.0+ $1,415.9= $2,257.9 billion
E. $8,542.8 + $2.084.6 + $2,257.9 + ($-693.6) = $12,191.7 billion

2.
A. $2,243.5+ 557.4+ 153.7= $2,954.6 billion
B. $6967.0+ 962.0 = $7,929.0 billion
C. $2,954.6 + 7,929.0 = $ 10,883.6 billion [The difference between the answer in 2C and 1E is attributable to some technical adjustments that are not covered in the textbook.]

3.A.

Company	Revenues	Cost of purchased inputs	Value added
Mr. Jones	$1,500	$0	1,500
Nevada Mill	$4,000	$1,500	$2,500
Mesa Company	$7,000	$4,000	$3,000

B. $7,000; total market value
C. $1,500; $2,500 + $3,000 = $5,500

D. 1,000 x $50 + 100 x $10,000 + 400 x $15,000 = $7,050,000; 1,500 x $60 + 50 x $12,500 +
    500 x $15,000 = $8,215,000; 1,000 x $50 + 100 x $10,000 + 400 x $15,000 = $7,050,000;
    1,500 x $50 + 50 x $10,000 + 500 x $15,000 = $8,075,000

4.
A. Working age population = number of persons employed + number of persons unemployed +
   number of persons not in the labor force (2000: 136,891+ 5,692+ 69,994= 212,577)
B. Labor force = number of persons employed + number of persons unemployed (for example,
   2000: 136,891+ 5,692= 142,583)
C. Unemployment rate = (number of persons unemployed divided by number of persons not in
   the labor force) times 100 (for example, 2000: (5,692/ 142,583) x 100 = 4.0%)
D. Participation rate = (number of persons in the labor force divided by Working age
   population) times 100 (for example, 2000: (142,583/212,577) x 100 = 67.1%)

Year	Employed	Unemployed	Not in Labor Force	Working Age Population	Labor Force	Unemployment rate (%)	Participation rate (%)
2000	136,891	5,692	69,994	212,577	142,583	4.0	67.1
2001	136,933	6,801	71,359	215,093	143,734	4.7	66.8
2002	136,485	8,378	72,707	217,570	144,863	5.8	66.6
2003	137,736	8,774	74,658	221,168	146,510	6.0	66.2
2004	139,252	8,149	75,956	223,357	147,401	5.5	66.0

Chapter 6
Measuring the Price Level and Inflation

I. Pretest: What Do You Really Know?
Circle the letter that corresponds to the best answer. (Answers appear immediately after the final question).

1. A measure of the average price of a given class of goods or services relative to the price of the same goods and services in a base year is called a
   A. real price.
   B. real quantity.
   C. rate of inflation.
   D. price level.
   E. price index.

2. The consumer price index for Planet Econ consists of only two items: books and hamburgers. In 1999, the base year, the typical consumer purchased 5 books for $20 each and 30 hamburgers for $1 each. In 2000, the typical consumer purchased 8 books for $22 each and 36 hamburgers for $1.50 each. The consumer price index for 2000 on Planet Econ equals
   A. 1.00
   B. 1.08
   C. 1.15
   D. 1.23
   E. 1.77

3. The CPI in year one equaled 1.45. The CPI in year two equaled 1.53. The rate of inflation between years one and two was _____ percent.
   A. 4.0
   B. 4.5
   C. 5.3
   D. 5.5
   E. 8.0

4. The situation when the price of most goods and services are falling over time is called
   A. inflation.
   B. disinflation.
   C. a boom.
   D. deflation.
   E. an expansion.

5. A quantity measured in terms of current dollar value is called a _____ quantity.
   A. nominal
   B. real
   C. deflated
   D. indexed
   E. relative

6. All of the following are real quantities EXCEPT the
   A. number of new cars produced in one year.
   B. tons of steel shipped to South America.
   C. millions of computer chips shipped to computer makers.
   D. billions of dollars invested in stocks.
   E. truckloads of oranges used to manufacture juice.

7. A college graduate in 1972 found a job paying $10,000. The CPI was 0.418 in 1972. A
   college graduate in 2000 found a job paying $30,000. The CPI was 1.68 in 2000. The 1972
   graduate's job paid ____ in nominal terms and _____ in real terms than the 2000 graduate's
   job.
   A. more; less
   B. more; more
   C. less; the same
   D. less, more
   E. less, less

8. The real wage is the wage
   A. measured in current dollars.
   B. required to maintain a minimum standard of living.
   C. employers are required to pay workers.
   D. measured in terms of purchasing power.
   E. the federal government sets as the minimum wage.

9. The CPI equals 1.00 in year one and 1.20 in year two. If the nominal wage is $15 in year one
   and a contract calls for the wage to be indexed to the CPI, what will be the nominal wage in
   year two?
   A. $12.50
   B. $15.00
   C. $15.20
   D. $17.25
   E. $18.00

10. If the Boskin Commission's conclusion that the CPI _____ the "true" inflation rate is correct, then indexing Social Security benefits to the CPI is ____ the federal government billions of dollars.
   A. understates; costing
   B. understates; saving
   C. measures; saving
   D. overstates; costing
   E. overstates; saving

Solutions and Feedback to Pretest
For each question you incorrectly answered, we strongly recommend taking the time to review the appropriate material before continuing. In the table below is listed for each question the pertinent Learning Objective from the following Key Point Review.

Correct Answer	Learning Objective
1. E	1
2. E	1
3. D	2
4. D	1
5. A	3
6. D	3
7. D	3
8. D	3
9. E	3
10. D	5

II. Key Point Review
The Forest

This chapter focuses on measuring the aggregate price level and inflation, adjusting dollar amounts to eliminate the effects of inflation, using a price index to maintain the constant real value of a variable, the costs of inflation, and the relationship between inflation and interest rates. The central questions you need to be able to answer are
   - How is the Consumer Price Index (CPI) constructed and used to calculate inflation?
   - How is the CPI used to adjust economic data to eliminate the effects of inflation?
   - To what extent does the CPI measure "true" inflation?
   - What are the costs of inflation?
   - What is the effect of inflation on interest rates?

The Trees

Learning Objective 1: Define price index, inflation and deflation, and explain how the Bureaus of Labor Statistics estimates the Consumer Price Index

The basic tool economists use to measure the price level and inflation in the U.S. economy is the consumer price index, or CPI. The CPI is a **price index**, a measure of the average price of a given class of goods or services relative to the price of the same goods and services in a base year. The **consumer price index** measures the cost, for any period, of a standard basket of goods and services relative to the cost of the same basket of goods and services in a fixed year, called the base year. The Bureaus of Labor Statistics (BLS) determines the goods and services to include in the standard basket through the Consumer Expenditure Survey. Then each month the BLS employees survey thousands of stores to determine the current prices of the goods and services. The formula for calculating the CPI is "cost of the base-year basket of goods and services in the current year" divided by the "cost of the base-year basket of goods and services in the base year."

Note: When calculating consumer price indices for a multi-year period, the denominator will be the **same** value (the cost of the base-year basket of goods and services) for each calculation.

Inflation measures how fast the average price level is changing over time. The rate of **inflation** is defined as the annual percentage rate of change in the price level, as measured, for example, by the CPI. **Deflation** is a situation in which the prices of most goods and services are falling over time, so that the rate of inflation is negative.

Learning Objective 2: Use the CPI to calculate the rate of inflation and explain why using the CPI to calculate the inflation rate may overstate the true inflation

The inflation rate is calculated for a specific time period (e.g., a year) by subtracting the price index of an earlier time period from the price index of a more recent time period (e.g., CPI in 2002 minus the CPI in 2001) and dividing the change in the price index by the price index in the earlier time period (e.g., CPI in 2001).

Hint: When calculating the inflation rate for different years, the denominator will **NOT** be the same value for each calculation. The inflation rate is calculated by dividing the change in the price index by the price index at the end of the previous year. Students sometimes confuse the calculation of inflation rates with calculating the CPI and mistakenly use the base year price index to calculate a series of inflation rates.

Using the CPI to measure inflation has not been without controversy. Because the CPI has been used to index Social Security benefits, the U.S. government commissioned a report on the subject. The Boskin Commission concluded that the official CPI inflation overstates the true inflation rate by as much as one to two percent per year. The CPI may overstate inflation because of the quality adjustment bias and the substitution bias. Quality adjustment bias refers to the inability of government statisticians to adequately adjust the data for changes in product quality. The substitution bias arises from the fact that the CPI is calculated from a fixed basket of goods and services and, thus, does not allow for the possibility that consumers can switch from products whose prices are rising to those whose prices are stable or falling.

Learning Objective 3: Define indexing and deflating
The CPI not only allows us to measure changes in the cost of living, but can also be used to adjust economic data to eliminate the effects of inflation, a process called **deflating**. To adjust a **nominal quantity**, a quantity that is measured at its current dollar value, we divide the nominal quantity by a price index for the period. The adjusted value is called a **real quantity**, that is, a quantity measured in physical terms. Such real quantities are also sometimes referred to as inflation-adjusted quantities. For example, nominal wages for two different periods can be adjusted using the CPI to determine the change in real wages over time. The **real wage** is the wage paid to workers measured in terms of real purchasing power. To calculate the real wage we divide the nominal (dollar) wage by the CPI for that period. The CPI can also be used to convert real quantities to nominal quantities. The practice of increasing a nominal quantity according to changes in a price index in order to prevent inflation from eroding purchasing power is called **indexing**. For example, some labor contracts provide for indexing of wages, using the CPI, in later years of a contract period.

Note: Deflating and indexing are essentially opposite means of compensating for inflation. Deflating removes the monetary value of past inflation, while indexing adds in the monetary value of potential future inflation.

Learning Objective 4: Distinguish between price level and relative price
The **price level** is a measure of the overall level of prices in the economy at a particular point in time, as measured by a price index (e.g., the CPI). The **relative price** of a specific good or service is its price in comparison to the prices of other goods and services. Inflation is an increase in the overall price level, not an increase in the relative price of a good or service. Understanding the difference between the price level and the relative price of a good or service is necessary in order to explain the costs of inflation.

Note: Changes in the price level are generally believed to impose costs on society with little or no benefits, while changes in relative prices are generally believed to be beneficial to the economy with little or no costs.

Learning Objective 5: Explain the five costs of inflation
When an economy suffers from inflation, the cost of holding cash increases and causes consumers and businesses to make more frequent trips to the bank, and to purchase cash-management systems. Banks will, therefore, hire more employees to handle the increased

transactions. These costs of economizing on cash have been called shoe-leather costs. Inflation also creates "noise" in the price system that obscures the information transmitted by prices, reduces the efficiency of the market system, and imposes costs on the economy. Similarly, inflation produces unintended changes in the tax people pay and distorts the incentives in the tax system that may encourage people to work, save, and invest. Another concern about inflation is that, if it is unanticipated, it arbitrarily redistributes wealth from one group to another (e.g., between lenders and borrowers, and workers and employers). As a result, a high inflation economy encourages people to use resources in trying to anticipate inflation to protect themselves against losses of wealth. The fifth cost of inflation is its tendency to interfere with the long-run planning of households and firms. While any inflation imposes some costs on the economy, **hyperinflation**, a situation in which the inflation rate is extremely high, greatly magnifies the costs.

Learning Objective 5: Explain the relationship between the inflation rate and interest rates
An important aspect of inflation is its effect on interest rates. To understand the relationship between inflation and interest rates, economists differentiate between the **nominal interest rate** and the **real interest rate.** The nominal interest rate (also called the market interest rate) is the annual percentage increase in the nominal value of a financial asset. The real interest rate is the annual percentage increase in the purchasing power of a financial asset, and is equal to the nominal interest rate minus the inflation rate. To obtain a given real interest rate, lenders must charge a higher nominal interest rate as the inflation rate rises. This tendency for nominal interest rates to rise when the inflation rate increases is called the **Fisher effect**.

> **Hint:** In order to correctly understand the relationship between the inflation rate and interest rates, it is important to recognize that the inflation rate is the independent variable (the causal factor) and the interest rate is the dependent variable (the effect). Thus, it is **not** correct to say that an increase in interest rates causes higher inflation rates.

III. Self-Test

Key Terms
Match the term in the right-hand column with the appropriate definition in the left-hand column by placing the letter of the term in the blank in front of its definition. (Answers are given at the end of the chapter.)

1. _____ The wage paid to workers measured in terms of real purchasing power.

2. _____ The tendency for nominal interest rates to be high when inflation is high and low when inflation is low.

3. _____ A measure of the overall level of prices at a particular point in time as measured by a price index such as the CPI.

4. _____ A situation in which the prices of most goods and services are falling over time so that inflation is negative.

5. _____ The practice of increasing a nominal quantity each period

a. consumer price index (CPI)

b. deflating (a nominal quantity)

c. deflation

d. Fisher effect

e. hyperinflation

by an amount equal to the percentage increase in a specified price index.

6. ____ A quantity that is measured in physical terms – for example, in terms of quantities of goods and services.

7. ____ The annual percentage increase in the nominal value of a financial asset.

8. ____ A situation in which the inflation rate is extremely high.

9. ____ For any period, measures the cost in that period of a standard basket of goods and services relative to the cost of the same basket of goods and services in a fixed year, called the base year.

10. ____ The annual percentage rate of change in the price level, as measured, for example by the CPI.

11. ____ A quantity that is measured in terms of its current dollar value.

12. ____ The process of dividing a nominal quantity by a price index (such as the CPI) to express the quantity in real terms.

13. ____ The annual percentage increase in the purchasing power of a financial asset.

14. ____ A measure of the average price of a given class of goods and services relative to the price of the same goods and services in a base year.

15. ____ The price of a specific good or service in comparison to the prices of other goods and services.

16. ____ A financial assets that pays the holder a nominal interest rate equal to the fixed real interest rate plus the actual rate of inflation each year.

f. indexing

g. inflation-protected bonds

h. nominal interest rate

i. nominal quantity

j. price index

k. price level

l. rate of inflation

m. real interest rate

n. real quantity

o. real wage

p. relative price

Multiple-Choice Questions
Circle the letter that corresponds to the best answer. (Answers are given at the end of the chapter.)

1. Inflation exists when
   A) and only when the prices of all goods and services are rising.
   B) the purchasing power of money is increasing.
   C) the average price level is rising, although some prices may be falling.
   D) the prices of basic necessities are increasing.
   E) wages and the price of oil are rising.

2. If the CPI is 125 at the end of 2004 and equals 150 at the end of 2005, then the inflation rate for 2005 would equal
   A) 15 percent.
   B) 20 percent.
   C) 25 percent
   D) 125 percent.
   E) 150 percent.

3. If the Consumer Price Index (CPI) overstates the true rate of inflation, the use of the CPI to adjust nominal incomes results in
    A) understating gains in real incomes.
    B) overstating gains in real incomes.
    C) an accurate statement of gains in real incomes.
    D) nominal values equaling real values.
    E) an arbitrary redistribution of income.

4. Which of the following statements is true about the relationship between a nominal quantity and a real quantity?
    A) A real quantity indicates the amount of money received, while a nominal quantity indicates the real quantity's purchasing power.
    B) A nominal quantity is measured in current dollar values, but a real quantity is measured in terms of physical quantity.
    C) A nominal quantity is adjusted for inflation; a real quantity is not.
    D) A real quantity minus a nominal quantity equals purchasing power.
    E) There is no difference; nominal quantity and real quantity are two different terms for the purchasing power of money.

5. If the Consumer Price Index (CPI) decreases
    A) the purchasing power of money decreases.
    B) a dollar will buy fewer goods and services.
    C) real income equals nominal income.
    D) there is inflation.
    E) there is deflation.

6. If you borrow money at what you believe is an appropriate interest rate for the level of expected inflation, but the actual inflation rate turns out to be much higher than you had expected, the
    A) loan will be paid back with dollars that have much higher purchasing power than you had expected.
    B) loan will be paid back with dollars that have the same purchasing power as the dollars you borrowed.
    C) borrower's and lender's wealth will have been destroyed by the higher inflation.
    D) borrower will gain from an intended redistribution of wealth.
    E) borrower will unintentionally redistribute wealth to the lender.

7. If, in a given period, the rate of inflation turns out to be lower than lenders and borrowers anticipated, the effect is that
    A) the real payments by the borrowers will be lower than expected.
    B) the nominal income of lenders will be higher than expected, but their real income will be lower than expected.
    C) the nominal income of the lenders will be as expected, but their real income will be higher than expected.
    D) both the nominal and real income of lenders will be higher than expected.

E) the real income of lenders will be higher than expected, but their nominal income will be lower than expected.

8. The Consumer Price Index is a measure of the change in prices of
   A) a standard basket of all goods and services.
   B) a standard basket of goods determined by the Consumer Expenditure Survey.
   C) a standard basket of agricultural goods determined by the Consumer Expenditure Survey.
   D) a standard basket of selected items in wholesale markets.
   E) a standard basket of machinery, tools, and new plant.

9. "Shoe leather" costs of inflation refer to the
   A) difficulty of interpreting the price signals in an inflationary environment.
   B) unintended changes in taxes caused by inflation.
   C) arbitrary redistribution of wealth from one group to another.
   D) costs of economizing on holding cash.
   E) interference of inflation on the long-run planning of households and businesses.

10. The CPI for a given year measures the cost of living in that year relative to
    A) what it was in the base year.
    B) what it was in the previous year.
    C) the cost of the basic goods and services need to sustain a typical household.
    D) the amount spent on goods and services by the randomly selected families in the Consumer Expenditure Survey.
    E) the cost of the basic goods and services in the base year.

11. When comparing the money wages of today's workers to money wages workers earned 10 years ago, it is necessary to adjust the nominal wages by
    A) indexing the money wages in each period to today's price index.
    B) deflating the money wages in each period with today's price index.
    C) indexing the money wages in each period with the price indexes of the respective periods.
    D) deflating the money wages in each period with the price indexes of the respective periods.
    E) deflating the money wages in each period with the price index of the past period.

12. The Boskin Commission reported that the official inflation rate, based on the CPI, might overstate true inflation. It identified two reasons, including the
    A) quality adjustment bias and the indexing bias
    B) quality adjustment bias and the substitution bias.
    C) substitution bias and the indexing bias.
    D) quality adjustment bias and the deflation bias.
    E) indexing bias and deflation bias.

13. During the last half of 1999 and first quarter of 2000, the members of the Organization of Petroleum Exporting Countries (OPEC) negotiated reductions in the global production of oil. As a result, the price of heating oil and gasoline increased dramatically in the United States

during that period. This led some analysts to predict an increase in the inflation rate in the United States. Drawing such a conclusion results from confusing

A) inflation with indexing.
B) inflation with deflation.
C) a change in the relative price of a good with a change in the price level.
D) a change in the relative price level with a change in the absolute price level.
E) indexing with deflating.

14. Inflation creates static or "noise" in the price system, making it difficult for

A) businesses and households to make long-term plans.
B) lenders and borrowers to determine an appropriate level of nominal interest rate on loans.
C) employers and workers to determine the appropriate level of money wages to be paid.
D) businesses to interpret the information being transmitted by price changes.
E) households and businesses to hold cash.

15. The real interest rate can be written in mathematical terms as

A) $r = i - \pi$
B) $r = \pi - i$
C) $r = i + \pi$
D) $r = \pi + i$
E) $r = i / \pi$

16. In the United States during the 1970s, nominal interest rates were

A) falling and real interest rates were falling.
B) rising and real interest rates were rising.
C) falling and real interest rates were rising.
D) rising and real interest rates were falling.
E) rising and real interest rates became negative.

17. If the Consumer Price Index is 135 at the end of 2004 and at the end of 2005 it is 142, then during 2005 the economy experienced

A) deflation
B) inflation
C) hyperinflation
D) indexing
E) deflating

18. Mr. Long is considering the purchase of a corporate bond with a yield (interest rate) of 6% per year, and he expects the inflation rate will average 4% per year during the period that he would hold the bond. Mr. Long has decided to purchase the bond only if the real rate of return is positive on the investment. If the tax rate on the interest income is

A) greater than 33.3%, he should buy the bond.
B) greater than 50%, he should buy the bond.
C) less than 33.3%, he should buy the bond.
D) less than 50%, he should buy the bond.
E) less than 33.3%, he should not buy the bond.

19. Ms. Savior bought 300 shares of stock in the Dot.com Company in 2000 for $1,000. In 2002 she sold the shares for $1,050, earning $50 in capital gains. She must pay a 20% capital gains tax, leaving her with a net gain of $40. During the two years that she held the stock the price level rose by 4%. As a result her real return on the stock was
    A) positive.
    B) negative.
    C) zero.
    D) greater than the nominal yield (interest rate).
    E) equal to the nominal yield (interest rate).

20. According to the Fisher Effect
    A) high interest rates will cause high inflation rates.
    B) high inflation rates will cause high interest rates.
    C) low interest rates will cause high inflation rates.
    D) low interest rates will cause low inflation rates.
    E) low inflation rates will cause high interest rates.

Short Answer Problems
(Answers and solutions are given at the end of the chapter.)

1. Consumer Price Index and Inflation
The data in the following table are taken from the U.S. Consumer Expenditure Survey conducted by the Bureau of Labor Statistics. The "Average Annual Expenditure" refers to the cost of purchasing the standard market basket of goods and services by the typical household in the United States in each year.

Year	Average Annual Expenditure	Consumer Price Index	Inflation rate (%)	After-tax Income	After-tax Real Income
2003	$40,817			$48,596	
2002	40,677			46,934	
2001	39,518			44,587	
2000	38,045			41,532	
1999	36,995			40,652	
1998	35,535			38,358	

A. Using 1998 as the base year, complete column 3 of the table by calculating the Consumer Price Index for 1997-2003.

B. Complete column 4 of the table by calculating the inflation rates for 1998-2003.

C. In the same survey, the BLS provides the average nominal income after paying taxes of the typical household, shown in column 5 of the table. Using the CPI to adjust the nominal income, complete column 6 of the table by calculating the after-tax real income of the typical household for 1997-2003.

D. In which of the years from 1997-2003 was the typical household in the United States economically best off? _____ .

E. In which of the years from 1997-2003 was the typical household in the United States economically worst off? _____

2. Costs of Higher Education

Deloitte and Touche, LLP (an accounting firm) estimated the average cost of college during 1994-95 for four-year public and private institutions. The data is shown in the table below.

Categories	Public Colleges	Private Colleges
Tuition and fees	$2,686	$11,709
Books and Supplies	578	585
Room and Board	3,826	4,976
Transportation	592	523
Other	1,308	991
Total Cost	$8,990	$18,784

A. In the year 2000-01, it has also estimated that the total cost of attending a public college was $14,266 and a private college was $33,277. Using 1994-95 as the base year, calculate the price index for attending public and private colleges. Price index for public college 1994-95 _____ ; price index for private college 1994-95 _____; price index for public college 2000-01_____ ; price index for public college 2000-01 _____ .

B. What was the percentage increase in the cost of attending a public college between 1994-95 and 2000-01? _____ percent. What was the percentage increase in the cost of attending a private college between 1994-95 and 2000-01? _____ percent.

C. Sam attended a public college in his home state beginning in 1994-95 and graduated in 2000-01. He paid the cost of his college education by working part time and summers as a firefighter. When he entered college his nominal (money) income was $13,000 and the year he graduated his nominal income had risen to $15,500. Because the cost of college includes all his living expenses, the price index for attending a public college represents his cost of living index. Thus, his real income (measured in 1994-95 dollars) in 1994-95 was $_____ and in 2000-01 it was $_____ .

D. Was Sam economically better off during the year he graduated or the first year he entered college? Explain your answer. _____

E. Sue attended a private college outside of her home state beginning in 1994-95 and she also graduated in 2000-01. She paid the cost of her college education by working part time and summers as a consultant to businesses designing web pages. When she entered college her nominal (money) income was $40,000. Because the cost of college includes all her living expenses, the price index for attending a private college represents her cost of living index. If her real income was to remain constant from 1994-95 through 2000-01, her nominal income in 2000-01 would have had to rise to $_____ .

3. Nominal and Real Interest Rates

Answer the questions below based on the data in the following table. The table shows the inflation rate in the United States, measured by the CPI, and nominal interest rate, measured by the yield on the 10-year Treasury bond.

Year	Inflation rate	Interest rate
2004	2.68	4.27
2000	3.38	6.03
1996	1.88	6.44
1992	2.75	7.01
1988	3.65	8.85

A. In what year was the real interest rate on the 10-year Treasury bond the highest? _____
B. In what year did the financial investors who bought the 10-year Treasury bonds get the best deal? _____
C. In what year was the real interest rate on the 10-year Treasury bond the lowest, but still positive? _____
D. In what year did the financial investors who bought the 10-year Treasury bonds get the worst deal? _____
E. What was the real interest rate on the 10-year Treasury bond in 1996? _____ %

IV. Becoming an Economic Naturalist: Case Study

In Economic Naturalist 6.1, the textbook authors discuss the political implications of the minimum wage not being indexed to inflation. The table below shows the historical nominal minimum wage and the CPI from 1960 to 2000. Answer the questions below using the data in the table to determine the economic implications of the minimum wage not being indexed to inflation.

Year	Nominal Minimum Wage	CPI ('82-84=100)	Year	Nominal Minimum Wage	CPI ('82-84=100)
1960	$1.00	29.6	1985	$3.35	107.6
1965	$1.25	31.5	1990	$3.80	130.7
1970	$1.60	38.8	1995	$4.25	152.4
1975	$2.10	53.8	2000	$5.15	172.2
1980	$3.10	82.4	2004	$5.15	188.9

In which of the years shown in the table was the real value of the minimum wage highest? In which of the years shown in the table was the real value of the minimum wage lowest? During which two periods was the real value of the minimum wage rising? During which time period was the real value of the minimum wage rising? In which year, 1960 or 2004, did minimum wage earners have the highest purchasing power?

Answer:

V. Self-Test Solutions

Key Terms
1. o
2. d
3. k
4. c
5. f
6. n
7. h
8. e
9. a
10. l
11. i
12. b
13. m
14. j

15. p
16. g

Multiple-Choice Questions

1. C
2. B The inflation rate = (150 – 125)/125 = 25/125 = .20 or 20%
3. A If the true inflation rate is less than the official measure of inflation, then the real income would be greater than the official data would suggest.
4. B
5. E
6. D The borrower gains from being able to pay back the loan in less valuable dollars.
7. C
8. B
9. D
10. A
11. D
12. B
13. C The changes in the prices of gasoline and heating oil are changes in relative prices, not changes in the price level that would indicate inflation.
14. D
15. A r = real interest rate; i = nominal, or market, interest rate; and π = inflation rate
16. E
17. B
18. C If the tax rate is 33.3% or greater, Mr. Long will pay the equivalent of 2% or more in income taxes, leaving him an after-tax nominal return of 4% or less. Subtracting the 4% expected inflation would result in a zero or negative real return on the investment. Since he decided to only invest if the real return was positive he should only buy the bond if the tax rate is less than 33.3%.
19. C The $40 after-tax return divided by the $1,000 price of the bond equals a nominal rate of return of 4%. Subtracting the inflation rate of 4% would give her a real return of zero.
20. B

Short Answer Problems

1.
A. CPI = (cost of the base-year basket of goods and services in the current year) divided by (cost of the base-year basket of goods and services in the base year) . For example, 2001 CPI = $39,518 / $35,535 = 1.11
B. inflation rate = (CPI in year – CPI in previous year) / CPI in previous year. For example, 2001 inflation rate = (1.11 – 1.07) / 1.07 = 3.74%
C. real income = nominal income / price index. For example, 2001 After tax real income = $44,587/ 1.11= $40,168.47

Year	Average Annual Expenditure	Consumer Price Index	Inflation rate (%)	After-tax Income	After-tax Real Income
2003	$40,817	1.15	0.88	$48,596	$42,257.39
2002	40,677	1.14	2.70	46,934	$41,170.18

2001	39,518	1.11	3.74	44,587	$40,168.47
2000	38,045	1.07	2.88	41,532	$38,814.95
1999	36,995	1.04	4.00	40,652	$39,088.46
1998	35,535	1.00	NA	38,358	$38,358.00

D. 2003
E. 1998

2.
A. price index = $8.990/$8,990 = 1.00; 1.00; $14,266/$8,990 = 1.59; 1.77
B. percentage change = ($14,266- $8,990)/ $8,990 =58.7%; 77.2%
C. real income = $13,000 / 1.00 = $13,000; ($15,500/1.59 =) $9,748.43
D. during his first year
E. To determine how much her income would need to rise by, you need to index her income during the first year of school by multiplying it times the price index for private college during year she graduated, (i.e., $40,000 x 1.77 = $70,800.00).

3.
A. 1988
B. 1988
C. 2004
D. 2004
E. 4.56% (= 6.4 – 1.88)

Chapter 7
Economic Growth, Productivity, and Living Standards

I. Pretest: What Do You Really Know?

Circle the letter that corresponds to the best answer. (Answers appear immediately after the final question).

1. The key indicator of a country's living standard and economic well being is
   A. the unemployment rate.
   B. the inflation rate.
   C. real GDP.
   D. real GDP per person.
   E. average labor productivity.

2. Real GDP per person in Westland is $15,000, while real GDP in Eastland is $20,000, However, Westland's real GDP per person is growing at 2.5 % per year and Eastland's is growing at 1.5% per year. If these growth rates persist indefinitely, then
   A. Westland's real GDP per person will increase until it equals, but does not exceed, Eastland's.
   B. Westland's real GDP per person will eventually be greater than Eastland's.
   C. Eastland's real GDP per person will always be greater than Westland's.
   D. Eastland's real GDP per person will decline until it equals Westland's.
   E. Eastland's real GDP per person will decline, but never be less than Westland's.

3. If real GDP per person equaled $1,000 in 1900 and grew at a 4 percent annual rate, what would real GDP equal 100 years later?
   A. $4,040
   B. $5,100
   C. $8,705
   D. $50,505
   E. $4,780,612

4. The payment of interest not only on the original deposit, but on all previously accumulated interest is called
   A. the real interest rate
   B. the nominal interest rate
   C. simple interest
   D. conflict of interest
   E. compound interest

5. If when you are 21 you put $1,000 in a bank deposit promising to pay 8 percent annual compound interest, how much will be in the account 45 years later when you retire at age 66?
   A. $4,600
   B. $13,765
   C. $31,920
   D. $48,600
   E. $86,962

6. Growth of real GDP per person is totally determined by the growth of average
   A. labor productivity and the proportion of the population employed.
   B. labor productivity and the proportion of the population in the labor force.
   C. labor force participation and the share of income going to capital.
   D. labor force participation and the share of the population employed.
   E. number of employed workers and population.

7. In Macroland 400,000 of the 1 million people in the country are employed. Average labor productivity in Macroland is $30,000 per worker. Real GDP per person in Macroland totals
   A. $1,000
   B. $12,000
   C. $15,000
   D. $30,000
   E. $42,000

8. Average labor productivity is determined by
   A. consumption, investment, government spending, and net exports.
   B. the number employed, unemployed, and the labor force participation rate.
   C. the quantity and quality of human capital, physical capital, technology, natural resources, entrpreneurship, and the legal and political environment.
   D. the real interest rate, the nominal interest rate, and the rate of inflation.
   E. the difference between government spending and revenues.

9. Mike and Tom debone chicken breasts for Ted's Chicken Co. Mike is new and can only debone 20 chicken breasts per hour, while Tom's experience allows him to debone 50 chicken breasts per hour. Both Mike and Tom work 40 hours per week. Their average hourly productivity as a team is ____ chicken breasts.
   A. 30
   B. 35
   C. 70

D. 90

E. 140

10. Countries with large amounts of capital per worker tend to have _____ levels of real GDP per person and _____ levels of average labor productivity.
   A. high; high
   B. high; low
   C. low; low
   D. low; average
   E. low; high

Solutions and Feedback to Pretest

For each question you incorrectly answered, we strongly recommend taking the time to review the appropriate material before continuing. In the table below are listed for each question the pertinent Learning Objective from the following Key Point Review.

Correct Answer	Learning Objective
1. D	1
2. B	2
3. D	2
4. E	2
5. C	2
6. A	3
7. B	3
8. C	4
9. B	3
10. A	4

II. Key Point Review
The Forest

This chapter focuses on the sources of economic growth and rising standards of living in the modern world. Secondary issues discussed include government policies to promote economic growth, the costs of rapid economic growth, and whether there may be limits to economic growth. The central questions you need to be able to answer are

- How does compound interest relate to living standards?
- GDP per person can be expressed as the product of what two variables?
- What determines the productivity of the average worker in a particular country?
- What are the costs of economic growth?
- What are some of the policies that promote economic growth?
- What are the arguments for and against indefinitely sustainable economic growth?

The Trees

Learning Objective 1: Compare rates of growth in real GDP per person among countries during the 19th and 20th centuries

Despite the recognition that it is an imperfect measure, economists have focused on real GDP per person as a key measure of a country's living standard and stage of economic development. As discussed in Chapter 18, real GDP per person is positively related to a number of pertinent variables, such as life expectancy, infant health, and literacy. During the 19th century, the annual percentage change in real GDP per person began to increase in a number of industrializing countries, and during the latter half of the 20th century the rate of economic growth increased again. While there was a noticeable slowdown in their growth rates during the 1970s and 1980s, since 1995 they have rebounded largely because of advances in information and communication technology. As a result of the power of compound interest, real GDP per person in these countries is anywhere from 5 to 28 times greater than it was a century and a third ago.

Learning Objective 2: Define compound interest and explain the effects of compound interest on living standards

The increases in the growth rates of real GDP during the last half of the 20th century were relatively small in comparison to the previous 80 years, but the power of compound interest resulted in large changes in real GDP over time. **Compound interest** is the payment of interest not only on the original deposit, but also on all previously accumulated interest. This is distinguished from simple interest in which interest is paid only on the original deposit. When interest is compounded, small differences in interest rates or growth rates matter a lot. As in the case of the industrializing countries during the late 19th and 20th centuries, relatively small differences in growth rates, among the countries and during different time periods, ultimately produced very different living standards.

Note: One way of grasping the power of compound interest is to apply what is often referred to as the "rule of 72." The rule of 72 is a quick way of estimating how long it will take for a country's real GDP to double as a result of a country's economic growth. For example, if GDP is growing at an average annual rate of two percent, by dividing 2 into 72 we find that the GDP will double in approximately 36 years. If growth increases to 3 percent, GDP will double in only 24 years.

Learning Objective 3: Discuss the relationship of real GDP per person to average labor productivity and share of working population

Real GDP per person can be expressed as the product of two terms: average labor productivity and the share of the population that is working. Real GDP per person can only grow if there is growth in worker productivity and/or the fraction of the population that is employed. In the United States, for example, during 1960-99 the fraction of the population employed increased as women entered the labor force in greater proportions, and as the coming of age of the "baby boomers" increased the share of the population that was of working age. This contributed to the increased growth in real GDP per capita in the United States during that time. In the long run, however, it is unlikely that this trend will continue as demographic changes take place. Average labor productivity is, therefore, the more important determinant of increases in living standards in the long run. In simple terms, the more people produce, the more they can consume.

Learning Objective 4: Discuss the determinants of average labor productivity
There are six factors that appear to account for the major differences in average labor productivity between countries and between generations. Human capital, i.e., the talents, education, training and skills of workers, is the *first* factor that affects average labor productivity. In general, people acquire additional education and skills when the difference in the additional wages paid (marginal benefit) to skilled workers is greater than the marginal cost of acquiring the skills. A *second* determinant of average labor productivity is physical capital, machines, equipment and buildings. More capital generally increases average labor productivity. There are, however, **diminishing returns to capital** (i.e., if the amount of labor and other inputs employed is held constant, then the greater the amount of capital already in use, the less an additional unit of capital adds to production).

> **Note:** Diminishing returns to capital is an illustration of the principle of increasing opportunity cost, or the low-hanging fruit principle. Capital will first be applied to the most productive activities available. Thus, as additional capital is applied the marginal return will eventually begin to decline.

The *third* determinant of average labor productivity is the availability of land and other resources. In general, an abundance of natural resources increases the productivity of the workers who use them. Because resources can be obtained through trade, countries need not possess large quantities of them within their own border to achieve economic growth. A *fourth* determinant is technology. A country's ability to develop and apply new, more productive, technologies will increase its workers' productivity.

> **Note:** Most economists would probably agree that new technologies are the single most important source of productivity improvements. Although a stable political and legal environment may be considered a prerequisite for a country to take advantage of the other five sources of productivity improvements.

Entrepreneurship and management are a *fifth* determinant of average labor productivity. **Entrepreneurs** are people who create new enterprises and who are critical to the introduction of new technologies into the production of goods and services. Managers also play an important role in determining average labor productivity as they work to introduce new technologies to better satisfy customers, organize production, obtain financing, assign workers to jobs and motivate them to work hard and effectively. Government, a *sixth* determinant, also has a role to play in fostering improved productivity. A key contribution of government is to provide a political and legal environment that encourages people to behave in economically productive ways. A stable government and well-defined property rights and free markets are important determinants of a nation's average labor productivity.

Learning Objective 5: Identify the costs of economic growth
While economic growth provides substantial benefits to society, it is not without costs. The high rate of investment in new physical and human capital requires that people save and, thus, consume less in the present. Also, reduced leisure time and, possibly, reduced workers' health and safety must be sacrificed in the present for workers to acquire the education and skills to build the capital infrastructure.

> **Note**: The fact that a higher living standard tomorrow must be purchased at the cost of current sacrifices is an example of the scarcity principle. The cost-benefit principle suggests that a nation should pursue additional growth only if the marginal benefits outweigh the marginal costs.

Learning Objective 6: Discuss potential government policies that may promote economic growth
If a society decides to try to increase its rate of economic growth, policymakers can help to achieve the goal by providing education and training programs or by subsidizing the provision of such programs by the private sector. In addition, governments can encourage high rates of saving and investment in the private sector through tax incentives. Governments can also directly contribute to capital formation through public investment in infrastructure. Government financing of research and development activities, especially in the area of basic scientific knowledge, and sharing the fruits of applied research in military and space applications can promote a higher rate of economic growth. Government also plays an essential role in providing the framework within which the private sector can operate productively, an area in which the poorest countries of the world lack adequate structural macroeconomic policies.

Learning Objective 7: Identify the issues raised in *The Limits to Growth*
While economic growth accelerated during the 19th and 20th centuries, an influential book, *The Limits to Growth*, published in 1972 reported the results of computer simulations that suggested continued growth would deplete natural resources, drinkable water, and breathable air. Critics of the limits to growth thesis point out that its underlying assumption is that growth implies producing more of the same type of goods. A second criticism is that it overlooks the fact that increased wealth expands a society's capacity to safeguard the environment. Additionally, it is argued that markets and government action can deal with the depletion of natural resources through new sources and conservation. Despite these shortcomings of the "limits to growth" perspective, most economists would agree that not all the problems created by economic growth can be dealt with effectively. Global environmental pollution will remain a problem unless international mechanisms are developed to deal with them. In particular, given that the relationship between pollution and real GDP per person is shaped like an inverted **U**, it is likely that as poorer countries become middle-income countries they will continue to pollute more until they become sufficiently wealthy to have the luxury of a clean environment.

III. Self-Test

Key Terms
Match the term in the right-hand column with the appropriate definition in the left-hand column by placing the letter of the term in the blank in front of its' definition. (Answers are given at the end of the chapter.)

1. ____ If the amount of labor and other inputs employed is held constant, then the greater the amount of capital already in use, the less an additional unit of capital adds to production.

    a. compound interest

2. ____ People who create new economic enterprises.

    b. diminishing returns to capital

3. ____ The payment of interest not only on the original deposit but on all previously accumulated interest.

    c. entrepreneur

Multiple-Choice Questions
Circle the letter that corresponds to the best answer. (Answers are given at the end of the chapter.)

1. Which country had the highest rate of growth in real GDP per person during 1870-2003 and 1950- 2003?
   A. Australia
   B. Canada
   C. Japan
   D. United Kingdom
   E. United States

2. Compound interest differs from simple interest in that compound interest is interest paid on
   A. the original deposit only, whereas simple interest is interest paid on not only on the original deposit but also on all previously accumulated interest.
   B. all previously accumulated interest, whereas simple interest is interest paid not only on the original deposit but also on all previously accumulated interest.
   C. the original deposit only, whereas simple interest is interest paid only on all previously accumulated interest.
   D. the original deposit and on all previously accumulated interest, whereas simple interest is interest paid on all previously accumulated interest .
   E. the original deposit and on all previously accumulated interest, whereas simple interest is interest paid on the original deposit only.

3. If on the day you were born, your parents deposited $1,000 into a savings account that would earn an annual compound interest rate of 5 percent, what would the value of the account be on your 20th birthday?
   A. $1,100.00
   B. $2,653.30
   C. $3,325,256.73
   D. $1,500.00
   E. $1,050.00

4. The increase in average labor productivity is important to the economy because
   A. without it, real GDP per person cannot increase.
   B. without it, real GDP per person must decrease.
   C. it is a key to improving living standards in the long run.
   D. the fraction of the total population that is employed is constant over time and, thus, real GDP per person is solely dependent upon average labor productivity.
   E. it implies more resources are being employed to produce less output.

5. International data on the relationship between the amount of capital per worker and average labor productivity indicate that there is a
   A. positive relationship between the two variables.
   B. negative relationship between the two variables.
   C. no relationship between the two variables.
   D. positive relationship between the two variables for some countries, but a negative relationship between the two variables for other countries.
   E. positive relationship between the two variables for some countries, but no relationship between the two variables for other countries.

6. An abundance of natural resources, such as arable land, raw materials, and energy,
   A. within a country's borders is necessary to achieve economic growth.
   B. increases the productivity of workers who use them.
   C. results in economic growth only if the population increases at least as rapidly.
   D. results in economic growth only if an economy obtains them through international trade.
   E. seldom contribute to economic growth, as measured by percentage increases in real GDP per person.

7. The investment in human capital that contributed to the rapid economic recovery in Germany and Japan after World War II was mainly achieved through
   A. a superior system of higher education.
   B. public education.
   C. an apprentice system and on-the-job training.
   D. subsidies provided by the U.S.-funded Marshall Plan.
   E. a large wage differential paid to skilled versus unskilled workers.

8. The faster the rate of technological change, the
   A. lower the rate of growth in productivity.
   B. lower the rate of economic growth.
   C. higher the rate of unemployment.
   D. higher the rate of productivity.
   E. higher the rate of capital accumulation.

9. For a given number of workers, as the amount of capital is increased output will
   A. increase at a diminishing rate.
   B. increase at an increasing rate.
   C. increase at a constant rate.

D. decrease at a diminishing rate.

E. decrease at an increasing rate.

10. Entrepreneurship is

   A. easy to teach in schools and colleges.

   B. not affected by government policies.

   C. more important than management in determining average labor productivity.

   D. mainly affected by individual factors rather than sociological factors.

   E. believed to have been largely absent in medieval China.

11. Using production function $Y = K^{1/2}L^{1/2}$, if K increases from 4 to 8, and L increases from 25 to 50, then Y will

   A. increase from 100 to 200.

   B. decrease from 200 to 100

   C. increase from 32 to 1250.

   D. increase from 10 to 20.

   E. be indeterminate (as there is not sufficient information to calculate the change in Y).

12. The scarcity principle implies that the cost of a higher economic growth rate is

   A. less future capital accumulation.

   B. less current consumption.

   C. greater future capital consumption.

   D. greater current consumption.

   E. greater future consumption.

13. The cost-benefit principle suggests that higher economic growth

   A. is always desirable.

   B. is seldom desirable.

   C. should be pursued only if the marginal benefits outweigh the marginal costs.

   D. should be pursued only if the marginal costs outweigh the marginal benefits.

   E. should be pursued only if the marginal benefits equal the marginal costs.

14. Most countries provide their citizens free public education through high school because

   A. the supply curve for education does not include all the social benefits of education.

   B. a market in equilibrium exploits all the gains achievable from collective action.

   C. the demand curve for education does not include all the social benefits of education.

   D. educational vouchers that help citizens purchase educational services in the private sector have not proven to increase human capital.

   E. direct government control over the standards and quality of education is necessary to increase human capital.

15. The U. S. government has promoted saving or investment in the economy by

   A. increasing the tax rates on Individual Retirement Accounts (IRAs).

   B. providing subsidies to the private sector to build infrastructure.

   C. reducing the amount of public investment in government-owned capital.

   D. providing funding during the early stages of the development of the internet.

E. eliminating all subsidies on Individual Retirement Accounts (IRAs).

16. In order to increase their rate of economic growth, most poor countries need to
A. establish political stability and the rule of law.
B. obtain greater financial support from the rich countries.
C. extract more of the natural resources that lie within their borders.
D. maintain the structural macroeconomic policies that they began to implement after World War II.
E. increase regulation of private sector monopolies.

17. The general thesis of the book, *The Limits to Growth*, is that continued pursuit of economic growth will soon
A. cease when all the workers are employed.
B. consume all available natural resources, drinkable water, and breathable air.
C. cause the principle of scarcity to no longer be an issue.
D. increase the living standard of the poorest nations to that of the richest nations.
E. limit our desire to increase the production of goods and services.

18. Critics of the "limits to growth" thesis argue that
A. economic growth will always take the form of more of what we have now, rather than newer, better, and cleaner goods and services.
B. the market is not capable of adjusting to shortages of resources.
C. clean air and water are luxury goods and the more economically developed a country becomes the more resources there are to keep the environment clean.
D. government action spurred by political pressure is the best way to avoid the depletion of natural resources and pollution of the environment that results from economic growth.
E. *all* the problems created by economic growth can be dealt with effectively through the market or the political process.

19. One criticism of the "limits to growth" thesis is that the market can deal with shortages of natural resources that may result from economic growth through price changes that induce
A. consumers to consume more and suppliers to produce less of the resources.
B. consumers to consume less and suppliers to produce more of the resources.
C. a slowdown in the rate of economic growth.
D. government actions to allocate public funds to preserve open space and reduce air pollution.
E. an optimal level of environmental quality on a global scale.

20. Empirical studies show that the relationship between pollution and real GDP per person takes the shape of an inverted U. This suggests that as countries move from very low levels of real GDP per person the level of pollution
A. tends to continuously worsen.
B. tends to continuously improve.
C. improves, but from middle-income to high-income levels pollution worsens.
D. worsens, but from middle-income to high-income levels pollution levels stabilize.
E. worsens at middle-income levels, but improves at high-income levels.

Short Answer Problems
(Answers and solutions are given at the end of the chapter.)

1. Compounding Economic Growth Rates
The table below shows the output per person for selected countries in 1998 and the economic growth rates of the countries for 1990-98. Use the data in the table to answer the following questions.

Country	1998 GNP per capita[1]	1990 - 1998 Growth Rate	2008 GNP per capita
Canada	$24,050	2.2%	
France	22,320	1.5%	
Germany	20,810	1.6%	
Italy	20,200	1.2%	
Mexico	8,190	2.5%	
New Zealand	15,840	3.2%	

Source: *World Development Report, 1999/2000*, Tables 1 and 11.
[1] Calculated in 1998 dollars and using the purchasing power parity method to adjust the value of output across countries.

A. Assuming that each countrys' economy continues to grow at the same rate that it did during 1990-98, complete column 4 of the table by calculating the GNP per capita (person) for 2008.

B. On the graph below, plot the level of GNP per capita for the remaining countries for 10, 20, 50, and 100 years later, assuming a compound growth rate equal to that of 1990-98,

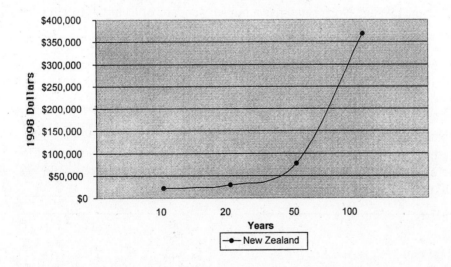

Compound Economic Growth

C. Approximately how many decades would it take for New Zealand's output per person to equal that of Canada's output per person? _____ decades.

D. Approximately how many decades would it take for Germany's output per person to equal that of France's output per person? _____ decades.

E. Approximately how many decades would it take for Mexico's output per person to equal that of Italy's output per person? _____ decades.

2. Why Nations Become Rich

This problem will help you understand the relationship between how much workers produce, how many people are working and the quantity of goods and services available to consume. The following table is comprised from data published by the U.S. Department of Labor' Bureau of Labor Statistics/ Office of Productivity and Technology. All data are for 1998 and the Real GDP and productivity are measured in 1998 dollars.

Country	Real GDP per person	Average Labor Productivity	Share of the population Employed
United States		$65,888	49.2
Canada	$25,496		47.5
France	$22,255	$56,722	
Japan	$24,170		51.2
Norway		$54,007	51.1

A. Complete the table above by calculating the value of real GDP per person for the United States and Norway, average labor productivity for Canada and Japan, and the share of the population employed in France during 1998.

B. The data indicate that workers in France produce considerable more output per year than do the workers in Norway, yet the average Norwegian has a higher standard of living. Explain why.

_____

C. A larger share of the population in Japan is employed than in the United States, yet the average American has a higher standard of living than the Japanese do. Explain why.

_____

D. The population in Japan is aging faster than the population in Canada and, thus, by the early 21st century the share of the population employed in Japan will decline as the elderly retire. If the share of the population employed in Japan falls to the level of Canada, which country would have the higher real GDP per capita, assuming no other changes? _____
Explain your answer. _____

IV. Becoming an Economic Naturalist: Case Study

The Economic Naturalist 7.5 discusses relationship between a country's level of income (real GDP per person) and the amount of air pollution in the country. The following table shows the classification by level of Real GDP per person of a limited number of countries in the *World Development Report 1999/2000*, and the graph shows the empirical relationship between air pollution and Real GDP per person.

Country	Ranking
Australia	High income
China	Low income
Mexico	Upper middle income
Namibia	Lower middle income

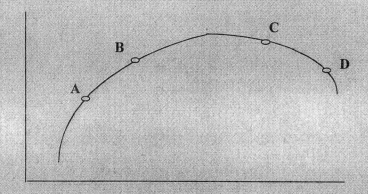

Real GDP per person

Identify each of the four countries listed in the table with one of the lettered points on the inverted U-shaped curve on the following graph. If the level of real GDP per person in Mexico increases so that it moves up to the next classification in future World Development Reports, will the amount of pollution likely increase or decrease? If the level of real GDP per person in China increases so that it moves up to the next classification in future World Development Reports, will the amount of pollution likely increase or decrease?

Answer:

V. Self-Test Solutions

Key Terms
1. b
2. c
3. a

Multiple-Choice Questions

1. C Compare the average annual growth rates for the countries in Table 20.1
2. E
3. B $\$1,000 \times 1.05^{20} = \$2,653.30$
4. C
5. A See Figure 20.4
6. B
7. C See Economic Naturalist 20.1
8. D
9. A
10. E
11. D $Y = \sqrt{100} = 10$ vs. $Y = \sqrt{400} = 20$
12. B
13. C
14. C
15. D
16. A
17. B
18. C
19. B
20. E

Short Answer Problems
(Answers and solutions are given at the end of the chapter.)

1.

A.

Country	1998 GNP per capita[1]	1990 - 1998 Growth Rate	2008 GNP per capita
Canada	$24,050.00	2.2%	$37,164.90
France	$22,320.00	1.5%	$30,061.80
Germany	$20,810.00	1.6%	$28,585.53
Italy	$20,200.00	1.2%	$25,642.57
Mexico	$8,190.00	2.5%	$13,420.27
New Zealand	$15,840.00	3.2%	$29,740.56

B.

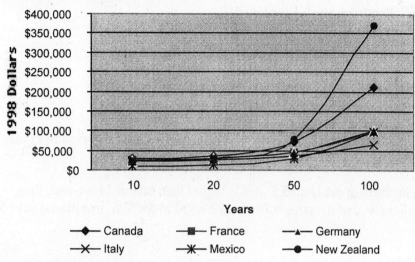

Compound Economic Growth

C. 5
D. 5
E. 6

2.
A.

Country	Real GDP per person	Average Labor Productivity	Share of the population Employed
US	$32,417	$65,888	49.2
Canada	$25,496	$53,676	47.5
France	$22,255	$56,722	39.2
Japan	$24,170	$47,207	51.2
Norway	$27,598	$54,007	51.1

B. Because a larger share of the population is employed in Norway than is employed in France, the average person in Norway has a higher standard of living than the French.

C. The average labor productivity in the United States is higher than that of Japan, and, thus, despite the fact that a smaller share of the population is employed in the U.S. its citizens have a higher standard of living.

D. Canada. If the share of the population employed in Japan declines to that of Canada, the standard of living for the average Canadian will be higher than that of the Japanese because of its higher average labor productivity.

2.

A.

Country	Real GDP per person	Average Labor Productivity	Share of the population Employed
US	$32,413	$65,888	49.2
Canada	$25,496	$53,702	47.5
France	$22,255	$56,722	39.2
Japan	$24,170	$47,232	51.2
Norway	$27,581	$54,007	51.1

B. Because a larger share of the population is employed in Norway than is employed in France, the average person in Norway has a higher standard of living than the French.

C. The average labor productivity in the United States is higher than that of Japan, and, thus, despite the fact that a smaller share of the population is employed in the U.S. its citizens have a higher standard of living.

D. Canada. If the share of the population employed in Japan declines to that of Canada, the standard of living for the average Canadian will be higher than that of the Japanese because of its higher average labor productivity.

Chapter 8
Workers, Wages, and Unemployment in the Modern Economy

I. Pretest: What Do You Really Know?

Circle the letter that corresponds to the best answer. (Answers appear immediately after the final question).

1. In the twentieth century, average real wages have risen substantially
    A. only in the United States.
    B. in industrial countries excluding the United States
    C. in industrial countries including the United States
    D. in neither the United States nor other industrial countries.
    E. in the United States, but not in other industrial countries.

2. In the United States the real wages of the least-skilled, least educated workers have ____ and the wages of best-educated, highest skilled workers have _____.
    A. increased; increased
    B. declined; increased
    C. increased; declined
    D. declined; declined
    E. declined; remained constant

3. In the last two decades of the twentieth century, the number of people with jobs in the United States:
    A. declined more rapidly than the population over sixteen.
    B. declined more slowly than the population over sixteen.
    C. remained approximately constant.
    D. grew more rapidly than the population over sixteen.
    E. grew more slowly than the population over sixteen.

4. According to the principle of diminishing returns to labor, if the amount of capital and other inputs are held constant, employing additional workers
   A. increases output at an increasing rate.
   B. increases output at a constant rate.
   C. increases output at a decreasing rate.
   D. decreases output at an increasing rate.
   E. decreases output at a decreasing rate.

5. High Tech, Inc. produces plastic chairs that sell for $10 each. The following table provides information about how many plastic chairs can be produced per hour. For simplicity assume that labor is the only input. How many workers will be hired, if the hourly wage for workers is $50?

Number of Workers	Chairs Produced per Hour
0	0
1	12
2	22
3	30
4	36
5	40

   A. 1
   B. 2
   C. 3
   D. 4
   E. 5

6. As the real wage increases the quantity of labor demanded _____ and the quantity of labor supplied _____.
   A. increases; increases
   B. increases; decreases
   C. decreases; decreases
   D. decreases; increases
   E. does not change; does not change

7. The slowdown in the growth of real wages in the United States since 1973, accompanied with job growth is consistent with _____ growth of labor demand and _____ growth of labor supply.
   A. slower; slower
   B. slower; faster
   C. slower; no change in
   D. faster; faster
   E. faster; slower

8. Initially workers in the shoe industry and the computer industry earn the same wage. Reductions in trade barriers give domestic consumers access to cheaper shoes produced abroad, so domestic shoe prices fall. At the same time foreign consumers purchase more computers, raising the relative price of computers. As a result of these changes, employment in the shoe industry ____ and employment in the computer industry _____.

A. increases; increases
B. increases; decreases
C. decreases; increases
D. decreases; does not change
E. decreases; decreases

9. Worker mobility is the
   A. demand for labor in different industries and firms.
   B. movement of workers between job, firms, and industries.
   C. process of increasing the size of the working-age population.
   D. attempt to increase workers' reservation prices.
   E. way to end globalization.

10. Skill-biased technological change affects the marginal products of _____ workers differently from those of _____ workers.
    A. male; female
    B. union; nonunion
    C. government; private-sector
    D. retail-industry; service-sector
    E. highly trained; low-skilled

Solutions and Feedback to Pretest

For each question you incorrectly answered, we strongly recommend taking the time to review the appropriate material before continuing. In the table below are listed for each question the pertinent Learning Objective from the following Key Point Review.

Correct Answer	Learning Objective
1. C	1
2. B	1
3. D	1
4. C	2
5. D	2
6. D	2, 4
7. B	3, 4
8. C	5
9. B	5
10. E	5

II. Key Point Review
The Forest

This chapter focuses on some important trends in the labor markets of industrialized countries, using supply and demand model to explain trends in real wages and employment. In addition, problems of unemployment, especially long-term unemployment, are discussed. The central questions you need to be able to answer are

- What are the five trends that have characterized the labor markets of industrialized countries during the 20th century?
- What factors determine the demand and supply of labor?
- What changes in the factors of supply and demand for labor explain the trends in real wages and employment in industrialized countries?
- What are the three types of unemployment?
- What are the major impediments to full employment?

The Trees

Learning Objective 1: Discuss international patterns in employment
The higher unemployment rates experienced by Western Europe over the past 20 years can be understood as a product of the structural features. Western European labor markets have a much higher degree of both government regulation and unionization compared to the United States. Globalization and skill-biased technological change, which caused low wage workers in the United States to see their wages fall, resulted in Western European employers permanently laying off workers *because wages could not fall*.

Learning Objective 2: Identify the factors that affect the demand for labor
The demand for labor is based on the two notions: how productive a given worker is and the value of the worker's production. As the firm hires additional workers, it is able to produce a greater amount of output. The key measure for labor demand analysis is not the total amount produced by 5 employees but the extra production associated with the hiring of the fifth worker. The extra output obtained by hiring an extra worker defines the marginal product of labor. The principle of **diminishing returns to labor** states that if other inputs like capital are fixed, the extra output from hiring an extra worker will decline at some point. However, knowing the marginal product of one's workers is not enough information to render a judgment about the optimal number to hire. Ultimately, the firm cares less about the amount each worker produces than about the additional revenue the extra production will generate. The benefit of hiring an extra worker is calculated as price of the product multiplied by the worker's marginal product, and is referred to as the value of marginal product. In fact, the value of marginal product is the firm's demand curve for labor.

> **Note:** The economic basis for the principle of diminishing returns to labor is related to the principle of increasing opportunity cost. A firm will use its available workers in the most productive way possible and, thus, will assign its first worker employed to its most productive job.

Learning Objective 3: Identify the factors that shift the labor demand curve
Two factors cause the labor demand curve to shift to the right or left. First, if the price of the firm's output increases, then the value to the firm of a given worker's marginal product grows, thus shifting labor demand to the right. Second, if the marginal productivity of workers rises due to technological change or training, then labor demand will increase, shifting to the right. Reductions in output price or marginal productivity cause decreases in labor demand. A decrease in the wage rate does not cause an increase in labor demand; it causes an increase in the quantity of labor demanded or a movement along the labor demand curve.

Learning Objective 4: Discuss the nature of labor supply and identify the factors that cause the labor supply curve to shift
The supply of labor shows the total number of people willing to work at each real wage rate. The real wage rate represents the opportunity cost of not working, for example, if the wage is $5 and one chooses to work one less hour, one has given up $5. The plausible assumption is made that the higher the real wage rate, the greater the number of people who will be willing to work. Increases and decreases in the supply of labor stem from changes in the size of the working age population and the percentage of working-age people who seek employment.

> **Note**: The decision of whether to work at any given wage is an application of the cost-benefit principle. In applying the cost-benefit principle to the employment decision, an additional worker should be employed only if the marginal benefit is at least equal to the marginal cost of employing the worker.

Learning Objective 5: Explain domestic and international patterns in real wages
The first trend, significant real wage growth over the entire twentieth century, has resulted from sustained productivity growth. For the industrial countries, technological progress and large increases in the stock of capital caused the productivity growth. Of course, the size of the working-age population expanded (a labor supply increase), but the increase in labor demand due to greater productivity was large enough to absorb the new entrants and to drive the real wage up.

The second trend, a distinct slowdown in real wage growth during the past 30 years, comes from a slowdown in productivity growth coupled with continued growth in the working-age population, particularly the rising participation of women. Unlike the first 70 years of the century, the increases in labor demand were large enough to accommodate the new entrants but not large enough to drive the real wage up markedly.

The third trend, increased wage inequality, is caused by two factors: globalization and technological change. Greater international trade has encouraged countries to further specialize in producing the goods for which they possess a comparative advantage, benefiting all consumers in all countries. When domestic markets are opened to trade, some markets will see an increase in demand for their output (the ones with a comparative advantage), while others will see a decrease in demand (those without a comparative advantage). As demand goes, so goes price. Thus, in the markets *lacking* a comparative advantage, the decrease in demand results in a lower price, translating into a decrease in the value for marginal product and, in turn, lower wages. In the markets *with* a comparative advantage, the reverse occurs, driving wages up. The United States enjoys comparative advantage in goods produced by highly skilled, high-wage workers but has difficulty competing with other countries in the production of goods requiring low-skilled, low-wage workers. The effects of trade then tend to drive the high-wage workers' wage up further while lowering the wages of low-wage workers, making wage inequality more pronounced. The free market solution involves **worker mobility**, the movement of worker's between jobs, firms, and industries. The higher wages in the high-skilled labor markets should draw new workers in while the lower wages in the low-skilled labor markets should cause workers to exit. However, the transition from one labor market to another, particularly from low skilled to high skilled, does not happen instantly, so government assistance to aid the process may be justified. The other issue propelling greater wage inequality is the nature of technological progress. While technological progress expands the size of the economic pie, it is not neutral in its influences. Unfortunately, it appears that skill-biased technological change – technological change favoring the marginal productivity of high skilled workers – characterizes recent decades. The effect of skill-biased technological change serves to increase the demand for high-skilled workers, resulting in higher wages for workers already receiving high wages. As a consequence, wage inequality worsens.

Learning Objective 6: Define frictional, structural, and cyclical unemployment

Economists have separated unemployment into three categories. **Frictional unemployment** results from the matching of workers and jobs and lasts for a relatively short period. Because workers and jobs are dissimilar or heterogeneous and the labor market is ever changing or dynamic, the process of matching workers and jobs takes time. So when a person quits one job, he or she may spend a few weeks or months finding the next one. Frictional unemployment is considered beneficial to the economy when a better match of worker and job occurs. Long-term and chronic unemployment that exists despite the normal operation of the economy is termed **structural unemployment**. The causes of structural unemployment take several forms: lack of skills, language barriers, or discrimination. Changes in the nature of the economy can also produce long-term unemployment. For example, the United States steel industry is in decline and many former steelworkers will never again work in the steel industry. Finally, structural features of the economy can cause chronic unemployment. Government programs may also contribute to structural unemployment. The minimum wage, as with any price floor, generates a surplus of workers, more commonly called unemployment. Unemployment insurance is a government transfer to unemployed workers, designed to lessen the burden of unemployment while searching for a new job. However, it may also lengthen the period of search and/or reduce the intensity of the search. Government regulations for workplace health and safety or discrimination tend to raise the cost of employing workers and reduce their productivity. Thus, firms wish to hire fewer workers than they would have in the absence of the regulations. Finally, labor unions "cause" unemployment by increasing the wage the firm must pay and hence the cost of hiring a worker. When the economy suffers a recession, the additional unemployment that results is called **cyclical unemployment**.

Note: While government regulations impose costs (i.e., higher structural unemployment), there are also benefits of the regulations (e.g., fewer injured workers). In order to achieve maximum economic efficiency, legislators should use the cost-benefit criterion when deciding which regulations to impose on the labor markets.

Learning Objective 7: Explain the costs associated with the different types of unemployment

The psychological and financial costs of frictional unemployment are relatively minor because of its short in duration. In fact, frictional unemployment is considered beneficial to the economy when a better match of workers and jobs occur. Structural and cyclical unemployment, on the other hand, impose heavy economic costs on workers and society, as well as psychological costs on workers and their families.

III. Self-Test

Key Terms

Match the term in the right-hand column with the appropriate definition in the left-hand column by placing the letter of the term in the blank in front of its' definition. (Answers are given at the end of the chapter.)

1. ____Technological change that affects the marginal products of higher-skilled workers differently from those of lower-skilled workers.   a. cyclical unemployment

2. ____ The extra unemployment that occurs during periods of recession.   b. diminishing returns to labor

3. ____ The movement of workers between jobs, firms and industries.   c. frictional unemployment

4. ____ If the amount of capital and other inputs in use is held constant, then the greater the quantity of labor already employed, the less each additional worker adds to production.   d. skill-biased technological change

5. ____ The short-term unemployment associated with the process of matching workers with jobs.   e. structural unemployment

6. ____ The long-term and chronic unemployment that exists even when the economy is producing at normal rates.   f. worker mobility

Multiple-Choice Questions

Circle the letter that corresponds to the best answer. (Answers are given at the end of the chapter.)

1. Which of the following statements is *not* supported by the data presented in the textbook?
   A. During the twentieth century, the industrial nations have experienced sizable real-wage growth.
   B. Real wages for skilled workers have risen dramatically over the past 20 years.
   C. The differential between skilled and unskilled workers' real wages has remained constant over the twentieth century.
   D. Real-wage inequality is less pronounced in Western Europe than in the United States.
   E. The average worker in the United States in 1999 has four times the purchasing power of the average worker in 1929.

2. Which of the following statements is *not* supported by the data presented in the textbook?
   A. Over the past several decades, the United States economy has generated a significant number of new jobs.
   B. Western European countries have experienced lower levels of unemployment than the United States in recent years.
   C. Job creation in Western European countries has been meager over the past two decades.
   D. In 1999, more than two-thirds of the over-16 population in the United States held a job.
   E. Of late, the United States economy has created jobs at a rate exceeding the rate of growth of the over-16 population.

3. When a firm hires 3, 4, and 5 workers, it observes that total output is 15, 25, and 30 units, respectively. The marginal product of the fourth worker, therefore, is ____ units.
   A. 40
   B. 25
   C. 15
   D. 10
   E. 5

4. Suppose the marginal products of the fifth, sixth, and seventh workers are 7, 4, and 1, respectively. One can infer that the firm
   A. is experiencing diminishing returns to labor.
   B. has hired too many workers.
   C. is profit maximizing.
   D. has selected low skilled workers.
   E. is experiencing negative returns to labor.

5. In order for a firm to determine the value of a particular worker, the firm must know
   A. the average amount of output the worker will produce.
   B. the extra amount of output the worker will produce.
   C. the price at which the output can be sold.
   D. the average amount of output the worker will produce and the price at which the output can be sold.
   E. the extra amount of output the worker will produce and the price at which the output can be sold.

6. The _____ is the firm's demand curve for labor because it illustrates the _____ for each extra worker.
   A. marginal product curve; extra output
   B. value of marginal product curve; the extra revenue
   C. value of average product curve; the average revenue
   D. value of marginal product curve; the extra profit
   E. value of marginal product curve; the extra cost

7. Which of the following events would not cause the demand curve for labor to shift?
   A. An increase in the productivity of labor.
   B. A decrease in demand for the output produced by the labor.

C. A decrease in the wage rate paid to laborers.

D. Introduction of new, inexpensive capital equipment designed to replace laborers.

E. An increase in demand for the output produced by the labor.

8. The reason the labor supply curve is thought to be upward sloping is that as the real wage rate rises,

A. the opportunity cost of not working increases.

B. the attractiveness of working declines.

C. the alternatives to working become more attractive.

D. the greed of individuals becomes more obvious.

E. more individuals are seduced into working when they would rather not.

9. The most important factor that shifts the labor supply curve is the

A. size of the real wage rate.

B. growth of the real wage rate.

C. the size of the under-16 population.

D. social norms about work.

E. the size of the working-age population.

10. In terms of the model of labor markets, the growth of real wages in the industrial countries during the twentieth century is best explained as a(n)

A. decrease in labor supply due to declining working-age populations.

B. increase in labor demand due to higher prices for consumer goods.

C. result of unions and government regulation of labor markets.

D. increase in labor demand due to technological change and the growth of capital stocks.

E. increase in labor supply due to increasing availability of educational opportunities.

11. The slowdown in real-wage growth that characterizes the past 30 years of the twentieth century is best explained as a(n)

A. nearly total lack of productivity growth.

B. combination of less rapid productivity growth and increased labor supply.

C. increase in labor supply.

D. combination of higher prices for consumer goods and decreased labor supply.

E. increased government regulation of the labor market.

12. The increased wage inequality in the United States caused by increased international trade stems from

A. foreign countries "dumping" products on the United States.

B. increased demand for domestically produced goods requiring low-skilled labor.

C. increased demand for domestically produced goods requiring high-skilled labor.

D. decreased demand for domestically produced goods requiring high-skilled labor.

E. the productivity of foreign labor being higher than the productivity of American labor.

13. As wages in United States decline for low-skilled workers and rise for high-skilled workers,
    A. the incentive to become a high-skilled worker is stronger, pulling more workers to the high-skill sector.
    B. the United States government should enact legislation to protect low–skilled workers from international competition.
    C. the United States government should compensate low-skilled workers with cash payments for the rest of their working life.
    D. no effective solution exists, so the growing inequality must just be accepted.
    E. allowing low-skilled workers to unionize is the only possible avenue to greater wage equality.

14. The technological change of the past 30 years seems to have
    A. benefited all workers equally.
    B. predominantly benefited low-skilled workers.
    C. harmed both low- and high-skilled workers.
    D. only benefited workers in the computer industry.
    E. predominantly benefited high-skilled workers.

15. To counteract the negative effects of both international trade and skill-biased technological change on the wages of low-skilled workers, the textbook proposes
    A. an end to international trade.
    B. governmental review of technologies with a ban on those that favor the highly skilled.
    C. assistance to retrain low-skilled workers and ease their transition to new labor markets.
    D. a hike in the minimum wage.
    E. subsidies to the industries that employ large numbers of low-skilled workers.

16. Generally speaking, _____ unemployment is thought to be the least costly because _____.
    A. cyclical; it is just part of the business cycle
    B. structural; as economies grow, some sectors gain and others lose
    C. cyclical; most of the layoffs are short term
    D. frictional; it results in a better match of workers with jobs
    E. frictional; it tends to last the longest

17. Which of the following features of labor markets in the United States does *not* contribute to long-term, chronic unemployment?
    A. Minimum wage legislation.
    B. Labor unions.
    C. Job search engines on the Internet.
    D. Unemployment insurance.
    E. Health and safety regulations.

18. According to the textbook, the best explanation for the chronically higher unemployment rates in Western Europe is
    A. a lack of retraining programs.
    B. a decline in demand for low-skilled workers.

C. structural features of the labor market that retard worker mobility.

D. excessive international trade.

E. a combination of a decrease in demand for low-skilled workers and more limited worker mobility.

19. The combination of greater international trade and skill-biased technological change in the United States during the past 30 years has

A. harmed low- and high-skilled workers equally.

B. dramatically increased the degree of wage inequality because the United States has a comparative advantage in goods requiring high-skilled workers.

C. not intensified the degree of wage inequality since the United States has a comparative advantage in goods that require both low- and high-skilled workers.

D. harmed low-skilled workers without providing any tangible benefit to consumers.

E. harmed low-skilled workers less than if only one of the two factors was present.

20. Which of the following proposals to assist low-skilled workers deals with the effects of international trade and skill-biased technological change would be most economically efficient?

A. A program to setup and provide access to an Internet-based job bank aimed at all industries.

B. Extension of the coverage period for unemployment insurance.

C. Tariffs on foreign goods produced using inexpensive foreign labor.

D. A public relations campaign to encourage consumers to buy American-made goods.

E. Demands that foreign countries pay their low-skilled workers more.

Short Answer Problems
(Answers and solutions are given at the end of the chapter.)

1. Labor Markets

Calculation of marginal product, the value of marginal product, and determining the profit maximizing level of labor usage are reviewed in this question. The data below show the relationship between labor usage and total output for a firm.

Employee-hours	Output	Price	Marginal Product	Value of Marginal Product
0	0	$2		
1	65	$2		
2	105	$2		
3	125	$2		
4	135	$2		
5	140	$2		

A. Calculate the marginal product and the value of the marginal product for the different levels of employee-hours.

B. Suppose the price the firm receives for its output rises from $2 to $3. As a result, the (marginal product/value of marginal product) _____ increases, implying the firm's demand for labor has (increased/decreased) _____.

C. Suppose that the efficiency of labor increases such that all employee-hours generate 10% more output, e.g., the first employee-hours now results in 71.5 units of output. The impact is that (only the marginal product/both the marginal product and the value of marginal product) _____ increase, shifting the labor demand curve to the (left/right) _____.

D. If the firm must pay a wage of $40 per employee-hour, the profit maximizing level of labor usage is (3/4) _____. If the wage rate were to fall to $20, the firm would increase its (labor demand/ quantity of labor demanded) _____ to (3/4) _____ hours.

2. Labor Market Dynamics I

This question assesses your ability to use the labor market model to explain the trends in wage and employment data presented at the beginning of the chapter. The graphs below show the market for two types of labor in the United States: workers A produce good X while workers B produce good Z. Presently, both occupations pay the same real wage to workers. Suppose a new trade agreement is signed to ease trading with other countries. Suppose further that in the international market, the United States has a comparative advantage in producing Z, and other countries have a comparative advantage in X.

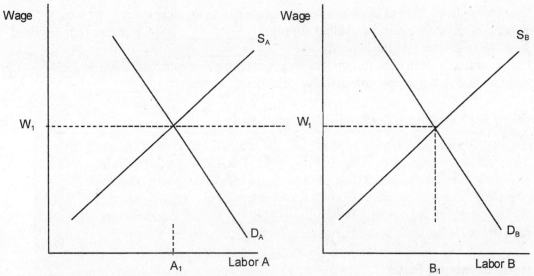

A. Illustrate the effects of the trade agreement on the wages of workers A and B.
B. Suppose that in addition to the trade agreement, recent technological innovations have favored workers B. Illustrate the effects, if any, on the wages of workers A and B.
C. A group, representing workers A, lobbies vigorously in opposition to the trade agreement on the grounds that workers would be harmed. Discuss who, if anyone, would be harmed by failing to sign the trade agreement.
D. Discuss an efficient way to assist workers A and have greater international trade.

3. **Labor Market Dynamics II**
This question also assesses your ability to use the labor market model to explain the trends in wage and employment, but rather than reasoning from the change to the effect, now the reasoning will run from effect to change. The table below presents hypothetical data on equilibrium real wages and employment for a national labor market.

Year	Real Wage	Employment
2002	$5.00	100
2003	$5.50	120
2004	$6.00	100
2005	$6.00	130
2006	$5.75	125

Hint: Draw a labor supply and demand graph that shows the equilibrium real wage and employment level for the initial year in each question. Then, identify the equilibrium real wage and employment level for the later year in the question and determine what type of change in supply or demand conditions would be necessary to achieve the change in equilibrium.

A. From 2002 to 2006, the data indicate that an (increase/decrease) _____ in the (supply of/demand for) _____ labor occurred.
B. Apparently, the (size of the working population/productivity of workers) _____ declined from 2003 to 2004, since the data are consistent with a decrease in the (supply of/demand for) _____ labor.

C. The change from 2004 to 2005 can best be explained as an increase in (just labor demand/both labor demand and labor supply) _____ because (employment grew/the real wage was unchanged) _____

D. The reduction in both equilibrium real wages and employment from 2003 to 2004 suggests that (labor supply increased/labor demand decreased) _____.

IV. Becoming an Economic Naturalist: Case Study

In Economic Naturalist 8.5, the textbook authors discuss the causes of the relatively high rates of unemployment in Western Europe. In an article entitled "Curbing Unemployment in Europe: Are There Lessons from Ireland and the Netherlands?" published in *Current Issues in Economics and Finance* (Vol. 7, No. 5 – May 2001), Cédric Tille and Kei-Mu Yi present the following graph showing unemployment rates for Ireland, the Netherlands and the European Union.

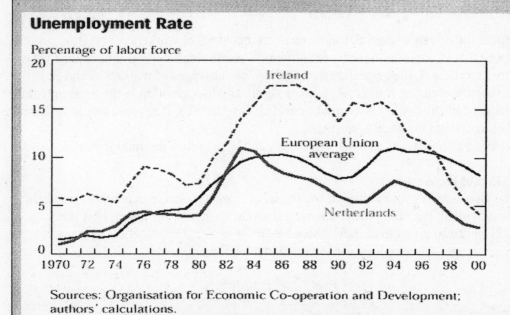

Unemployment Rate

Percentage of labor force

Sources: Organisation for Economic Co-operation and Development; authors' calculations.

What conclusions can be drawn about the structural rigidities of the labor markets in these countries during 1970 through the mid-1980s compared to the mid-1980s through 2000?

Answer:

Self-Test Solutions

Key Terms
1. d
2. a
3. f
4. b
5. c
6. e

Multiple-Choice Questions
1. C
2. B
3. D Total output with 4 workers is 25 while total output with 3 workers is 15 so adding the fourth worker increases total output by 10 units.
4. A
5. E The firm need to know the value of the marginal product ($P*MP$) for each worker.
6. B
7. C A wage change would cause a movement along the labor demand curve.
8. A
9. E
10. D
11. B
12. C
13. A
14. E
15. C
16. D
17. C
18. E
19. B
20. A

Short Answer Problems
1.
A. See table.

Employee-hours	Output	Price	Marginal Product	Value of Marginal Product
0	0	$2		
1	65	$2	65	$130
2	105	$2	40	$80
3	125	$2	20	$40
4	135	$2	10	$20
5	140	$2	5	$10

A. value of marginal product; increased
B. both the marginal product and the value of the marginal product; right
C. 3; quantity of labor demanded; 4

2.

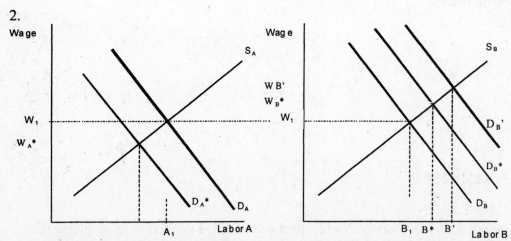

A. The demand for good X declines due to trade and, thus, the demand for labor A declines (D_A*), lowering employment and wages. Demand for Z increases with trade, which increases demand for B workers (D_B*) driving employment and wages up.

B. The technological change further stimulates demand for labor B (D_B'), causing an added increase in wages and employment.

C. Failing to sign the trade agreement harms consumers and workers producing good Z.

D. Sign the agreement and use tax revenues to assist the unemployed laborers in A to get new training and locate new jobs.

3.

A. increase; demand for

B. size of the working population; supply of

C. both labor demand and labor supply; the real wage was unchanged

D. labor demand decreased

Chapter 9
Saving and Capital Formation

I. Pretest: What Do You Really Know?

Circle the letter that corresponds to the best answer. (Answers appear immediately after the final question).

1. The saving rate equals saving divided by
   A. wealth.
   B. assets.
   C. liabilities.
   D. income.
   E. investment.

2. Charles has the following assets and liabilities:

Two cars	$10,000
House	$300,000
Mortgage	$100,000
Cash	$1,000
Car loans	$4,000
Checking account balance	$2,000
Credit card balance	$1,000

   What is Charles's wealth?
   A. $206,000
   B. $208,000
   C. $210,000
   D. $312,000
   E. $416,000

3. Which of the following is a stock?
   A. saving
   B. income
   C. consumption
   D. wealth
   E. investment

4. Saving is a(n) _____ and wealth is a(n) _____.
  A. flow; flow
  B. flow; stock
  C. asset; liability
  D. liability; asset
  E. stock; flow

5. Saving for protection against unexpected setbacks, such as the loss of a job or a medical emergency, is called _____ saving.
  A. public
  B. national
  C. precautionary
  D. life-cycle
  E. bequest

6. Saving done for the purpose of leaving an inheritance is called _____ saving.
  A. public
  B. national
  C. precautionary
  D. life-cycle
  E. bequest

7. Life-cycle saving is saving
  A. to meet long-term objectives, such as retirement, college attendance, or the purchase of a home.
  B. for protection against unexpected setbacks, such as the loss of a job or a medical emergency.
  C. for the purpose of leaving an inheritance.
  D. to pay life-insurance premiums.
  E. by older people to induce younger people to care for them.

8. Saving by households and businesses is called _____ saving.
  A. private
  B. public
  C. national
  D. aggregate
  E. bequest

9. _____ saving equals _____ saving plus _____ saving.
  A. National; private; public
  B. Public; national; private
  C. Private; national; public
  D. Life-cycle; bequest; precautionary
  E. Precautionary; bequest; life-cycle

10. Public saving is negative when
    A. there is a government budget surplus.
    B. there is a government budget deficit.
    C. the government's budget is balanced.
    D. after-tax income of households and businesses is greater than consumption expenditures.
    E. after-tax income of households and businesses is less than consumption expenditure.

Solutions and Feedback to Pretest
For each question you incorrectly answered, we strongly recommend taking the time to review the appropriate material before continuing. In the table below are listed for each question the pertinent Learning Objective from the following Key Point Review.

Correct Answer	Learning Objective
1. D	1
2. B	1
3. D	1
4. B	1
5. C	2
6. E	2
7. A	2
8. A	4
9. A	4
10. B	4

II. Key Point Review
The Forest

This chapter focuses on saving and its links to the formation of new capital. The central questions you need to be able to answer are

- How are saving and wealth related?
- Why do people save?
- What are the components of national saving?
- What is the relationship between national saving and investment?

The Trees

Learning Objective 1: Define saving, saving rate, wealth, assets, liabilities, stocks, flows, capital gains, capital losses, and explain the link between saving and wealth

Saving by an economic unit (e.g., a household, business, or nation) is its current income minus its spending on current needs. It can be expressed as a **saving rate** by dividing the amount of saving by the amount of income. Saving by an economic unit is closely related to its **wealth**, the value of its assets minus its liabilities. **Assets** are anything of value that is owned, while **liabilities** are the debts that are owed. Accountants list the assets and liabilities of an economic unit on a balance sheet to determine its net worth. Saving and wealth are related because saving contributes to wealth. This relationship is best understood by distinguishing between stocks and flows. A **flow** is a measure that is defined per unit of time, and a **stock** is a measure that is defined at a point in time. In many cases, a flow is the rate of change in a stock. For example, the flow of saving causes the stock of wealth to change at the same rate. Higher rates of saving, therefore, lead to faster accumulation of wealth and a higher standard of living. Although saving increases wealth, it is not the only factor that determines wealth. Wealth also changes because of changes in the values of the real and financial assets owed by an economic unit. If the value of an existing asset increases, the owner has a **capital gain**, but if the value of an existing asset decreases, then there is a **capital loss**. In summary, changes in wealth equal the amount of saving plus capital gains minus capital losses.

> **Hint:** Use the bathtub analogy to help you remember the concepts of stock and flow. The amount of water in the bathtub at any specific moment is the "stock" of water, while turning on the tap adds a "flow" of water. The more water flowing in per minute, the higher the rate of change in the stock of water in the bathtub. Opening the drain will cause a flow of water out of the tub and, therefore, will reduce the stock of water in the tub.
>
> Similarly, the stock and flow concepts can be applied to economic variables. For example, wealth is a stock of assets and saving is a flow of assets. If a family currently owns assets, say a house (valued at $100,000), a Picasso painting ($250,000) and $50,000 in certificates of deposit (CDs), its total wealth equals $400,000. If the family saves $10,000 during the next year, its wealth at the end of next year will be $410,000. The higher one's rate of saving (flow), the faster one's (stock of) wealth increases. If the family then takes $20,000 out of its CDs to pay for a vacation the following year, then its wealth at the end of that year would fall to $390,000.

Learning Objective 2: Identify the three broad reasons why people save and explain the relationship between the amount of saving and interest rates

People save part of their income rather than spending all they earn for three reasons. First, they save to meet certain long-term objectives, such as retirement or the purchase of a home. This is called **life-cycle saving**. A second reason people save is called **precautionary saving**, saving to protect against unexpected setbacks. The third reason for saving is **bequest saving**, saving for the purpose of leaving an inheritance. Although most people save for one of these three reasons, the amount that they save depends on the economic environment. The economic variable that is most important in saving decisions is the real interest rate, r. The real interest rate is the reward for saving. Because of the power of compound interest in the long run, a higher real interest rate causes a dramatic increase in the real value of a saver's wealth. On the other hand, a higher real interest rate reduces the amount people need to save each year to reach a given wealth target. Nonetheless, empirical evidence suggests people are willing to save more the higher the real interest rate, all else being equal.

Learning Objective 3: Discuss the reasons why U.S. household saving rate is low
There are some who argue that, despite these rational reasons for saving, some people lack the self-control to do what is in their own best interest. Despite having good intentions to save, for example, some lack the necessary self-control to put aside as much of their income as they would like. This so-called self-control hypothesis suggests that consumer credit arrangements that make borrowing and spending easier may reduce the amount that people save. Similarly, the demonstration effect suggests that additional spending by some people causes others to spend more to maintain a lifestyle commensurate with their peer group. These hypotheses, in addition to the generous government assistance for the elderly, may explain why household saving in the U.S. has declined recently.

Learning Objective 4: Define national saving, private saving, public saving, and government budget deficit and surplus.
The above discussion pertains to individual saving, but macroeconomists are interested primarily in saving and wealth for the country as a whole. Similar to any economic unit, a nation's saving equals its current income less its spending on current needs. The current income of a country is its GDP (Y), the value of the final goods and service produced within the country's borders during the year. Identifying the part of total expenditures that corresponds to a country's current needs is more difficult. Because investment spending is done to improve the future productive capacity, it is clearly not a part of spending on current needs. For consumption and government spending, some portion is for current needs while another portion is for future needs. Determining how much should be attributed to each portion is extremely difficult. For this reason, the U.S. government statistics has for some years treated all of consumption expenditures and government spending as spending on current needs. The textbook authors follow this convention, with the caveat that this will understate the true amount of national saving. **National saving** (S), therefore, equals GDP less consumption expenditures and government purchases of goods and services, or $S = Y - C - G$ (this excludes the international sector, which is discussed in a later chapter).

To better understand national saving, one can divide it into two major components: private saving by households and businesses, and public saving by the government. To distinguish these two components, the above equation is expanded to incorporate taxes and payments made by the government to the private sector. Government payments to the private sector include transfer payments and interest paid to individuals and institutions that hold government bonds. **Transfer payments** are payments the government makes to the public for which it receives no current goods or services in return (e.g., social security benefits). If T represents taxes paid by the private sector to the government less transfer payments and government interest payments, it can be called net taxes. **Private saving** can, thus, be expressed as $S_{private} = Y - T - C$, or private sector after-tax income minus its consumption spending. Private sector saving can be further broken down into household saving and business saving. **Public saving**, or saving of the government sector, is equal to net tax payments minus government purchases ($S_{public} = T - G$). A **government budget deficit**, the excess of government spending over tax collections ($G - T$), implies that public saving is negative, while a **government budget surplus**, the excess of government tax collections over spending ($T - G$), means public saving is positive.

Note: To conclude that the adverse effects of low household saving on the family implies that low household saving is a problem for nation is to commit the "fallacy of composition." The fallacy of composition states, what is true for one part of a whole is not necessarily true for the whole. For example, if you alone stand up at a football game, you can see the game better. It does not follow, however, that if everyone at the game stands up, everyone can see better. Thus, while a low household saving rate may cause microeconomic problems for a family (such as insufficient funds to pay for college or to retire), it is not necessarily a macroeconomic problem for the nation.

Learning Objective 5: Discuss why low U.S. household saving is not a macroeconomic problem, but may be a microeconomic concern

In recent years, decreases in private household saving in the United States have been partially offset by increases in public saving. The relatively low U.S. household saving rate is not a problem from a macroeconomic perspective because national saving, not household saving, determines the capacity of an economy to invest in new capital goods and continue to improve its standard of living. Although U.S. household saving is low, saving by business firms is significant, and, during the 1990s, government budget surpluses have approximately offset the fall in household saving. Overall, despite the fact that it is low by international standards, the U.S. national saving rate has been reasonably stable and sufficient to allow it to become one of the most productive economies in the world. From a microeconomic perspective, however, the low household saving rate does exacerbate the problem of large and growing inequality in wealth among U.S. households. Saving patterns are increasing this inequality as better-off households not only save more, but, as business owners and stockholders, they also are the ultimate beneficiaries of the saving by businesses.

Learning Objective 6: Apply cost-benefit analysis to the investment decision and identify the factors that affect the costs and benefits of investment

From the point of view of the economy as a whole, the importance of national saving is that it provides the funds needed for investment. Investment is the creation of new capital goods and housing and is critical to increasing average labor productivity and improving standards of living. Firms' willingness to invest depends on the expected cost of using the capital and the expected benefit, measured as the marginal product, of the capital. On the cost side, two important factors are the price of capital goods and the real interest rate. The more expensive the capital goods, the less willing businesses are to invest in them. The real interest rate measures the opportunity cost of a capital investment. Since an increase in the real interest rate increases the opportunity cost of investing in new capital, it lowers the willingness of firms to invest. On the benefit side, the key factor in determining business investment is the value of the marginal product of the new capital, calculated net of operating costs, maintenance expenses, and taxes paid on the revenues the capital generates. The value of the marginal product of capital is affected by several factors, including technological improvement and the relative price of the good or service that the capital is used to produce. Technological improvements and increases in the price of the good or service raise the marginal product of capital and increase the willingness of businesses to invest.

Learning Objective 7: Apply the supply and demand model to analyze the issue of national saving

The factors that affect the costs and benefits of investment can be analyzed in a supply and demand model. In an economy without international borrowing and lending, national saving must equal investment. The supply of national savings and the demand for savings are equalized through the workings of financial markets. The supply of saving shows the relationship between the real interest rate and the quantity of national saving. It is an upward-sloping curve because empirical evidence suggests that increases in the real interest rate stimulate saving, all other things equal. The demand for saving shows the relationship between the real interest rate and the quantity of investment in new capital. It is a downward-sloping curve because higher real interest rates raise the opportunity cost of capital and reduce the willingness of firms to invest, all other things equal. Holding aside the possibility of borrowing from foreigners, a country can only invest those resources that its savers make available.

In equilibrium, desired investment (the quantity demanded of saving) and national saving (the quantity supplied of saving) must be equal. Desired saving is equated with desired investment through adjustments in the real interest rate, which functions as the price of saving. Changes in factors other than the real interest rate that affect the supply of or demand for saving will shift the curves, leading to a new equilibrium in the financial market. Technological improvements and changes in the price of the good or service produced by the capital will shift the demand for saving. The supply of saving is affected by changes in private and public saving. In particular, an increase in the government budget deficit shifts the supply of saving curve to the left and the equilibrium quantity of saving and investment will decrease. This tendency of government budget deficits to reduce investment spending is called **crowding out**.

Hint: The financial markets are a mechanism for rationing the limited national saving in an economy among the many possible investment opportunities. Essentially, markets ration the national savings first to those individual investors whose projects generate the greatest profits and, therefore, can afford to pay the highest price (i.e., the highest interest rate) to obtain the loans. When the government runs a budget deficit, it must borrow funds to cover the excess expenditures. It pays back the loans, however, with tax revenues rather than with profits.

You can think of the financial markets as a queue with private sector borrowers lined up to get their projects funded. The investors with the highest potential for earning profits are at the front of the line and those with lower profit potential behind. Then, the government representatives come along and they "cut" in line. As a result, they push further back in the queue some private sector investors. If some private sector investors fail to get to the front of the line before the national saving runs out, they will not get their projects funded. Thus, they are crowded out.

III. Self-Test

Key Terms
Match the term in the right-hand column with the appropriate definition in the left-hand column by placing the letter of the term in the blank in front of its' definition. (Answers are given at the end of the chapter.)

1. ____The excess of government spending over tax collections (G – T).

2. ____The saving of the entire economy, equal to GDP less consumption expenditures and government purchases of goods and services, or Y – C – G.

3. ____The debts that one owes

4. ____Decreases in the value of existing assets.

5. ____Saving that is identical to the government budget surplus.

6. ____Payments the government makes to the public for which it receives no current goods or services in return.

7. ____After-tax income of the private sector minus its consumption spending (Y – T – C).

8. ____Saving done for the purpose of leaving an inheritance.

9. ____A measure that is defined per unit of time.

10. ___Saving divided by income.

11. ___A measure that is defined at a point in time.

12. ___Saving to meet long-term objectives, such as retirement, college attendance, or purchase of a home.

13. ___Current income minus spending on current needs.

14. ___Saving to protect against unexpected setbacks, such as the loss of a job or a medical emergency.

15. ___The tendency of increased government deficits to reduce investment spending.

16. ___The value of assets minus liabilities.

17. ___Anything of value that one owns.

18. ___Increases in the value of existing assets.

19. ___The excess of government tax collections over government spending (T – G).

20. ___A list of an economic units assets and liabilities on a specific date.

a. assets

b. balance sheet

c. bequest saving

d. capital gains

e. capital losses

f. crowding out

g. flow

h. government budget deficit

i. government budget surplus

j. liabilities

k. life-cycle saving.

l. national saving

m. precautionary saving

n. private saving

o. public saving

p. saving

q. saving rate

r. stock

s. transfer payments

t. wealth

Multiple-Choice Questions
Circle the letter that corresponds to the best answer. (Answers are given at the end of the chapter.)

1. Luis had accumulated $5,000 in wealth at the end of a year. At the beginning of the next year he deposits $50 in a saving account that will earn 10% interest per year. If there are no changes in his liabilities, at the end of the next year his wealth will have
   A.   increased by $50.
   B.   decreased by $50.
   C.   increased by $55.
   D.   decreased by $55.
   E.   not changed.

2. The strong U.S. bull market of the late 1990s ended (at least temporarily) in early 2000, as the stock market indexes fell 25% or more during the second quarter of 2000. As a result, many Americans
   A.   suffered capital losses and increases in their wealth.
   B.   suffered capital losses and decreases in their wealth.
   C.   enjoyed capital gains and increases in their wealth.
   D.   enjoyed capital gains and decreases in their wealth.
   E.   suffered capital losses and decreases in their liabilities.

3. If the real interest rate on saving account increases from 3% to 5%, all other things equal
   A.   business investment spending for new capital will increase.
   B.   business investment spending for new capital will remain unchanged.
   C.   people will be less willing to save.
   D.   people will be more willing to save.
   E.   the amount people will save will remain unchanged.

4. Which of the following hypotheses is a plausible explanation for why U.S. households save so little?
   A.   Interest rates in the United States are typically lower than they are in the rest of the world.
   B.   Most American already own homes and, therefore, have less need for life-cycle saving.
   C.   The highly developed financial markets in the United States have reduced the need for precautionary saving by Americans.
   D.   Government assistance to low-income U.S. households has increased the demonstration effects on spending by the poor.
   E.   Government assistance to the elderly has reduced the need for life-cycle saving.

5. If net taxes paid by households increase,
   A.   private saving will decrease.
   B.   private saving will increase.
   C.   public saving will decrease.
   D.   transfer payments to households will decrease.
   E.   transfer payments to households will increase.

6. The low and declining U.S. household saving rate is
    A. a macroeconomic problem because it reduces the amount of funds available for
        investment and, thus, reduces the standard of living.
    B. not a macroeconomic problem because the national saving rate has been stable and
        sufficient.
    C. a microeconomic problem because it reduces the amount of funds available for
        investment and, thus, reduces the standard of living.
    D. not a microeconomic problem because the national saving rate has been stable and
        sufficient.
    E. not a microeconomic problem because the booming stock market has increased the
        wealth of Americans and reduced income inequality.

7. Joe's Taco Hut can purchase a delivery truck for $20,000 and Joe estimates it will generate a
   net income (i.e., after-taxes and maintenance and operating costs) of $2,000 per year. He
   should
    A. purchase the truck if the real interest rate is less than 2%.
    B. not purchase the truck if the real interest rate is greater than 2%.
    C. purchase the truck if the real interest rate is greater than 10%.
    D. purchase the truck if the real interest rate is less than 10%.
    E. purchase the truck if the real interest rate is less than 3%.

8. The investment demand curve indicates that there is a(n)
    A. positive relationship between the real interest rates and the level of investment spending,
        all other things equal.
    B. inverse relationship between the real interest rates and the level of investment spending,
        all other things equal.
    C. direct relationship between the real interest rates and the level of investment spending,
        all other things equal.
    D. inverse relationship between the determinants of investment and the level of investment
        spending, holding interest rates constant.
    E. positive relationship between the determinants of investment and the level of investment
        spending, holding interest rates constant.

9. Rafael's current income is $100 more per month than his current consumption needs. He
   decides to use the $100 to reduce his credit card debt. As a result, his
    A. liabilities will decrease and his wealth will increase.
    B. liabilities and his wealth will decrease.
    C. assets will decrease and his wealth will increase.
    D. assets and his wealth will decrease.
    E. assets and his wealth will increase.

10. If, in a given year, the saving rate in an economy decreases by an amount equal to the net
    capital gains, the economy's
    A. wealth will decrease.
    B. wealth will increase.

C. wealth will remain unchanged.
D. assets will decrease.
E. liabilities will decrease.

11. One reason that household saving in Japan is higher than household saving in the U.S. is
    A. that the average Japanese income is higher than it is in the United States.
    B. housing in the United States is more expensive and, therefore, Americans spend more of
       their income on housing and save less.
    C. because Japanese workers continue working until they are much older and, therefore,
       they can save more.
    D. the Japanese save more for precautionary reasons because they have, in general, less job
       security than American workers.
    E. the higher cost of housing and larger down payments required to purchase a house in
       Japan results in higher life-cycle saving.

12. During a conversation with her mother about her financial circumstances, Sylvia complained
    that she could not afford to save because she wanted to maintain a lifestyle similar to that of
    her friends. Her mother suggested that if she would save more now, she would not only have
    more wealth, but she would also have a higher standard of living than her friends in the
    future. Her mother's argument was
    A. incorrect, because if she saved her standard of living would be lower than that of her
       friends.
    B. incorrect, and probably an attempt to confuse her daughter in order to get her to begin
       saving some of her income.
    C. correct, because of the power of compound interest her income would increase to a level
       that would allow her to save and consume more.
    D. correct, because the more saving, the higher the standard of living.
    E. irrelevant, because daughters never listen to what their mother tells them.

13. Household saving in the United States
    A. is low relative to previous periods, but approximately equal to the rate in other
       countries.
    B. decreased through the 1990s and became negative in 1998.
    C. had decreased since the 1960s, but, because the economy was so strong during the
       1990s, has recently increased.
    D. is low relative to other countries and has declined since the 1960s.
    E. is low relative to other countries, but has increased during the 1990s.

14. Private saving
    A. can be broken down into household saving and business saving.
    B. can be broken down into transfers and household saving.
    C. rises when net taxes increase.
    D. falls when income rises.
    E. rises when government spending decreases.

15. An increase in net taxes (i.e., taxes paid by the private sector to the government minus transfer payments and interest payments made by the government to the private sector) will
    A. increase private saving.
    B. decrease public saving.
    C. increase public saving.
    D. reduce investment in new capital equipment.
    E. cause crowding out.

16. Public saving is
    A. increased when the government budget deficit rises.
    B. identical to the government budget surplus.
    C. less important to national saving than private saving.
    D. more important to national saving than private saving.
    E. unimportant in determining the capacity of an economy to invest in new capital.

17. Samantha has $5,000 in a CD account paying 10% interest. It will mature in a few weeks and the bank told her that interest rates on CDs were decreasing. She is thinking of spending it on a new computer and software that she will use to start a bookkeeping service. If she were to do so, she would have to quit her job where she makes $15,000 per year in after-tax income. She has estimated that the bookkeeping service will earn a net income of $15, 250 after taxes, and maintenance and operating costs.
    A. Since the interest rate is declining, Samantha would be better off using the money to buy the computer.
    B. If the interest rate on the new CD is 7% or greater she should leave the money in the CD.
    C. If the interest rate on the new CD is 2.5% or greater she should buy the computer.
    D. If the interest rate on the new CD is 2% or less she should leave the money in the CD.
    E. If the interest rate on the new CD is 5% or greater she should leave the money in the CD.

18. As the cost of capital goods increases relative to other prices, the
    A. demand for investment in new capital will shift to the left.
    B. demand for investment in new capital will shift to the right.
    C. amount of investment in new capital will increase.
    D. amount of saving will rise.
    E. amount of saving will fall.

19. A decrease in the capital gains tax on income generated through investment in new capital will
    A. shift the demand for investment curve to the left.
    B. shift the demand for investment curve to the right.
    C. shift the supply of saving curve to the left.
    D. shift the supply of saving curve to the right.
    E. decrease real interest rates.

20. The introduction of a new technology that raises the marginal product of new capital will
   A. decrease real interest rates and increase the equilibrium quantity of saving supplied and demanded.
   B. decrease real interest rates and the equilibrium quantity of saving supplied and demanded.
   C. increase real interest rates and the equilibrium quantity of saving supplied and demanded.
   D. increase real interest rates and decrease the equilibrium quantity of saving supplied and demanded.
   E. decrease real interest rates and the equilibrium quantity of saving supplied and demanded will remain unchanged.

Short Answer Problems
(Answers and solutions are given at the end of the chapter.)

1. Savings and Wealth
In this problem you will identify an individual's assets and liabilities to determine his wealth. You will also calculate the effect of saving on wealth over time.

At the end of the year 2000, Franklin prepared for the new millenium by writing down all his assets and liabilities. His list included a car with a market value of $7,500, but with $6,000 left on the car loan; his home with a market value of $125,000 and a mortgage of $122,500; a checking account with a $750 balance; a credit card balance of $1,000; 8,000 shares of the ABC Corporation with a current price of $12 per share; and a debt of $2,500 on a student loan.

A. Construct Franklin's balance sheet below, and calculate his wealth.

Franklin's Balance Sheet

Assets	Liabilities
Total	Total
	Net Worth

B. Upon returning to work in January 2001, his boss informed him that he had been awarded a bonus of $1,000. He decided he would not spend it on consumption, but rather used it to increase his wealth. His alternatives were to put it into a CD account paying 7.5% annual interest, pay off his credit card debt that had an annual interest charge of 11%, or pay off his student loan that had a 7% annual interest charge. What would you recommend that he do with his bonus to maximize the increase in his wealth? _____
Why? _____

C. After reviewing his net worth, Franklin decided that he has insufficient wealth to achieve his goal of retiring in 20 years. He decided he would begin saving $500 per year in a 401K account (a retirement account that is not subject to taxes until after he retires). After investigating all the options, Franklin settled on depositing his 401K funds into a money market account paying 5% annual interest. Assume that Franklin deposits $500 on the 1st of January in each year, and calculate the value of his retirement account at the end of each of the following periods: 1 year _____, 2 years _____, 3 years _____ , 4 years _____, 5 years _____ .

D. At the end of the 5th year, Franklin reviews his retirement account and discovers that had he deposited the 401K funds in a stock fund rather than the money market account, he would have earned an average of 10% in capital gains each year. Recalculate the value that his retirement account would have reached, if he had chosen the stock fund, at the end of 1 year _____, 2 years _____, 3 years _____ , 4 years _____, and 5 years _____ .

2. Cost-Benefit Analysis for Investment Decisions

This problem focuses on the use of cost-benefit analysis in making investment decisions. You will calculate the marginal product of capital, determine the marginal benefit and marginal cost of capital, and decide whether to make an investment. You will also analyze the effects of changes in taxation, the cost of capital, and expected income on the investment decision.

Thelma is thinking of going into the business of translating documents for international businesses. In order to do so, she needs to borrow $5,000 to the buy computer equipment. She has estimated that she will earn a profit of $25,000 per year, after deducting operating and maintenance costs. The tax rate on her business profit each year would be 15%, and the annual interest rate on the loan would equal 12%. Her best job alternative would be teaching Spanish in high school with an after-tax income of $20,000.

A. Assume the computer equipment does not lose value over time. Calculate the marginal product of the computer equipment. $ _____

B. Calculate the amount of the annual interest that Thelma would have to pay on the loan. $_____

C. Should Thelma choose to invest in the computer equipment and start the translation business? _____ Why or why not? _____
_____

D. If the government increases the tax rate on business profits to 19%, and the computer equipment does not lose value over time, calculate the marginal product of the computer equipment. $ _____

E. After the tax increase in Question D, should Thelma to buy the computer equipment and start the translation business? _____ Why? _____
_____

F. If the cost of the computer equipment decreased to $2,000, should Thelma buy the computer equipment and start the translation business? _____ Why or why not? _____
_____

G. If the computer equipment was less productive than Thelma thought, so that her profit was $22,500 per year, should Thelma buy the computer equipment and start the translation business? _____ Why or why not? ? _____
_____

3. The Supply and Demand for Saving

In this problem you will use the supply and demand model to analyze the financial market for saving and investment. You will determine the equilibrium real interest rate and quantity of saving and determine the effects of changes in the government budget and technology on the market equilibrium.

Answer the questions below based on the following the supply and demand curves for saving.

Real Interest Rate (%)

($ billions)

A. The equilibrium real interest rate is _____ % and the equilibrium quantity of saving/ investment is $_____ billion.

B. An increase in the government budget surplus would cause the (supply/demand) _____ curve for saving to (increase/decrease) _____ . On the above graph, draw a new curve that would reflect the change caused by the increased government budget surplus.

C. As a result of the increased government budget surplus, the equilibrium real interest rate _____ and the equilibrium quantity of saving/investment _____ .

D. The introduction of new technologies that increase the marginal product of new capital would cause the (supply/demand) _____ curve for saving to (increase/decrease) _____ . On the above graph, draw a new curve that would reflect the change caused by the new technologies.

E. As a result of the new technologies, the equilibrium real interest rate _____ and the equilibrium quantity of saving/investment _____ .

IV. Becoming an Economic Naturalist: Case Study

Economic Naturalist 9.5 discusses alternative tax mechanisms (income vs. consumption taxes) to increase national savings in the U.S. In 2001, the U.S. Congress legislated lower income tax rates on capital gains and dividends, in part, "to promote saving and economic growth." These lower tax rates, however, are temporary and will expire in 2008 without further legislation. President Bush has proposed in his 2006 budget to make the tax cuts permanent. But some oppose his proposal arguing that it will reduce our national saving. Discuss the implicit assumptions of those who support the President's proposal and those opposed regarding the impact of the tax cuts on the private and public components of national saving.

Answer:

V. Self-Test Solutions

Key Terms
1. h
2. l
3. j
4. e
5. o
6. s
7. n
8. c
9. g
10. q
11. r
12. k
13. p
14. m
15. f
16. t
17. a
18. d
19. i
20. b

Multiple-Choice Questions

1. C His wealth increases by an amount equal to the saving plus the interest earned on the saving. Thus, $50 + $5 ($50 x .10) = $55
2. B
3. D
4. E
5. A
6. B
7. D If the interest rate is less than 10%, then the financial cost of the capital (equal to the amount of the loan times the interest rate) will be less than the financial benefit of the capital (equal to the net income earned with the capital).
8. B
9. A Debt is a type of liability, and reducing liabilities increase wealth.
10. C
11. E
12. C
13. D
14. A
15. C
16. B
17. E The financial benefit of the computer is $250. If the interest rate on the CD were less than 5%, the financial cost of the capital ($5,000 times the interest rate) would be less than the financial benefit of the computer. Therefore, if the interest rate on the CD is less than 5%, she should buy the computer.
18. A
19. B
20. C

Short Answer Problems

1.

A.

Franklin's Balance Sheet

Assets		Liabilities	
Car	$7,500	Car loan	$6,000
Home	125,000	Mortgage	122,500
Checking account	750	Credit card balance	1,000
ABC Corp. shares	96,000	Student loan	2,500
Total	$ 229,250	Total	$132,000
		Net Worth	$ 97,250

B. He should pay off his credit card debt because it will reduce his liabilities and, thus, increase his wealth. The credit card debt has a higher opportunity cost (interest rate) than the student loan and he will save more in interest payments than he would earn on the CD account.

C. $525(= $500 + [$500 x.05]); $1,076.25 (= 525 + 500 + [1,025 x .05]); $1,655.06; $2,262.81; $2,900.95

D. $550; $1,155; $1,820.50; $2,552.55; $3,357.80

2.
A. $1,250 (Thelma would have to pay $3,750 [$25,000 x .15] in profit taxes, leaving her an after-tax income of $25,000 – $3,750 = $21,250. Subtracting the Spanish teacher salary [$20,000] that she must forego to start the translating business from the after-tax income [$21,250] equals the marginal product of the computer equipment.)
B. $600 (= $5,000 x .12)
C. Yes; Because the financial cost ($600 interest payment) is less than the financial benefit ($1,250 marginal product of the computer equipment).
D. $250 (The solution is the same as in 2A, except the tax rate is now .19.)
E. No; Because the financial cost ($600) is greater than the financial benefit ($250).
F. Yes; Because the financial cost ($240) is less than the financial benefit ($250).
G. No; Because the financial benefit ($ –1,775) is less than the financial cost.

3.
A. 4; $1,000 billion
B. supply; increase;

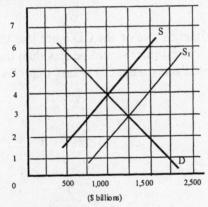

C. decreased; increased
D. demand; increase;

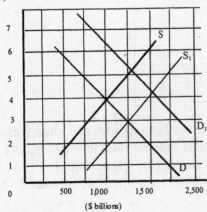

E. increased; increased

Chapter 10
Money, Prices and the Federal Reserve

I. Pretest: What Do You Really Know?
Circle the letter that corresponds to the best answer. (Answers appear immediately after the final question).

1. Money is
   A. the same as income.
   B. all financial assets.
   C. any asset used to make purchases.
   D. the sum of assets minus debts.
   E. the market value of all final goods and services produced in a country in a year.

2. The functions of money include
   A. medium of exchange, diversification of risk, and store of value.
   B. medium of exchange, unit of value, and store of account.
   C. medium of value, unit of exchange, and store of account.
   D. medium of account, store of value, and unit of exchange.
   E. medium of exchange, unit of account, and store of value.

3. M1 consists of
   A. all currency and balances held in checking accounts.
   B. currency outstanding and balances held in checking accounts.
   C. M2 plus savings deposits, small-denomination time deposits, and money market mutual funds.
   D. currency outstanding, balances in checking accounts plus savings deposits, small-denomination time deposits, and money market mutual funds.
   E. M2 minus balances in checking accounts, savings deposits, small-denomination time deposits, and money market mutual funds.

4. Banks reserves are

    A. cash or similar assets held for the purpose of meeting depositor withdrawals and payments.

    B. cash or similar assets held for the purpose of insuring bank deposits.

    C. cash or similar assets held for the purpose of making loans.

    D. cash or similar assets held for the purpose of ensuring that loans are repaid and depositors funds are not depleted.

    E. cash or similar assets held for the purpose of facilitating monetary policy.

5. A fractional-reserve banking system

    A. allows bank reserves to circulate as part of the money supply.

    B. requires banks to hold reserves equal to 100 percent of their deposits.

    C. allows banks to expand the money supply by lending some of their deposits.

    D. is illegal in most countries because banks are required to maintain reserves equal to their deposits.

    E. enables banks to lend 100 percent of their reserves.

6. The primary responsibility of the Federal Reserve System is to

    A. regulate the stock market.

    B. enable banks to make affordable mortgages.

    C. print currency.

    D. conduct monetary policy.

    E. insure bank deposits.

7. The most important, most convenient, and most flexible way in which the Federal Reserve affects the supply of bank reserves is through

    A. conducting open-market operations.

    B. changing the Federal Reserve discount rate.

    C. printing currency.

    D. changing interest rates.

    E. conducting bank examinations.

8. If the Federal Reserve wants to decrease the money supply, it should

    A. print more currency.

    B. print less currency.

    C. conduct open-market purchases.

    D. conduct open-market sales.

    E. decrease interest rates.

9. Deposit insurance is a system in which the government guarantees that

    A. depositors will not lose any money even if their bank goes bankrupt.

    B. people can have deposits at commercial banks.

    C. commercial banks will not go bankrupt.

    D. depositors of commercial banks can obtain low-cost life insurance.

    E. commercial banks will not lose any deposits.

10. In the long run, a higher rate of growth in the money supply will cause a higher rate of inflation
   A. if the velocity of money increases.
   B. because the larger amount of money in circulation will allow people to bid up the prices of goods and services.
   C. because the higher velocity of money will allow people to bid up the prices of goods and services.
   D. because the larger quantity of transactions will allow people to bid up the prices of goods and services.
   E. if the velocity of money increases and the quantity of transactions is constant.

Solutions and Feedback to Pretest

For each question you incorrectly answered, we strongly recommend taking the time to review the appropriate material before continuing. In the table below are listed for each question the pertinent Learning Objective from the following Key Point Review.

Correct Answer	Learning Objective
1. C	1
2. E	2
3. B	3
4. A	4
5. C	4
6. D	5
7. A	6
8. D	6
9. A	7
10. B	8

II. Key Point Review
The Forest

This chapter focuses on the role of money in modern economies. The central questions you need to be able to answer are:

- What is money and what are the functions of money?
- How is the money supply measured?
- How is money created?
- What is the structure and responsibilities of the Federal Reserve Banking System?
- What is the relationship between the money supply and inflation in the long run?

The Trees

Learning Objective 1: Define money and barter

Money is any asset that can be used in making purchases. Without money, all economic transactions would have to be in the form of **barter**, that is the direct trade of goods and services for other goods and services. Barter is inefficient because it requires that both parties to a trade have something the other party wants, a so-called double coincidence of wants. Money facilitates more efficient transactions and permits individuals to specialize in producing particular goods and services.

Learning Objective 2: Define the three functions of money

Money has three principal uses: it serves as a medium of exchange, a unit of account, and a store of value. Money serves as a **medium of exchange** when it is used to purchase goods and services. As a **unit of account**, money is the basic yardstick for measuring economic value. As a **store of value** money serves as a means of holding wealth.

> **Note:** The store of value function of money is undermined by inflation because inflation erodes the purchasing power of money. When you hold some of your wealth in the form of money and the economy experiences inflation, what you can purchase with those dollars decreases over time. It make sense then that, as the purchase power of your money decreases, you will choose to hold less of your wealth in the form of money (and, thus, more of your wealth in some other form, e.g., land). During periods of hyperinflation (rapidly escalating inflation), the medium of exchange function of money can also be undermined. That is, people will prefer to not accept money in exchange for goods and services and may revert to a barter system, or give preference to some non-domestic currencies (e.g., dollars rather than rubles).

Learning Objective 3: Calculate the amount of M1 and M2

When measuring the quantity of money in the economy, economists vary as to how they define the concept of money. The narrowest definition of the amount of money in the United States is called **M1**, the sum of currency outstanding and balances held in checking accounts. A broader measure of the money supply is **M2**, which includes all the assets in M1 plus savings deposits, small-denomination time deposits, and money market mutual funds. Because the definition of the money supply includes both currency and bank deposits, the amount of money in the economy depends in part on the behavior of commercial banks and their depositors. When households or businesses deposit currency into a bank, the currency becomes a part of the bank reserves.

> **Hint:** Because the money measures are cumulative, when calculating M2 be sure to remember to begin with the value of M1 (or the amounts of the components that make of M1) before adding in the value of the non-M1 components.

Learning Objective 4: Define bank reserves, 100% reserve banking, reserve/deposit ratio, and fractional reserve banking system

Bank reserves are cash or similar assets held by commercial banks for the purpose of meeting depositor withdrawals and payments. When banks must keep bank reserves equal to the amount of their deposits, it is referred to as a **100% reserve banking system**. If banks can maintain a **reserve/deposit ratio** (bank reserves divided by deposits) of less than 100%, then it is referred to as a **fractional-reserve banking system**. In a fractional-reserve banking system the amount of the money supply is expanded when banks make loans in the form of new deposits.

Learning Objective 5: Define the Federal Reserve System, Board of Governors, and Federal Open-Market Committee and discuss the structure of each component of the Fed

The **Federal Reserve System**, often called the Fed, is the central bank of the United States and is responsible for monetary policy, as well as oversight and regulation of financial markets. The leadership of the Fed is provided by its **Board of Governors**, consisting of seven members appointed by the President to staggered fourteen-year terms. Decisions about monetary policy are made by the **Federal Open Market Committee** (FOMC), which is made up of the seven members of the Board of Governors, the President of the Federal Reserve Bank of New York, and four of the presidents of the other Federal Reserve Banks. The Fed's primary responsibility is making monetary policy, which involves decisions about the appropriate size of the nation's money supply. The Fed controls the money supply indirectly by changing the amount of reserves held by commercial banks. The Fed affects the amount of reserves through open-market operations, discount window lending, and changing reserve requirements.

Learning Objective 6: Explain how the Fed uses open market operations to change the amount of bank reserves and the money supply

Open-market operations are the most important tool of monetary policy. When the Fed wants to increase the money supply, the Fed buys government bonds (an **open-market purchase)** from the public. The seller of the bond receives a check in exchange for its bonds and deposits some, or all, of the amount of the check in a bank account. As a result, the bank's reserves increase allowing the bank to make new loans and increase the money supply. **Open-market sales** of government bonds to the public are used to reduce bank reserves and the money supply. When the buyer writes a check to pay for the bond, banks reserves are decreased and, thus, the bank lending eventually is reduced.

Learning Objective 7: Explain the Fed's role in stabilizing financial markets

Besides controlling the money supply, the Fed has the responsibility (along with other government agencies) of ensuring that financial markets operate smoothly. Historically, in the United States, banking panics were the most disruptive type of recurrent financial crisis. A banking panic is an episode in which depositors, spurred by news or rumors of the imminent bankruptcy of one or more banks, rush to withdraw their deposits from the banking system. The Fed, established in 1913 in response to a particularly severe banking panic in 1907, was given the power to supervise and regulate banks to create greater confidence in banks, and was allowed to lend cash to banks to help them meet withdrawals during a bank panic. Following the creation of the Fed there were no bank panics until 1930. During 1930-33, however, the United States experienced the worst and most protracted series of bank panics in its history. The inability of the Fed to stop the bank panics of the 1930s caused Congress to institute a system of deposit insurance. Under a system of deposit insurance, the government guarantees depositors that they will get their money back even if the bank goes bankrupt, eliminating the incentive of depositors to withdraw their deposits when rumors of financial trouble are circulating.

Learning Objective 8: Explain the relationship between money and prices in the long run
In the long run, the rate of growth of the money supply and the inflation rate are positively related. That is, a higher rate of growth in the money supply will cause a higher rate of inflation because the larger amount of money in circulation will allow people to bid up the prices of goods and services. Velocity measures the speed at which money circulates and is calculated as the value of transactions (or nominal GDP) divided by the supply of money. The definition of velocity can be rewritten as the quantity equation, or M x V = P x Y. The quantity equation shows that, if velocity and output are constant, a given percentage increase in the money supply will lead to the same percentage increase in the price level.

> **Hint:** The key to understanding the relationship between the change in the money supply and the inflation rate is to recognize that the quantity equation refers to **amounts** of money supply and price **level**, whereas the last sentence in the above paragraph refers to a **change** in the money supply and the **change** in the price level.

III. Self-Test

Key Terms
Match the term in the right-hand column with the appropriate definition in the left-hand column by placing the letter of the term in the blank in front of its' definition. (Answers are given at the end of the chapter.)

1. _____ A basic measure of economic value.

2. _____ Any asset that can be used in making purchases.

3. _____ Bank reserves divided by deposits.

4. _____ The sum of currency outstanding and balances held in checking accounts.

5. _____ A situation in which banks' reserves equal 100 percent of their deposits.

6. _____ Cash or similar assets held by commercial banks for the purpose of meeting depositor withdrawals and payments.

7. _____ An asset used in purchasing goods and services.

8. _____ An asset that services as a means of holding wealth.

9. _____ All the assets in M1 plus some additional assets that are usable in making payments but at greater cost or inconvenience than currency or checks.

10. _____ The direct trade of goods or services for other goods or services.

a. bank reserves

b. banking panic

c. barter

d. Board of Governors

e. deposit insurance

f. Federal Open Market Committee (or FOMC)

g. Federal Reserve System (or Fed)

h. fractional-reserve banking system

i. M1

j. M2

11.____ The leadership of the Fed, consisting of seven governors   k. medium of exchange
appointed by the President to staggered 14-year terms.

12.____ A banking system in which bank reserves are less than   l. money
deposits so that the reserve-deposit ration is less than 100 percent.

13.____ The committee that makes decisions concerning monetary   m. 100 percent reserves
policy.   banking

14.____ The central bank of the United States.   n. open-market operations

15.____ Open-market purchases and open-market sales.   o. open-market purchases

16.____ A system under which the government guarantees that   p. open-market sale
depositors will not lose any money even if their bank goes
bankrupt.

17.____ The sale by the Fed of government bonds to the public for   q. quantity equation
the purpose of reducing bank reserves and the money supply.

18.____ A measure of the speed at which money circulates.   r. reserve-deposit ratio

19.____ Money times velocity equals nominal GDP.   s. store of value

20.____ An episode in which depositors, spurred by news or   t. unit of account
rumors of the imminent bankruptcy of one or more banks, rsuh to
withdraw their deposits from the banking system.

21.____ The purchase of government bonds from the public by the   u. velocity
Fed for the purpose of increasing the supply of bank reserves and
the money supply.

Multiple-Choice Questions
Circle the letter that corresponds to the best answer. (Answers are given at the end of the chapter.)

1. Double coincidence of wants is avoided if money is used as a
    A. medium of exchange.
    B. measure of value.
    C. standard of deferred payment.
    D. store of value
    E. tool of monetary policy.

2. Money serves as a basic yardstick for measuring economic value (i.e., a unit of account), allowing
    A. people to hold their wealth in a liquid form.
    B. governments to restrict the issuance of private monies.
    C. easy comparison of the relative prices of goods and services.
    D. goods and services to be exchanged with a double coincidence of wants.
    E. private money to be issued for local use.

3. In the United States, money is issued
    A. only by the Fed.
    B. by the Fed and all commercial banks.
    C. mainly by the c Fed, but also is issued privately in some communities.
    D. once per year by the Fed.
    E. by the U.S. Congress

4. M1 differs from M2 in that
   A. M1 includes currency and balances held in checking accounts, which are not included in M2.
   B. M2 includes savings deposits, small-denomination time deposits, and money market mutual funds which are not included in M1
   C. M2 includes small savings accounts, large time deposits, and money market mutual funds that are not included in M1.
   D. M1 is a broader measure of the money supply than M2.
   E. the assets in M2 are more liquid than the assets in M1.

5. The difference between a fractional-reserve banking system and a 100 percent reserve banking system is that a fractional reserve banking system
   A. only allows banks to lend a fraction of their reserves, whereas a 100 percent banking system allows banks to lend 100 percent of their reserves.
   B. only allows the money supply to increase by a fraction of banks' reserves, whereas a 100 percent banking system allows the money supply to increase by 100 percent of their reserves.
   C. does not allow banks to lend their reserves, but a 100 percent reserve banking system does allow banks to lend their reserves.
   D. allows banks to lend some of their reserves, but a 100 percent reserve banking system does not allow banks to lend any of their reserves.
   E. does not allow for growth in the money supply through bank lending, while a 100 percent reserve banking system does allow for growth in the money supply through bank lending.

6. When a bank makes a loan by crediting the borrower's checking account balance with an amount equal to the loan
   A. money is created.
   B. the bank gains new reserves.
   C. the bank immediately loses reserves.
   D. money is destroyed.
   E. the Fed has made an open-market purchase.

7. If a bank's desired reserve/deposit ratio is .33 and it has deposit liabilities of $100 million and reserves of $50 million, it
   A. has too few reserves and will reduce its lending.
   B. has too many reserves and will increase its lending.
   C. has the correct amount of reserves and outstanding loans.
   D. should increase the amount of its reserves.
   E. should decrease the amount of its reserves.

8. If the reserve/deposit ratio is .25 and the banking system receives an additional $10 million in reserves, bank deposits can increase by a maximum of
   A. $10 million.
   B. $250 million.
   C. $400 million.
   D. $4 million.
   E. $40 million.

9. Decisions about the United States' monetary policy are made by the
   A. U.S. Congress.
   B. President of the United States.
   C. Fed's Board of Governors.
   D. Federal Open Market Committee (FOMC).
   E. 12 presidents of the regional Federal Reserve Banks.

10. The most important tool of monetary policy is
    A. reserve requirement ratios.
    B. the discount rate.
    C. open-market operations.
    D. the minimum net worth required of banks.
    E. market interest rates.

11. When the Fed sells government securities, the banks'
    A. reserves will increase and lending will expand, causing an increase in the money supply.
    B. reserves will decrease and lending will contract, causing a decrease in the money supply.
    C. reserve requirements will increase and lending will contract, causing a decrease in the money supply.
    D. reserves/deposit ratio will increase and lending will expand, causing an increase in the money supply.
    E. reserves/deposit ratio will decrease and lending will contract, causing an increase in the money supply.

12. An open-market purchase of government securities by the Fed will
    A. increase bank reserves, and the money supply will increase.
    B. decrease bank reserves, and the money supply will increase.
    C. increase bank reserves, and the money supply will decrease.
    D. decrease bank reserves, and the money supply will decrease.
    E. increase bank reserves, and the money supply will not change.

13. The FOMC consists of
    A. seven members appointed by the President of the United States, subject to confirmation by the Senate.
    B. 12 regional Federal Reserve Bank presidents.
    C. the seven Fed governors, the president of the Federal Reserve bank of New York, and four presidents of other regional Federal Reserve Banks.
    D. the Fed chairman, the secretary of the U.S. Treasury and 12 regional Federal Reserve Bank presidents.
    E. the President of the United States, the Fed chairman, and the secretary of the U.S. Treasury.

14. When an individual deposits currency into a checking account
    A. bank reserves increase, which allows banks to lend more and, ultimately, increases the money supply.
    B. bank reserves decrease, which reduces the amount banks can lend thereby reducing the growth of the money supply.
    C. bank reserves are unchanged.
    D. bank reserves decrease, which increases the amount banks can lend, thereby increasing the growth of the money supply.
    E. bank reserves increase, which reduces the amount banks can lend, thereby reducing the growth of the money supply.

15. Deposit insurance for banks
    A. helped the Fed combat the bank panics of 1930-33.
    B. was first legislated by the Federal Reserve Bank Act of 1913.
    C. may induce the managers of banks to take more risks.
    D. guarantees the interest payments on depositors' checking accounts.
    E. is a perfect solution to the problem of bank panics.

16. Holding money as a store of wealth has the advantage of being useful as a medium of exchange and being anonymous. The disadvantages of holding your wealth in the form of money are that it
    A. may be stolen or lost, and people may think you're a smuggler or drug dealer.
    B. is difficult to trace and may be lost or stolen.
    C. may be lost or stolen and usually pays no interest.
    D. pays no interest and is difficult to trace.
    E. pays no interest and people may think you're a smuggler or drug dealer.

17. During the bank panic of 1930-33, the public withdrew deposits from the bank preferring to hold currency. As a result,
    A. bank reserves decreased but were offset by an equal increase in currency, with no net effect on the money supply.
    B. bank reserves increased by less than the increase in currency, causing the money supply to decrease.
    C. bank reserves decreased by more than the increase in currency, causing the money supply to decrease.
    D. bank reserves decreased by less than the increase in currency, causing the money supply to increase.
    E. bank reserves decrease by an amount equal to the increase in currency, causing the money supply to decrease.

18. From a macroeconomic perspective, a major reason that control of the supply of money is important is that,
    A. in the long run, the higher the rate of inflation, the higher the rate of growth of the money supply.
    B. in the long run, the higher the rate of growth of the money supply, the higher the rate of inflation.

C. in the short run, the higher the rate of growth of the money supply, the higher the rate of inflation.
D. in the long run, the lower the rate of growth of the money supply, the higher the rate of inflation.
E. in the long run, the higher the rate of growth of the money supply, the higher velocity of money.

19. The measure of the speed at which money circulates, or velocity, is equivalent to
A. value of transactions divided by nominal GDP.
B. nominal GDP times price divided by money supply.
C. price times money supply divided by nominal GDP.
D. nominal GDP divided by money supply.
E. total value of transactions divided by nominal GDP.

20. The quantity equation
A. states that the velocity of money is equal to the money supply times nominal GDP.
B. implies that if velocity and real output are constant, an increase in inflation will cause an equal increase in the money supply in the long run.
C. implies that if velocity and real output are constant, an increase in the money supply will cause an equal increase in inflation in the long run.
D. implies that if velocity and real output are constant, an increase in the money supply will cause an equal increase in inflation in the short run.
E. implies that if velocity and real output are constant, an increase in inflation will cause an equal increase in the money supply in the short run.

Short Answer Problems
(Answers and solutions are given at the end of the chapter.)

1. Measuring the Money Supply
In this problem you will practice calculating the measures of the U.S. money supply—Ml and M2.

Month/ Year	Currency	Savings deposits	Demand and other checkable deposits	Money market mutual funds	Small time deposits
Mar. '05	$703.9	$3.548.3	$667.6	$702.4	$850.2
Apr. '05	704.4	3,542.9	649.7	706.6	865.6
May '05	706.1	3,516.3	659.7	704.5	883.8
June '05	709.0	3,535.8	656.2	701.7	900.3

Source: Federal Reserve Board of Governors Statistical Release July 14, 2005. All figures are in billions of dollars.

A. Use the preceding data to complete the following table, calculating the amounts for Ml and M2 for January through April 2000.

Month/Year	M1	M2
Aug-02		
Sep-02		
Oct-02		
Nov-02		

B. If the public transfers funds from their (small) savings accounts at the Township Savings and Loan Association to their checking accounts at the Village Bank, this will (increase/decrease/leave unchanged)_____ M1, and (increase/decrease/leave unchanged) _____ M2.

C. If the public deposits currency into their checking accounts at Village Bank, this will (increase/decrease/leave unchanged) _____ Ml, and (increase/ decrease/leave unchanged) _____ M2.

2. Reserve/Deposit Ratio, Open-Market Operations, and Money Creation

In this problem you will calculate reserve/deposit ratios, determine how much a bank can lend based on its reserves, deposit liabilities and reserve/deposit ratio, and determine the effect of open-market sales and purchases of government securities on a bank's ability to lend and create money. Each question refers back to balance sheet of The Bank of Haute Finance shown below (i.e., do not take into account the transaction indicated in Questions 3A-3C when answering Questions 3B-3D).

Balance Sheet of
The Bank of Haute Finance

Assets	Liabilities
Currency (= reserves) $10,000	Deposits $10,000

A. If The Bank of Haute Finance has a desired reserve/deposit ratio of 10%, it can make new loans of $_____ in the form of new _____. After making the new loans The Bank of Haute Finance will have total deposit liabilities of $_____ , currency (= reserves) of $_____, and outstanding loans of $_____ . Its total assets will then equal $_____ and its total liabilities will equal $_____ .

B. If the Fed imposes a minimum reserve/deposit ratio in the form of a 20% reserve requirement, the maximum amount of new loans The Bank of Haute Finance could make would be $_____ . After making the new loans The Bank of Haute Finance would have total deposit liabilities of $_____ , currency (= reserves) of $_____ and outstanding loans of $_____ . Its total assets would then equal $_____ and its total liabilities would equal $_____ .

C. Assume the Federal Reserve System buys $3000 of government securities from Susan Slavin and she deposits the $3000 in her checking account at The Bank of Haute Finance. Following the deposit, The Bank of Haute Finance would have currency (= reserves) of $_____ and deposit liabilities of $_____ . Assuming the Fed maintains a minimum reserve/deposit ratio of 20%, The Bank of Haute Finance could make new loans of $_____ . By doing so it would (increase/decrease) _____ the money supply by $_____ .

D. Assume the Federal Reserve System sells $3000 of government securities to The Bank of Haute Finance which it pays for out of its reserves. After the sale of the government securities, The Bank of Haute Finance would have currency (= reserves) of $_____ and deposit liabilities of $_____ . Assuming the Fed maintains a minimum reserve/deposit ratio of 20%, The Bank of Haute Finance could make new loans of $_____ . By doing so it would (increase/decrease) _____ the money supply by $_____ .

E. In comparing the answers to Questions 3B and 3D, by selling $3,000 of government securities to The Bank of Haute Finance, the Fed would be able to reduce the growth in the supply of money by $_____ .

3. Quantity Equation

This problem focuses on the relationship between the rate of growth of the money supply and inflation rates. You will practice calculating velocity and analyzing the relationship between growth in the money supply and inflation rates.

Date	M1	M2	Nominal GDP	Velocity of M1	Velocity of M2
June 2004	$1,336.8	$6,276.5	$11,657.5		
Sept. 2004	$1,351.8	$6.334.4	$11,814.9		
Dec. 2004	$1,365.6	$6,422.1	$11,994.8		
Mar. 2005	$1,371.4	$6,472.3	$12,191.7		

Sources: M1 and M2 data are from the Federal Reserve Board of Governors Statistical Release July 14, 2005, and Nominal GDP data are from the web site of the Bureau of Economic Analysis at http://www.bea.gov/bea/dn/home/gdp.htm. All figures are in billions of dollars.

A. Complete the above table by calculating the velocity of M1 and M2 for June 2004, September 2004, December 2004, and March 2005 (round your answer to the nearest hundredth).

Dates	M1 Growth Rate	Inflation Rate
1961-70	51.9	33.6
1971-80	89.4	116.8
1981-90	100.6	53.8
1991-00	56.5	40.2

Source: The data were calculated from the Federal Reserve Economic Data (FRED II) available through the Federal Reserve Bank of St. Louis web site at http://research.stlouisfed.org/fred2/

B. Does the above data on the U.S. inflation rate and M1 growth rate support the conclusion that an increase in the supply of money will cause an exact increase the inflation rate in the long run.

_____

C. Does the above data support the weaker conclusion that higher rates of growth in the money supply will cause higher inflation rates_____

_____

IV. Becoming an Economic Naturalist: Case Study

In the Economic Naturalist 10.1, it is explained that privately issued monies, such as Ithaca Hours and LETS (local electronic trading system), are alternative media of exchange in some communities where the law allows. The common characteristic of Ithaca Hours and LETS is that they function as a medium of exchange and, thus, facilitate trade. Credit cards are also issued by privately owned companies, typically banks, and are used to facilitate the purchase of goods and services. Discuss whether credit cards are privately issued monies.

Answer:

V. Self-Test Solutions

Key Terms
1. t
2. l
3. r
4. i
5. m
6. a
7. k
8. s
9. j
10. c
11. d
12. h
13. f
14. g
15. n
16. e
17. p
18. u
19. q
20. b
21. o

Multiple-Choice Questions

1. A
2. C
3. C
4. B
5. D
6. A
7. B With $50 million in reserves and $100 million in deposits, its reserve/deposit ratio of 1/2 is greater than its desired ratio. It would, therefore, increase its deposits to $150 million by making new loans.
8. E $10 million in new reserves divided by $40 million in new deposits equals .25 (the reserve/deposit ratio)
9. D
10. C
11. B
12. A
13. C
14. A
15. C
16. C
17. E Because each dollar of bank reserves translates into several dollars of money supply, the decrease in bank reserves is equal to the increase in currency caused the money supply to decrease.
18. B
19. D
20. C

Short Answer Problems

1.
A.

Month/Year	M1	M2
Mar. '05	$1,371.50	$6,472.40
Apr. '05	$1,354.10	$6,469.20
May '05	$1,365.80	$6,470.40
June '05	$1,365.20	$6,503.00

B. increase; leave unchanged (because the components of M1 are also included in M2)
C. leave unchanged; leave unchanged (currency and checking deposits are included in both M1 and M2. Thus, depositing currency into a checking account does not change the amount of M1 or M2.)

2.
A. $90,000 (Because the desired reserve/deposit ratio is .10 the $10,000 in reserves can support $10,000/.10 = $100,000 in deposits. Thus, $100,000 minus the existing $10,000 in deposits = $90,000); checking deposits; $100,000; $10,000; $90,000; $100,000; $100,000

B. $40,000 (Now that the Fed has imposed a reserve requirements of .20, the $10,000 in reserves can support $10,000/.2 = $50,000. Thus, the bank can make new loan of $40,000); $50,000; $10,000; $40,000; $50,000; $50,000

C. $10,000 + $3,000 = $13,000; $13,000; $52,000 ($13,000/.2 = $65,000 from which the existing $13,000 is subtracted, allowing new loans of $52,000); increase; $52,000

D. $10,000 - $3,000 = $7,000; $7,000/.2 = $35,000 from which the existing $10,000 is subtracted, allowing new loans of $25,000; increase; $25,000

$50,000 - $25,000 = $25,000

3.
A.

Date	M1	M2	Nominal GDP	Velocity M1	Velocity M2
June 2004	$1,336.8	$6,276.5	$11,657.5	8.72	1.86
Sept. 2004	$1,351.8	$6.334.4	$11,814.9	8.74	1.87
Dec. 2004	$1,365.6	$6,422.1	$11,994.8	8.78	1.87
Mar. 2005	$1,371.4	$6,472.3	$12,191.7	8.89	1.88

B. No, the data does not support the extreme conclusion that an increase in the growth rate of money will lend to an exact increase in the inflation rate

C. With the exception of 1981-90, higher growth in M1 did lead to higher inflation in the U.S. Thus, the weaker conclusion that higher growth in the money supply will cause higher inflation is partially supported by the data.

Chapter 11
Financial Markets and
International Capital Flows

I. Pretest: What Do You Really Know?

Circle the letter that corresponds to the best answer. (Answers appear immediately after the final question).

1) Financial intermediaries are firms that
   A. extend credit to borrowers using funds from savers.
   B. match buyers and sellers of stocks.
   C. match buyers and sellers of bonds.
   D. conduct open market operations.
   E. issue currency in exchange for government debt.

2) A legal promise to repay a debt is called
   A. equity.
   B. stock.
   C. a bond.
   D. a dividend.
   E. the principal amount.

3) Stockholders receive returns on their financial investment in the form of _____ and _____.
   A. interest payments; dividends
   B. interest payments; deposits
   C. coupon payments; capital gains
   D. capital gains; interest payments
   E. capital gains; dividends

4) To the individual investor, a major advantage of mutual funds is
   A. increased interest income.
   B. increased diversification.
   C. increased riskiness.
   D. decreased diversification.
   E. increased dividends.

5) If domestic saving is greater than domestic investment, then a country will have a _____ and _____ net capital inflows.
   A. trade deficit; negative
   B. trade deficit; positive
   C. trade balance; zero
   D. trade surplus; negative
   E. trade surplus; positive

6) Purchases of foreign assets by domestic firms or households is called a(n)
   A. import.
   B. export.
   C. capital outflow.
   D. capital inflow.
   E. protectionism.

7) When a U.S. exporter sells software to France and uses the proceeds to buy stock in a French company, U.S. exports _____ and there is a capital _____ to/from the United States.
   A. increase; outflow
   B. increase; inflow
   C. do not change; outflow
   D. decrease; outflow
   E. decrease; inflow

8) In an open economy, a decrease in capital inflows _____ the equilibrium domestic real interest rate and _____ the quantity of domestic investment.
   A. increases; increases
   B. increases; decreases
   C. decreases; does not change
   D. decreases; increases
   E. decreases; decreases

9) If the United States has a $500 billion net capital inflow, then there must be a
   A. trade surplus of $500 billion.
   B. trade deficit of $500 billion.
   C. no trade surplus or trade deficit.
   D. net capital outflow of $1,000 billion.
   E. trade surplus of $1,000 billion.

10) At each value of the domestic interest rate, a decrease in the riskiness of domestic assets _____ capital inflows, _____ capital outflows, and _____ net capital inflows.
   A. increase; increase; increase
   B. increase; increase; decrease
   C. increase; decrease; increase
   D. decrease; decrease; decrease
   E. decrease; increase; decrease

Solutions and Feedback to Pretest
For each question you incorrectly answered, we strongly recommend taking the time to review the appropriate material before continuing. In the table below are listed for each question the pertinent Learning Objective from the following Key Point Review.

Correct Answer	Learning Objective
1. A	2
2. C	3
3. E	4
4. B	5
5. D	6, 7
6. C	7
7. A	7
8. B	7
9. B	7
10. C	8

II. Key Point Review
The Forest

This chapter focuses on the major financial markets and institutions, and their role in directing saving to productive uses, as well as the international dimension of capital and saving. The central questions you need to be able to answer are:

- What are the major financial institutions and how does the financial system allocate saving to alternative productive uses?
- What factors determine international capital flows and how are international capital flows related to net exports?
- What is the relationship between international capital flows and domestic saving and investment?

The Trees

Learning Objective 1: Explain how market-oriented financial systems improve the allocation of saving
A successful economy not only saves but also uses its' saving to invest in projects that are likely to be the most productive. In a market economy like that of the United States, savings are allocated by means of a decentralized, market-oriented financial system. A market-oriented financial system improves the allocation of savings by providing savers information about the uses of their funds that are most likely to prove productive, and by helping savers share the risks of individual investment projects. Three key components of a market-oriented financial system are discussed in this chapter: (1) the banking system, (2) the bond market, and (3) the stock market.

Learning Objective 2: Define financial intermediaries and explain the role of financial intermediaries in a market economy

Financial intermediaries are firms that extend credit to borrowers using funds raised from savers. The most important financial intermediaries in the banking system are the commercial banks. They are privately owned firms that accept deposits from individuals and businesses and use those deposits to make loans. Savers are willing to hold bank deposits because banks (and other financial intermediaries) have a comparative advantage in information-gathering about lending opportunities that results in lower costs and better results than individual savers could achieve on their own. Banks also make it easier for households and business to make payments for goods and services.

> **Note**: Banks and other financial intermediaries have gained experience in evaluating potential borrowers and monitoring borrowers' activities. This not only benefits the banks and savers, but also helps the borrowers by providing access to credit that may otherwise not be provided.

Learning Objective 3: Explain how bond markets can be a source of funds for businesses; define bond, principal amount, maturation date, coupon rate and coupon payment

In addition to obtaining funds from banks, corporations and governments can obtain funds in the bond market. Corporations and governments frequently raise funds by issuing bonds and selling them to savers. A **bond** is a legal promise to repay a debt, usually including the **principal amount** (the amount originally lent), **maturation date** (the date at which the principal will be repaid) and regular interest payments. The promised interest rate when a bond is issued is called the **coupon rate**, which is paid to the bondholder in regular interest payments called **coupon payments**. The coupon rate must be sufficiently attractive to savers, depending upon the term, or length of time before the debt is fully repaid, and the risk that the borrower will not repay the debt. Bonds also differ in terms of their tax treatment. The interest on municipal bonds, issued by local governments, is exempt from federal income taxes and, thus, typically pays a lower coupon rate than do other comparable bonds. Bondholders do not have to hold bonds until they are to be repaid by the issuer because they can sell them in the bond market. The price (or market value) of a bond at any point in time is inversely related to interest rates being paid on comparable newly issued bonds.

> **Hint**: Because bond prices and interest rates are inversely related, if interest rates on new bond issues rise, the price a bond holder will received for an outstanding bond will fall. That is, if you are holding a bond that pays an interest rate of six percent annually, and new bond issues are now paying seven percent annually, you will only be able to sell the bond to another investor if you price the bond sufficiently low to allow the investor to earn the seven percent rate of return that the investor could currently earn elsewhere. The price would be below what you paid for the bond and would result in a capital loss.

Learning Objective 4: Explain the role of the stock markets; define stock dividend and risk premium

Another important way of raising funds, but one that is restricted to corporations is issuing stock to the public. A share of **stock**, also called equity, is a claim to partial ownership of a firm. Stockholders receive returns on their financial investment in a firm through dividend payments and capital gains (the increase in the price of the stock). A **dividend** is a regular payment received by stockholders for each share that they own, as determined by the firm's management and is usually dependent on the firm's recent profits. The price of a share of stock at any point in time depends on the expected future dividends and capital gain, adjusted for the risk premium. **Risk premium** is the rate of return that financial investors require to hold risky assets minus the rate of return on safe assets.

Learning Objective 5: Define diversification and explain the role of mutual funds

Like banks, bond and stock markets provide a means of channeling funds from savers to borrowers with productive investment opportunities. Savers and their financial advisors search for high returns in the bond and stock markets and, thus, provide a powerful incentive to potential borrowers to use the funds productively. The markets also give savers a means to diversify their financial investments. **Diversification** is the practice of spreading one's wealth over a variety of different financial investments in order to reduce overall risk. From society's perspective, diversification makes it possible for risky but worthwhile projects to obtain funding without individual savers having to bear too much risk. For the typical saver, a convenient way to diversify is buy stocks and bonds indirectly through mutual funds. A **mutual fund** is a financial intermediary that sells shares to the public, then uses the funds raised to buy a wide variety of financial assets.

Note: In the past, small investor with limited funds would find it very difficult to achieve a diversified portfolio of investments by directly purchasing individual stocks and bonds. Most small investors, therefore, did little more than put their wealth into saving accounts. But in recent years with the rapid growth in the number of stock and bond mutual funds, small investors have increasingly been able to reduce the risks of investing and simultaneously increase their rate of return by purchasing shares of stock and bond mutual funds.

Learning Objective 6: Define trade balance, trade surplus, and trade deficit and capital flows

When an economy is open to trade, its **trade balance**, the value of a country's exports minus the value of its imports in a particular period, may be positive or negative. A country is said to have a **trade surplus** for a period when the value of its exports exceeds the value of its imports. Alternatively, a country is said to have a **trade deficit** for a period, when the value of its imports exceeds the value of its exports. In addition to the trade of goods and services that is captured in the trade balance, trade among countries occurs in real and financial assets.

Learning Objective 7: Discuss the relationships among international capital flows, and domestic saving and investment
Purchases or sales of real and financial assets across international borders are known as **international capital flows**. From the perspective of a particular country, purchases of domestic assets by foreigners are called **capital inflows**, and purchases of foreign assets by domestic households and firms are called **capital outflows**. Capital inflows are related to real interest rates and investment risk in a country. The higher the real interest rate in a country, and the lower the risk of investing there, the higher its capital inflows. Capital inflows expand a country's pool of saving, allowing for more domestic investment and economic growth. A potential drawback, however, to using capital inflows to finance domestic investment is that the interest and dividends on the borrowed funds must be paid to foreign savers rather than domestic residents.

Learning Objective 8: Explain the link between the trade balance and capital flows
There is a precise link between the trade balance and international capital flows. In any given period, the trade balance and net capital inflows add up to zero, or NX (net exports) + KI (net capital inflows) = 0. This link suggests the primary cause of a trade deficit is a country's low rate of national saving. A low-saving, high-spending country is likely to import more and export less than a high-saving, low-spending country. A low-saving, high-spending country is also likely to have higher real interest rates in order to attract capital inflows. Because the sum of the trade balance and capital inflows is zero, a high level of net capital inflows is consistent with a large trade deficit.

Note: In theory, it is impossible for a country to continuously run a trade deficit because the capital inflows will eventually decrease the value of its currency vis-à-vis other currencies. As this happens, the cost of imports will increase and it will import less, and its exports will become more competitive and its exports will grow. As a result, net exports will rise and its trade deficit will decline.

III. Self-Test

Key Terms
Match the term in the right-hand column with the appropriate definition in the left-hand column by placing the letter of the term in the blank in front of its' definition. (Answers are given at the end of the chapter.)

1. _____ Firms that extend credit to borrowers using funds raised from savers.   a. bond

2. _____ A regular payment received by stockholders for each share that they own.   b. capital inflows

3. _____ The value of a country's exports less the value of its imports in a particular period (quarter or year).   c. capital outflows

4. _____ When imports exceed exports, the difference between the value of a country's imports and the value of its exports in a given period.   d. coupon payment

5. ____ A legal promise to repay a debt, usually including both the principal amount and regular interest payments.

6. ____ the practice of spreading of one's wealth over a variety of different financial investments to reduce overall risk.

7. ____ When exports exceed imports, the difference between the value of a country's exports and the value of its imports in a given period.

8. ____ A financial intermediary that sells shares in itself to the public, then uses the funds raised to buy a wide variety of financial assets.

9. ____ The amount originally lent.

10. ____ A claim to a partial ownership of a firm.

11. ____ Purchases or sales of real and financial assets across international borders.

12. ____ The interest rate promised when a bond is issued.

13. ____ Purchases of foreign assets by domestic households and firms.

14. ____ The rate of return that financial investors require to hold risky assets minus the rate of return on safe assets.

15. ____ Regular interest payments made to the bondholder.

16. ____ The date at which the principal of a bond will be repaid.

17. ____ Equal to foreign purchases of domestic assets minus domestic purchases of foreign assets.

18. ____ Purchases of domestic assets by foreign households and firms.

e. coupon rate

f. diversification

g. dividend

h. financial intermediaries

i. international capital flows

j. maturation date

k. net capital inflows

l. mutual fund

m. principal amount

n. risk premium

o. stock

p. trade balance (or net exports)

q. trade deficit

r. trade surplus

Multiple-Choice Questions
Circle the letter that corresponds to the best answer. (Answers are given at the end of the chapter.)

1. A market-oriented financial system improves the allocation of savings by providing
   A. information about savers and helping savers share the risks of individual investment projects.
   B. information to savers about the risks of individual investment projects and helping investors reduce the risks of individual investment projects.
   C. information to savers about alternative productive uses for funds and helping savers share the risks of individual investment projects.
   D. banks with a comparative advantage over small savers in evaluating and monitoring prospective borrowers.
   E. information to financial intermediaries, stock and bond markets about alternative productive uses for funds and by reducing the risk to savers through diversification.

2. Banks and other financial intermediaries are necessary because they
   A. have a comparative advantage in evaluating the quality of borrowers.
   B. shift the risk of investing from borrowers to savers.
   C. facilitate the direct lending of funds by savers to borrowers.
   D. diversify the risk of saving.
   E. eliminate the need to gather information about borrowers.

3. A feature common to all financial intermediaries is that they
   A. buy and sell information about savers and borrowers.
   B. have a comparative advantage in gathering and evaluating information about borrowers.
   C. act as agents for buyers and sellers in the money market.
   D. shift the risk of investing from borrowers to savers.
   E. collect funds from a few savers and distribute the funds to many borrowers.

4. Which of the following sources of funds are available to large and well-established corporations but not to the typical small borrower?
   A. Financial intermediaries and bond markets
   B. Municipal bond and stock markets
   C. Financial intermediaries, stock and bond markets
   D. Stock and corporate bond markets
   E. All sources of funds are available to both large and well-established corporations and the typical small borrower.

5. In comparison to a corporate bond, a municipal bond of the same term and credit risk will have a
   A. higher risk premium.
   B. higher coupon payment.
   C. higher coupon rate.
   D. lower coupon rate.
   E. same coupon rate.

6. During the 1990s, the Japanese banking system
   A. experienced severe financial problems that contributed to a severe economic downturn in Japan.
   B. acquired corporate stocks and made loans to real estate developers that contributed to an economic boom in Japan.
   C. experienced severe financial problems that created a "credit crunch" for large corporations in Japan.
   D. experienced severe financial problems that created a global "credit crunch" for small- and medium-sized businesses.
   E. experienced severe financial problems that has forced the Japanese government to nationalize the banking system to return it to a healthy financial condition.

7. The price of a share of corporate stock varies over time depending upon stockholders' expectations about the future
   A. coupon rate, risk premium, and coupon payment.
   B. dividend, stock price, and coupon rate.
   C. coupon payment, dividend and risk premium.

D. coupon rate, coupon premium and dividend.

E. dividend, stock price, and risk premium

8. The informational role of the stock and bond markets provides incentives for savers and their financial advisors to

A. direct funds to those borrowers that appear to have the safest investments.

B. direct funds to those borrowers that appear to have the most productive investments.

C. diversify their investments by purchasing mutual funds.

D. shift the risk of investing to the borrowers.

E. avoid the cost of paying the financial intermediaries by going directly to the borrowers to make loans.

9. Antonio holds a two-year bond issued by the Jetson Corporation with a principal amount of $10,000. The annual coupon rate is 6 percent. He considered selling it after receiving the first coupon payment a week ago at a price of $9,390. Since that time, the coupon rate on new bond issues has risen from 6.5% to 7.0%. If he were to sell the bond today, the price would be

A. $10,000.

B. higher than it was a week ago.

C. the same at it was a week ago.

D. lower than it was a week ago.

E. impossible to determine from the information given.

10. When American investors pay cash for shares of stock in a French corporation, from the perspective of

A. the United States, it is a capital inflow.

B. France, it is a capital outflow.

C. the United States, it is a capital outflow.

D. France, it is a trade deficit.

E. the United States, it is a trade deficit.

11. If interest rates in Japan increase relative to international interest rate levels, all else being equal, Japan's net capital

A. inflows will tend to increase, and the pool of funds for domestic investment will tend to decrease.

B. inflows will tend to increase, and the pool of funds for domestic investment will tend to increase.

C. outflows will tend to increase, and the pool of funds for domestic investment will tend to decrease.

D. outflows will tend to increase, and the pool of funds for domestic investment will tend to increase.

E. inflows will tend to decrease, and the pool of funds for domestic investment will tend to decrease.

12. The sum of national saving and capital inflows from abroad must equal
    A. domestic investment in new capital goods.
    B. capital outflows.
    C. aggregate demand.
    D. the trade deficit.
    E. the trade surplus.

13. The U.S. trade deficit is mainly caused by
    A. production of inferior goods in the country.
    B. unfair trade restrictions imposed by other countries on imports.
    C. a low rate of national saving.
    D. cheap labor in other countries.
    E. inadequate safety and environmental protections in other countries.

14. Which of the following transactions would cause a capital inflow to a country?
    A. exports of goods or services
    B. import of goods or services
    C. purchasing financial assets (e.g., a corporate bond) from abroad
    D. purchasing real assets (e.g., a factory) abroad
    E. lending money abroad

15. The illegal drug trade has increased the political instability in Colombia and has
    A. reduced net capital outflows from Colombia.
    B. reduced net capital inflows to Colombia.
    C. increased net capital inflows to Colombia.
    D. increased Colombia's trade deficit.
    E. decreased Colombia's trade surplus.

16. An increase in net capital inflows to a country will
    A. increase its real interest rates.
    B. increase its imports.
    C. decrease its exports.
    D. decrease its real interest rates.
    E. decrease its investment in new capital.

17. During the 1960s and 1970s, the U.S. trade balance was close to zero, but during the 1980s
    the trade deficit ballooned to unprecedented levels due to
    A. an inability of U.S. companies to compete in the international market.
    B. a decline in private saving that resulted from an upsurge in consumption.
    C. a decline in national saving without a corresponding decrease in investment.
    D. a worldwide recession that made it difficult for U. S. companies to sell their products
    abroad.
    E. unfair protectionist policies imposed by the United State's major trade partners.

18. A country's trade balance and its net capital inflows
    A. Add up to zero.
    B. determine the size of the pool of saving available for capital investment.
    C. must always equal the sum of the four components of aggregate demand.
    D. must equal domestic investment in new capital goods.
    E. are identical in open and closed economies.

19. Capital inflows used to finance capital investment in some developing countries have
    A. decreased domestic saving.
    B. benefited domestic savers because of higher interest rates paid on saving accounts.
    C. caused debt crises because the returns on the investments were less than the interest cost of the capital.
    D. caused debt crises because the returns on the investments were greater than the interest cost of the capital.
    E. had economic benefits without costs.

20. The Argentine economic collapse in 2001-02 was caused by:
    A. an increase in domestic savings rates and a corresponding decline in domestic consumption spending that led to a collapse in production.
    B. an insufficient level of skilled and educated workers to work in the growing high tech industries.
    C. the International Monetary Fund's refusal to provide additional loans to the Argentine government to pay its foreign debt.
    D. Argentina defaulting on its foreign debt and the subsequent unwillingness of foreign lenders to make additional loans.
    E. Argentina defaulting on its foreign debt because the Argentine government's spending exceeded its tax revenues.

Short Answer Problems
(Answers and solutions are given at the end of the chapter.)

1. Bond and Stock Prices
This problem will require you to calculate the effects of various factors on the price of bonds and stocks.

A. Carley has purchased a newly issued bond from the SimonSays Corp. for $10,000. The SimonSays Corp. will pay the bondholder $750 at the end of years 1-4 and will pay $10,750 at the end of year 5. The bond has a principal amount of $_____, a term of _____ years, a coupon rate of _____ %, and a coupon payment of $_____ .

B. After receiving coupon payments 1 through 4, Carley has decided to sell the bond. What price should she expect to receive if the one-year interest rate on comparable financial assets is 5%? $_____ What price should she expect to receive if the one-year interest rate on comparable financial assets is 8%? $_____

C. Justin has decided to buy 100 shares of stock in The Boot Company. He expects the company to pay a dividend of $3 per share in one year and expects the price of the shares will be $40 at that time. How much should he be willing to pay today per share if the safe rate of interest is 7% and The Boot Company carries no risk? $_____

D. How much should Justin be willing to pay today per share if the safe rate of interest is 5% and The Boot Company carries no risk? $_____

E. How much should Justin be willing to pay today per share if the safe rate of interest is 5% and he requires a risk premium of 2%? $_____

2. International Capital Flows

This problem focuses on the determinants of international capital flows, including risks and domestic and international interest rates.

A. The graph below shows the net capital inflows to the United States for 2006. What level of domestic interest rate is necessary for net capital inflows to be positive? _____ percent

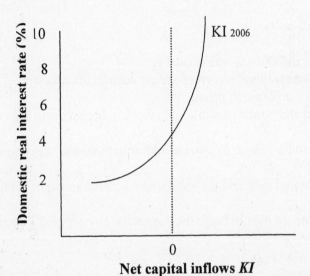

Net capital inflows KI

B. On the graph above, show the impact of increased riskiness of domestic assets (label the new curve KI₁).

C. On the graph above, show the impact of an increase in real interest rates abroad (label the new curve KI₂).

D. On the graph above, show the impact of an increase in riskiness of assets abroad (label the new curve KI₃).

3. Saving, Investment and Capital Flows in an Open Economy

This problem expands upon the saving-investment diagram for a closed economy by focusing on the effects of international capital flows on domestic interest rates and investment.

A. In an open economy the amount of investment must be equal to _____ plus

_____ .

B. The graph below shows domestic saving (S) and domestic investment curves. Draw a new curve that would show the impact of opening the domestic financial markets to capital inflows (label the new curve S+KI).

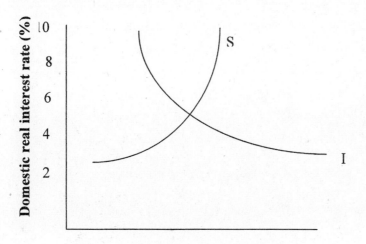

Saving and Investment

C. As a result of opening the domestic economy to capital inflows, the domestic equilibrium interest rate will (decrease/increase/remain unchanged) _____ and the equilibrium level of saving and investment will (decrease/increase/remain unchanged)

_____ .

D. As the economy is opened, if capital inflows allow the level of investment to exceed the amount of national saving, then the country must also have a trade (surplus/deficit)

_____ .

IV. Becoming an Economic Naturalist: Case Study

In Economic Naturalist 11.4, the relationship between the U.S. trade deficit and the level of national saving and investment is explained. It is noted that the large U.S. trade deficits since the late 1970s, particularly during the mid-1980s and the latter part of the 1990s, correspond to periods in which investment in the U.S. exceeded national saving. More recently, since the economic recovery began in 2002, investments in residential housing and business capital have grown rapidly, while national saving has been restrained by increases in the government budget deficit. Given these trends in U.S. investment and saving, what would you expect to find in terms of the U.S. trade balance during this period? Is the actual data on the U.S. trade balance during 2002-05 consistent with your prediction?

Answer:

V. Self-Test Solutions

Key Terms
1. h
2. g
3. p
4. q
5. a
6. f
7. r
8. l
9. m
10. o
11. i
12. e
13. c
14. n
15. d
16. j
17. k
18. b

Multiple-Choice Questions
1. C
2. A
3. B
4. D
5. D Because municipal bonds are exempt from federal income taxes, they have a lower coupon rate than comparable non-municipal bonds.
6. A
7. E
8. B
9. D
10. C
11. B
12. A
13. C
14. A
15. B
16. D
17. C
18. A
19. C
20. D

Short Answer Problems

1.
A. $10,000; 5; 7.5%; $750
B. $10,750 / 1.05 = $10, 238.10; $9,953.70
C. $43 / 1.07 = $40.19
D. $43 / 1.05 = $40.95
E. $43 / (1.05 + .02) = $40.19

2.
A. 4
B.

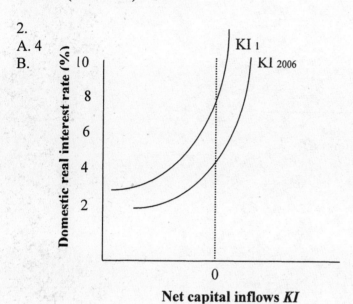

C.

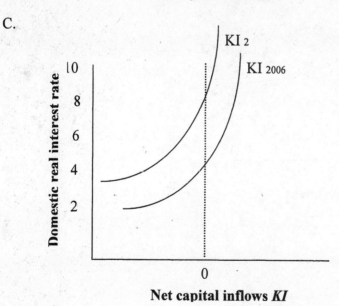

D.

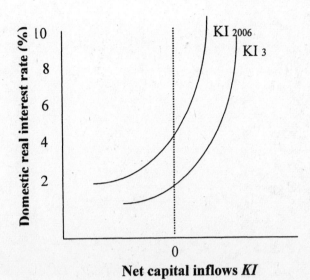

3.
A. saving; capital inflows
B.

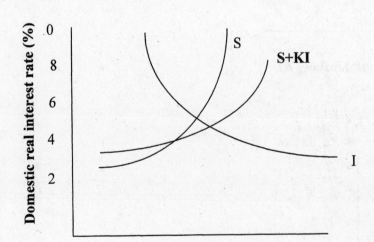

C. decrease; increase
D. deficit

Chapter 12
Short-term Economic Fluctuations:
An Introduction

I. Pretest: What Do You Really Know?

Circle the letter that corresponds to the best answer. (Answers appear immediately after the final question).

1) Since the end of World War II, recessions in the U.S have _____ than expansions.
   A. occurred more frequently
   B. been shorter in duration, on average,
   C. been longer in duration, on average,
   D. generated more inflation
   E. been more predictable

2) Economic activity moves from a trough into a period of _____ until it reaches a _____ and then into a period of _____.
   A. expansion; trough; recession.
   B. recession; trough; expansion
   C. expansion; peak; recession
   D. recession; peak; expansion
   E. expansion; trough; expansion

3) In reference to short-term economic fluctuations, the "peak" refers to
   A. a period in which the economy is growing at a rate significantly above normal.
   B. the high point of economic activity prior to a downturn.
   C. the low point of economic activity prior to a recovery.
   D. a particularly strong and protracted expansion.
   E. a particularly severe and protracted recession.

4) An expansion is
   A. a period in which the economy is growing at a rate significantly below normal.
   B. a period in which the economy is growing at a rate significantly above normal.
   C. the high point of economic activity prior to a downturn.
   D. the low point of economic activity prior to a recovery.

E. a particularly severe or protracted recession.

5) The following data give the dates of successive turning points in U.S. economic activity and
    the corresponding levels of real GDP at the time:

Turning Point	Date	Real GDP(1996 $ billions)
(A)	Jan. 1980	4958.9
(B)	July 1980	4850.3
(C)	July 1981	5056.8
(D)	Nov. 1982	4912.1
(E)	July 1990	6731.7

Which of the following periods is a recession?
A. Jan. 1980 through July 1980
B. Jan. 1980 through July 1981
C. July 1980 through July 1981
D. July 1980 though Nov. 1982
E. Nov. 1982 through July 1990

6) All of the following are characteristics of short-term economic fluctuations EXCEPT
    A. expansions and recessions are felt throughout the economy.
    B. expansions and recessions are irregular in length and severity
    C. unemployment falls sharply during recessions.
    D. durable-goods industries are more sensitive to short-term fluctuations than service and
        non-durable industries.
    E. recessions tend to be followed by a decline in inflation.

7) Which of the following workers is most likely to lose his/her job during a recession?
    A. construction worker
    B. baker
    C. farmer
    D. barber
    E. police officer

8) The difference between the economy's potential output and its actual output at a point in time
    is called the
    A. budget deficit.
    B. trade deficit.
    C. output gap.
    D. full-employment rate.
    E. cyclical peak.

9) If potential output equals $5 billion and actual output equals $3.5 billion, then this economy
    has a(n)
    A. budget deficit.
    B. trade deficit.
    C. expansionary gap.
    D. recessionary gap.

E. value-added gap.

10) In Macroland potential GDP equals $8 trillion and real GDP equals $7.6 trillion. Macroland
has a(n) _____ gap equal to _____ percent of potential GDP.
   A. expansionary; -5
   B. expansionary; 5
   C. recessionary; -5
   D. recessionary; 5
   E. recessionary; 6

Solutions and Feedback to Pretest
For each question you incorrectly answered, we strongly recommend taking the time to review
the appropriate material before continuing. In the table below are listed for each question the
pertinent Learning Objective from the following Key Point Review.

Correct Answer	Learning Objective
1. B	1
2. C	1
3. B	1
4. B	1
5. A	1
6. B	2
7. A	2
8. C	3
9. D	3
10. D	3

II. Key Point Review
The Forest

This chapter focuses on the history, characteristics and causes of short-run fluctuations in
economic conditions, and concludes with preview of the causes of recessions and expansions.
The central questions you need to be able to answer are
   - What are the four stages of the business cycle?
   - What are the primary characteristics of recessions and expansions?
   - What are the two types of output gaps and how are they measured?
   - How is the natural rate of unemployment defined and how is it related to cyclical
     unemployment?
   - What is Okun's Law?

The Trees

Learning Objective 1: Define recession, depression, expansion, boom, peak, and trough
The short-run fluctuations in economic conditions are commonly known as recessions and
expansions. A **recession**, or contraction, is a period in which the economy is growing at a rate
significantly below normal. An extremely severe or protracted recession is called a **depression**.

A more informal definition of a recession (often used by the mass media) is a period during which real GDP falls for at least two consecutive quarters. While the "two consecutive quarters" rule would not classify a slow-growth episode as a recession, many economists would argue that a period in which real GDP growth is significantly below normal should be counted as a recession. The beginning of a recession is called a **peak**, the high point of economic activity prior to a downturn. The end of a recession, marking the low point of economic activity prior to a recovery, is called the **trough**. By far the longest and most severe recession in the United States was during 1929-33. Since World War II, U.S. recessions have generally been short, lasting between six and sixteen months. The opposite of a recession is an **expansion**; a period in which the economy is growing at a rate that is significantly above normal. A particularly strong and protracted expansion is called a **boom**. On average, expansions have lasted longer than recessions. The two longest expansions were during 1961-69, and 1990-2001 (in February, 2000 this boom broke the all-time record for the duration of a U.S. expansion).

Learning Objective 2: Discuss the characteristics of short-term economic fluctuations
Expansions and recessions are not new, as they have been a feature of industrial economies since at least the late 18th century. Short-run economic fluctuations, although they are sometimes referred to as business cycles, or cyclical fluctuations, do not recur at predictable intervals but rather are quite irregular in their length and severity. This irregularity makes it extremely hard to predict the dates of peaks and troughs. Expansions and recessions are felt throughout the economy, and even globally. Unemployment is a key indicator of short-term fluctuations, typically rising during recessions and falling (although more slowly) during expansions. Cyclical unemployment is the type of unemployment associated with recessions. In addition to rising unemployment, labor market conditions become more unfavorable during recessions, with real wages growing more slowly and workers less likely to receive promotions or bonuses. Inflation also follows a typical pattern during recessions and expansions, though not as sharply defined. Recessions tend to be preceded by increases in inflation, and followed soon after by a decline in the rate of inflation. Durable goods industries tend to be more affected by recessions and expansions, while services and nondurable goods industries are less sensitive to short-term economic fluctuations.

Learning Objective 3: Define potential output, output gap, recessionary gap and expansionary gap
Economists measure expansions and recessions by determining how far actual output is from potential output. **Potential output** (also known as potential GDP or full-employment output) is the maximum sustainable amount of output (real GDP) that an economy can produce. Actual output (real GDP) may be below or above potential output at any point in time. The difference between potential output and actual output is called the **output gap**. The output gap is expressed in symbols as $Y^* - Y$. A positive output gap, when actual output is below potential output and resources are not fully utilized, is called a **recessionary gap**. A negative output gap, when actual output is above potential output and resources are utilized at above-normal rates, is called an **expansionary gap**.

Note: Be careful to not become confused by the terminology regarding output gaps. Sometimes students mistakenly think that because actual output is below potential the output gap should be negative. When actual output is below potential output there is a **positive** output gap. When actual output is above potential output there is a **negative** output gap.

Learning Objective 4: Define the natural rate of unemployment and explain its relationship to cyclical unemployment

Recessionary gaps are associated with below normal utilization of labor resources. This is another way of saying there is extra unemployment during recessions. Specifically, in addition to the frictional and structural unemployment, which are always present in the labor market, cyclical unemployment is present during recessions. Economists call that part of the total unemployment rate that is attributable to frictional and structural unemployment the **natural rate of unemployment**. The natural rate of unemployment can vary over time because of changes in frictional and/or structural unemployment. The natural rate of unemployment is the unemployment rate that prevails when cyclical unemployment is zero. Cyclical unemployment can, therefore, be calculated as the difference between the actual unemployment rate (u) and the natural rate of unemployment ($u*$). During recessions cyclical unemployment is positive, and during expansions it is negative.

Hint: The concept of a "natural" rate of unemployment is intended to reflect the fact that there is always some amount of unemployment in the economy, i.e., it is a *natural* state of the economy. Thus, it is virtually impossible for the unemployment rate to ever equal zero.

Learning Objective 5: Define Okun's Law and explain its importance to understanding short-run fluctuations in the economy

A rule of thumb called Okun's Law helps economists quantify the relationship between the amount of cyclical unemployment and the output gap. **Okun's Law** states that each extra percentage point of cyclical unemployment is associated with about a two-percentage point increase in the output gap. The output losses calculated according to Okun's Law suggest that recessions have significant costs (which are reflected, for example, in the importance that short-run economic fluctuations have on presidential elections in the United States).

Note: Be careful to not mistakenly attribute Okun's Law to indicate that the change in unemployment causes the output gap. The cause-and-effect works in the opposite direction. That is, an increase in output gap causes unemployment to rise. It is, however, much easier to observe changes in unemployment than changes in output gaps. Thus, Okun's Law is more of a rule of thumb than an analytical theory.

Learning Objective 6: Explain why short-run fluctuations occur
In the short run, prices do not always adjust immediately to changing demand or supply as some producers vary the quantity of output rather than price, meeting the demand at a preset price. In the short run, therefore, changes in economy-wide spending are the primary cause of output gaps. In the long run, however, prices will adjust to their market-clearing levels, as producers better understand the information provided by the market, and output will equal potential output. The quantities of inputs, and the productivity with which they are used, are the primary determinants of economic activity in the long run. While total spending in the economy affects output in the short run, in the long run its main effects are on prices.

III. Self-Test

<u>**Key Terms**</u>
Match the term in the right-hand column with the appropriate definition in the left-hand column by placing the letter of the term in the blank in front of its' definition. (Answers are given at the end of the chapter.)

1. ____A particularly strong and protracted expansion.
2. ____ The maximum sustainable amount of output (real GDP) that an economy can produce.
3. ____ Each extra percentage point of cyclical unemployment is associated with about a 2 percentage point increase in the output gap, measured in relation to potential output.
4. ____ An extremely severe or protracted recession.
5. ____ A negative output gap, which occurs when actual output is above potential output
6. ____ The end of a recession, the low point of economic activity prior to a recovery.
7. ____The difference between the economy's potential output and its actual output at some point in time.
8. ____ A period in which the economy is growing at a rate significantly below normal.
9. ____ The part of the total unemployment rate that is attributable to frictional and structural unemployment.
10.____ The beginning of a recession, (the high point of economic activity prior to a downturn).
11.____ A period in which the economy is growing at a rate that is significantly above normal.
12.____ A positive output gap, which occurs when potential output exceeds actual output.

a. boom
b. depression
c. expansion
d. expansionary gap
e. natural rate of unemployment
f. Okun's Law
g. output gap
h. peak
i. potential output
j. recession
k. recessionary gap
l. trough

Multiple-Choice Questions
Circle the letter that corresponds to the best answer. (Answers are given at the end of the chapter.)

1. The longest and most severe recession in the United States was during
   A. August 1957 to February 1961, initiating what became known as the Great Depression.
   B. November 1973 to March 1975, initiating what became known as the Great Depression.
   C. May 1937 to June 1938, initiating what became known as the Great Depression.
   D. January 1980 to November 1982, initiating what became known as the Great Depression.
   E. August 1929 to March 1933, initiating what became known as the Great Depression.

2. Short-term economic fluctuations
   A. recur at predictable intervals.
   B. have a limited impact on a few industries or regions.
   C. contain peaks and troughs that are easily predicted by the professional forecasters.
   D. are irregular in their length and severity.
   E. have little impact on unemployment and inflation.

3. Unemployment typically
   A. is unaffected by recessions and expansions.
   B. rises during recession and falls during expansions.
   C. falls during recessions and rises during expansions.
   D. rises during recessions and falls during expansions, as does inflation.
   E. falls during recessions and rises during expansions, as does inflation.

4. The Japanese economy slowed markedly during the 1990s due to
   A. faster growth in potential output combined with a significant output gap.
   B. slower growth in potential output, and actual output equal to potential output.
   C. slower growth in potential output combined with a significant output gap.
   D. faster growth in potential output, and actual output equal to potential output.
   E. normal growth in potential output combined with a significant output gap.

5. As the average age of U.S. workers has increased since 1980
   A. frictional unemployment has fallen and the natural rate of unemployment has decreased.
   B. cyclical unemployment has fallen and the natural rate of unemployment has decreased.
   C. structural unemployment has fallen and the natural rate of unemployment has decreased.
   D. frictional unemployment has risen and the natural rate of unemployment has increased.
   E. cyclical unemployment has risen and the natural rate of unemployment has increased.

6. If cyclical unemployment rises to 2.5% and potential output (GDP) equals $9,000 billion, the output gap would equal
   A. $22,500 billion.
   B. $225 billion.
   C. $9,000 billion.
   D. $8,775 billion.
   E. $9,225 billion.

7. The firm behavior known as "meeting the demand, " refers to
    A. firms adjusting prices from moment to moment in response to changes in demand.
    B. firms adjusting prices continuously in order to ensure that the quantity supplied equals the quantity demanded.
    C. changes in economy-wide spending as the primary cause of output gaps.
    D. price changes that eliminate output gaps in a self-correcting market.
    E. firms adjusting prices only periodically, while in the short run varying the quantity of output.

8. A recessionary gap occurs when
    A. total spending is abnormally high.
    B. total spending is at normal levels, but potential output is growing at abnormally high levels.
    C. total spending is low for some reason.
    D. potential output is less than actual output.
    E. actual output is greater than potential output.

9. The self-correcting market mechanism eliminates output gaps over time though price
    A. decreases if demand exceeds potential output.
    B. increases if demand is less than potential output.
    C. decreases if an expansionary gap exists.
    D. decreases if recessionary gap exists.
    E. increases if recessionary gap exists.

10. The longest expansion in the U.S. economy
    A. began in August 1929, at the trough of the Great Depression.
    B. lasted 106 months.
    C. began in March 1991, at the trough of the 1990-91 recession.
    D. lasted 92 months.
    E. began in February 1961, at the trough of the 1960-61 recession.

11. On average, recessions in the United States have been
    A. shorter than expansions.
    B. longer than expansions.
    C. longer and more severe during the post-WWII period than prior to WWII.
    D. shorter but more severe during the post-WWII period than prior to WWII.
    E. equal in duration to expansions.

12. During short-term economic fluctuations, inflation tends to
    A. rise following an economic peak and fall soon after the trough.
    B. fall following an economic peak and rise soon after the trough.
    C. rise following an economic peak and rise soon after the trough.
    D. fall following an economic peak and rise soon after the trough.
    E. move in the same direction as unemployment.

13. An economy grows significantly below its maximum sustainable output when
    A. actual output is above potential output.
    B. actual output equals potential output, but potential output is growing very slowly.
    C. actual output equals potential output, but potential output is growing very rapidly.
    D. actual output is below potential output and potential output is growing very rapidly.
    E. actual output is above potential output and potential output is growing very rapidly.

14. An expansionary gap implies that resources are
    A. not being fully utilized and the unemployment rate would be above the natural rate of unemployment.
    B. being utilized at above-normal rates and the unemployment rate would be above the natural rate of unemployment.
    C. not being fully utilized and the unemployment rate would be below the natural rate of unemployment.
    D. being utilized at above-normal rates and cyclical unemployment is positive.
    E. being utilized at above-normal rates and cyclical unemployment is negative.

15. In some markets, such as the market for grain, price-setting by auction occurs, but in other markets it does not because
    A. there are not enough auctioneers to announce prices for all the markets.
    B. auctions are inefficient when there are a small number of customers and low sales volume at any given time.
    C. auctions are inefficient when a market has a large number of buyers and sellers and a large volume of standardized goods.
    D. auctions are not feasible when the goods are perishable (e.g., ice cream).
    E. the economic benefits of auctions are less than the economic costs of auctions in markets for perishable goods.

16. In the long run
    A. prices adjust to market-clearing levels, and output equals potential output.
    B. prices adjust to market-clearing levels, and output is less than potential output.
    C. prices adjust to market-clearing levels, and output is greater than potential output.
    D. output is primarily determined by economy-wide spending.
    E. the main effect of total spending is on output.

17. During the period1960-1999, inflation was at its highest level in the United States during the
    A. boom of 1961-69.
    B. expansion of 1982-90.
    C. expansion of 1990-99.
    D. recession of 1981-82.
    E. recession of 1973-75.

18. Recessions and expansions have a greater impact on
    A. inflation than on unemployment.
    B. frictional unemployment than on cyclical unemployment.
    C. structural unemployment than on cyclical unemployment.

D. industries that produce durable goods than on service and nondurable goods industries.

E. industries that produce services and nondurable goods than on durable goods industries.

19. The difference between the total unemployment rate and the natural rate of unemployment
    A. is positive during a recession.
    B. is negative during a recession.
    C. is positive during an expansion.
    D. represents that portion of total unemployment that economists call frictional
    unemployment.
    E. represents that portion of total unemployment that economists call structural
    unemployment.

20. Online job services have made labor markets more efficient and, thus, have contributed to
    A. a decline in cyclical unemployment.
    B. an increase in cyclical unemployment.
    C. a decline the natural rate of unemployment.
    D. an increase in the natural rate of unemployment.
    E. an increase in structural and frictional unemployment.

Short Answer Problems
(Answers and solutions are given at the end of the chapter.)

1. Actual Output and Potential Output
This problem utilizes data on real GDP and potential GDP for the United States for the years
1994-1999, in billions of 1992 dollars, and will help you become more familiar with the concept
of output gaps (recessionary and expansionary gaps).

Year	Real GDP	Potential GDP	Output Gap	Expansionary or Recessionary Gap?
1998	$9,611	$9,777		
1999	9,762	9,955		
2000	9,995	10,138		
2001	10,720	10,325		
2002	10,553	10,517		
2003	10,883	10,714		

A. Complete column 4 of the above table by calculating the size of the output gap for 1998
through 2003 (be sure to include a plus sign if a positive gap, or a minus sign if negative gap).
B. In column 5 of the above table, identify whether the output gap was a recessionary gap or an
expansionary gap for each year.

IV. Becoming an Economic Naturalist: Case Study

Economic Naturalist 12.3 discusses the monetary policy decisions of the Federal Reserve during 1999-2000 to counteract the perceived threat of increasing inflation brought on by a growing expansionary gap. By early 2001, the U.S. economy had stalled and fell into a recession and the Fed reversed course, taking measures to eliminate the recessionary gap. Go to the Federal Reserve web site at http://www.federalreserve.gov/fomc/ and review the FOMC's policy decisions since 2001 to determine how long the Fed continued the policy begun in early 2001. What does the most recent policy decisions indicate is the Fed's current economic concern, expansionary or recessionary gap?

Answer:

V. Self-Test Solutions

Key Terms

1. a
2. i
3. f
4. b
5. d
6. l
7. g
8. j
9. e
10. h
11. c
12. k

Multiple-Choice Questions

1. E
2. D
3. B
4. C
5. A
6. B $9,000 billion times .025 = $225 billion
7. E
8. C
9. D
10. C
11. A
12. D
13. B
14. E
15. B
16. A

17. D
18. D
19. A
20. C

Short Answer Problems
1.
A. and B.

Year	Real GDP	Potential GDP	Output Gap	Expansionary or Recessionary Gap?
1998	$9,611	$9,777	+$166	Recessionary gap
1999	9,762	9,955	+$193	Recessionary gap
2000	9,995	10,138	+$143	Recessionary gap
2001	10,720	10,325	-$395	Expansionary gap
2002	10,553	10,517	-$36	Expansionary gap
2003	10,883	10,714	-$169	Expansionary gap

Chapter 13
Spending and Output
in the Short Run

I. Pretest: What Do You Really Know?

Circle the letter that corresponds to the best answer. (Answers appear immediately after the final question).

1. The two key assumptions of the basic Keynesian model are that aggregate demand _____ and that in the short run firms _____.
   A. is constant; meet demand at preset prices
   B. fluctuates; adjust prices to bring sales in line with capacity
   C. increases with the general level of prices; meet demand at preset prices
   D. is constant; adjust prices to bring sales in line with capacity
   E. fluctuates; meet demand at preset prices

2. Firms do not change prices frequently because
   A. there are legal prohibitions against doing so.
   B. it is easier to change the quantity of capital used in production.
   C. it is costly to do so.
   D. customers will refuse to patronize firms that change prices frequently.
   E. managers are lazy.

3. If firms sell more output than expected, planned investment
   A. is greater than actual investment.
   B. is less than actual investment.
   C. equals actual investment.
   D. equals zero.
   E. equals aggregate demand.

4. Dave's Mirror Company expects to sell $2,000,000 worth of mirrors and to produce $2,250,000 worth of mirrors in the coming year. The company purchases $500,000 of new equipment during the year. Sales for the year turn out to be $1,900,000. Actual investment by Dave's Mirror Company equals _____ and planned investment equals _____.
   A. $500,000; $500,000

  B. $500,000; $750,000
  C. $750,000; $850,000
  D. $850,000; $500,000
  E. $850,000; $750,000

5. The consumption function is relationship between consumption and
  A. aggregate demand.
  B. total spending.
  C. investment.
  D. its determinants, such as disposable income.
  E. unplanned changes in spending, particularly inventory investment.

6. If consumption increases by $90 when after-tax disposable income increases by $100, the marginal propensity to consume (mpc) equals
  A. 0.1
  B. 0.9
  C. 1.0
  D. 90
  E. 100

7. Autonomous expenditure is the portion of planned aggregate expenditure that
  A. equals aggregate output.
  B. equals planned spending.
  C. equals induced aggregate demand.
  D. is determined within the model.
  E. is determined outside the model.

8. In Macroland autonomous consumption equals 200, the marginal propensity to consume equals 0.6, net taxes are fixed at 50, planned investment is fixed at 100, government purchases are fixed at 200, and net exports are fixed at 30. Short-run equilibrium output in this economy equals
  A. 1,100
  B. 1,175
  C. 1,250
  D. 1,325
  E. 1,400

9. If planned aggregate expenditure in an economy can be written as: AD= 4000 + .8 Y, what is the short-run equilibrium level of output in this economy?
  A. 5,000
  B. 5,800
  C. 9,000
  D. 20,000
  E. 25,000

10. For an economy starting from potential output, a decrease in planned investment in the short run results in a(n)
    A. expansionary output gap.
    B. recessionary output gap.
    C. increase in potential output.
    D. decrease in potential output.
    E. increase in cyclical unemployment.

Solutions and Feedback to Pretest

For each question you incorrectly answered, we strongly recommend taking the time to review the appropriate material before continuing. In the table below are listed for each question as the pertinent Learning Objective from the following Key Point Review.

Correct Answer	Learning Objective
1. E	1
2. C	1
3. A	3
4. E	3
5. D	4
6. B	4
7. E	5
8. C	6
9. D	6
10. B	7

II. Key Point Review
The Forest

This chapter focuses on the basic Keynesian model (also known as the Keynesian Cross) showing how recessions and expansions may arise from fluctuations in aggregate spending. The central questions you need to be able to answer are
- What are the key assumptions of the Keynesian model and what are the four components of planned aggregate expenditure?
- What factors affect the consumption function and what is the relationship between the consumption function and planned aggregate expenditure?
- What determine the short-run equilibrium output?
- What is the income-expenditure multiplier and how can a change in planned spending can cause a change in the short-run equilibrium output?
- What stabilization policies are derived from the Keynesian analysis?

The Trees

Learning Objective 1: Identify the key assumption of the model
The Keynesian model is based on the ideas first developed by John Maynard Keynes (1883-1946) and published in *The General Theory of Employment, Interest and Money* (1936). The key assumption of the basic Keynesian model is that, in the short run, firms meet the demand for

their products at preset prices. Firms change prices only if the benefits of doing so outweigh the **menu costs**, (i.e., the costs of changing prices).

> **Note**: the decision by a firm whether to change price is an application of the cost-benefit principle. Firms will only change the price of a product if the marginal benefit is at least equal to the marginal cost.

Learning Objective 2: Define planned aggregate expenditure (PAE) and identify the four components of PAE

The most important concept of the basic Keynesian model is planned aggregate expenditure. **Planned aggregate expenditure** (PAE) is the total planned spending on final goods and services. PAE is composed of four components: (1) consumer expenditures, or simply consumption (C), is spending by domestic households on final goods and services; (2) investment (I) is spending by domestic firms on new capital goods, residential investment, and increases in inventories; (3) government purchases (G) is spending by domestic governments (federal, state and local) on goods and services; and (4) net exports (NX), or exports minus imports, is sales of domestically produced goods and services to foreigners less purchases by domestic residents of goods and services produced abroad which have been included in C, I, and G, but must be subtracted because they do not represent domestic production.

Learning Objective 3: Explain why planned spending may differ from actual spending

Planned spending (or PAE) may differ from actual spending. If, for example, a firm sells more of its output than it planned to sell, actual investment will be less than planned investment and total actual spending will be greater than total planned spending. Assuming that actual spending for consumption, government purchases, and net exports equals planned spending, but that actual investment may not equal planned investment, the equation for planned aggregate expenditure is $PAE = C + I^p + G + NX$, where I^p is planned investment spending.

> **Note:** If a firm's actual sales are greater than it's expected sales, actual investment will be less than planned investment because there will be an unexpected decrease in inventories. Since, changes in inventory are one component of investment, an unexpected decrease will reduce actual investment below the planned level of investment.

Learning Objective 4: Define consumption function and marginal propensity to consume

Consumption, the largest component of *PAE*, is affected by many factors, the most important being after-tax income, or disposable income. The relationship between consumption spending and its determinants, is referred to as the **consumption function** and is expressed by the equation $C = \overline{C} + c(Y - T)$, where $\overline{C}$ is a constant term intended to capture factors other than disposable income, and $(Y - T)$ represents disposable income, and mpc is a fixed number called the marginal propensity to consume. The **marginal propensity to consume**, or mpc, is the amount by which consumption rises when disposable income rises by one dollar, and is greater than 0 but less than 1 (i.e., $0 < c < 1$). The consumption function can also be show graphically, in which case $\overline{C}$

represents the intercept of the consumption function on the vertical axis and the mpc is the slope of the consumption function. The consumption function indicates that as disposable income rises, consumption spending will increase, but by a lesser amount.

Learning Objective 5: Explain the relationship between the consumption function and planned aggregate expenditure
Incorporating the consumption function into the equation for planned aggregate expenditure results in the expanded equation $PAE = [C + c(Y - T)] + I^p + G + NX$. Grouping together those terms that depend on output (Y), and those that do not, yields the equation $PAE = [C + cT + I^p + G + NX] + cY$. This equation captures the key idea that as planned aggregate expenditure changes real output changes with it, in the same direction. It also shows that planned aggregate expenditure can be divided into two parts, one portion that is determined outside the model called **autonomous expenditure** ($[C + cT + I^p + G + NX]$), and a second portion that is determined within the model (because it depends on output) called **induced expenditure** (cY).

> **Hint:** It will be important that you are able to calculate changes in the amount of autonomous expenditure because changes in autonomous expenditure cause changes in the equilibrium level of output. If you do not know the components of autonomous expenditure, you will not be able to calculate changes in autonomous expenditure and, thus, will not be able to determine the impact on the equilibrium level of output.

Learning Objective 6: Define short-run equilibrium output
In the basic Keynesian model, the **short-run equilibrium output** is the level at which output, Y, equals planned aggregate expenditure, PAE, and is the level of output that prevails during the period in which prices are predetermined. The short-run equilibrium output can be determined numerically by comparing possible levels for short-run equilibrium output to the value of planned aggregate expenditure at each level of output. The short-run equilibrium output is determined where $Y = PAE$, or equivalently $Y - PAE = 0$. The short-run equilibrium output can also be determined graphically where the 45° line intersects the expenditure line. If output is less (greater) than the equilibrium level in the short run, when prices are pre-set and firms are committed to meeting their customers' demand, output will rise (fall). Lastly, we can use algebra to determine the short-run equilibrium output (this is explained in detail in Appendix A of the textbook chapter).

Learning Objective 7: Explain how a decrease in planned spending can lead to a recession
A decrease in one or more of the components of autonomous planned aggregate expenditure will cause short-run equilibrium output to fall. When the short-run equilibrium output is less than the potential output, the result is a recessionary gap. According to the basic Keynesian model, inadequate spending is an important cause of recessions in the economy.

Learning Objective 8: Define the income-expenditure multiplier
A change in one or more of the components of autonomous planned aggregate expenditure will cause a larger change in the short-run equilibrium output. The impact on output is larger than the

initial change in spending because of the multiplier effect. The effect of a one-unit increase or decrease in autonomous planned spending on the short-run equilibrium output is called the **income-expenditure multiplier,** or the multiplier for short. In the basic Keynesian model, the multiplier is inversely related to the marginal propensity to consume.

Learning Objective 9: Discuss the use of fiscal policy to stabilize planned spending
To fight recessions caused by insufficient planned aggregate expenditure, policymakers can use stabilization policies. **Stabilization policies** are government policies that are used to affect planned aggregate expenditure, with the objective of eliminating output gaps. There are two major types of stabilization policy, monetary policy and fiscal policy. This chapter focuses on fiscal policy, i.e., government spending and taxes. Keynes felt that changes in government spending were probably the most effective tool for reducing or eliminating output gaps. He argued that a recessionary gap could be eliminated by increases in government spending. Alternatively, a decrease in taxes (payments from the private sector to government) could eliminate a recessionary gap. Government spending can be in the form of government purchases of goods and services or transfer payments (payments from government to the private sector). Changes in government purchases directly change the amount of PAE, whereas transfer payments and taxes only indirectly change PAE by altering the amount of disposable income. The change in PAE is equal to the change in taxes (or transfer payments) times the mpc. Because the mpc is a fraction, the change in taxes or transfer payments must be larger than the change in government purchases to cause the same change in PAE.

Learning Objective 10: Discuss three qualifications related to the use of fiscal policy as a stabilization tool
While the basic Keynesian model suggests that fiscal policy can be used quite precisely to eliminate output gaps, in the real world it is more complicated than that. Using fiscal policy as a stabilization tool is complicated by the fact that fiscal policy may affect potential output as well as planned aggregate expenditure. Government spending, for example, on investments in public capital, (e.g., roads, airports, and schools) can play a major role in the growth of potential output. Taxes and transfer payments may affect the incentives, and thus the economic behavior, of households and firms that, in turn, affect potential output. A second qualification is the need to avoid large and persistent government budget deficits. The need to keep deficits under control may make it more difficult to increase government spending or cut taxes to fight a recession. The third qualification is that fiscal policy is not always flexible enough to be useful for stabilization. Changes in government spending or taxation must usually go through a lengthy legislative process making it difficult to respond in a timely way to economic conditions. In addition, policymakers have many objectives besides stabilizing planned aggregate expenditure.

III. Self-Test

Key Terms
Match the term in the right-hand column with the appropriate definition in the left-hand column by placing the letter of the term in the blank in front of its' definition. (Answers are given at the end of the chapter.)

1. _____ The tendency of changes in asset prices to affect households' wealth and thus their spending on consumption goods.
2. _____ The portion of planned aggregate expenditure that depends on output.
3. _____ The portion of planned aggregate expenditure that is independent of output.
4. _____ Government policies that are used to affect planned aggregate expenditure, with the objective of eliminating output gaps.
5. _____ The level of output at which output equals planned aggregate expenditure.
6. _____ Government policy actions designed to reduce planned spending and output.
7. _____ The costs of changing prices.

8. _____ The effect of a 1-unit increase in autonomous expenditure on short-run equilibrium output.
9. _____ Total planned spending on final goods and services.
10.___ The relationship between consumption spending and its determinants, in particular, disposable (after-tax) income.
11.___ The amount by which consumption rises when disposable income rise by one dollar.
12.___ Provisions in law that imply automatic increases in government spending or decreases in taxes when real output declines.
13.___ Government policy actions intended to increase planned spending and output.

a. automatic stabilizers
b. autonomous expenditure
c. consumption function
d. contractionary policies
e. expansionary policies
f. induced expenditure
g. income-expenditure multiplier
h. marginal propensity to consume (mpc)
i. menu costs
j. planned aggregate expenditure
k. short-run equilibrium output
l. stabilization policies
m. wealth effect

Multiple-Choice Questions
Circle the letter that corresponds to the best answer. (Answers are given at the end of the chapter.)

1. Which of the following is a key assumption of the basic Keynesian model?
   A. Total spending fluctuates.
   B. In the short run, firms meet the demand for their products at preset prices.
   C. In the long run, firms meet the demand for the products at preset prices.
   D. In the short run, firms adjust price to changes in planned aggregate expenditure so as to clear the market.
   E. In the long run, firms adjust price to changes in planned aggregate expenditure so as to clear the market.

2. When firms apply the core principle of cost-benefit analysis to price changing decisions, they change the prices of their goods if
   A. menu costs are greater than or equal to the benefits of changing prices.
   B. menu costs are greater than or equal to the additional revenue derived from changing prices.
   C. additional revenue derived from changing prices is less than the menu costs.
   D. additional revenue derived from changing prices is greater than the menu costs.

E. additional revenue derived from changing prices is less than or equal to the menu costs.

3. In *The General Theory of Employment, Interest, and Money*, John Maynard Keynes explained
    A. how economies always operate at the natural rate of employment.
    B. the causes of expansionary gaps and recommended the use of monetary policy to combat the resulting high inflation.
    C. how economies can remain at low levels of output for long periods and recommended increased government spending to combat the resulting high unemployment.
    D. that attempts to extract large reparation payments from Germany after World War I would prevent economic recovery of Germany and likely lead to another war.
    E. the key elements of the post-WWII international monetary and financial institutions.

4. Planned aggregate expenditure is the sum of desired or planned
    A. consumption expenditures, investment, government purchases, and net exports.
    B. consumption expenditures, investment, government purchases, and exports.
    C. consumption expenditures, investment, government purchases, and net imports.
    D. consumption expenditures, net investment, government purchasers, and net exports.
    E. consumption expenditures, net investment, government expenditures, and net exports.

5. If a firm's actual sales are greater than expected sales
    A. actual inventories will be greater than planned inventories, and actual investment will be greater than planned investment.
    B. actual inventories will be less than planned inventories, and actual investment will be less than planned investment.
    C. actual inventories will be greater than planned inventories, and actual investment will be less than planned investment.
    D. actual inventories will be less than planned inventories, and actual investment will be greater than planned investment.
    E. planned inventories will be less than actual inventories, and planned investment will be greater than actual investment.

6. A decrease in consumers' disposable income will cause a(n)
    A. decrease in the consumption function and an increase in output.
    B. increase in the consumption function and a decrease in output.
    C. decrease in the consumption function and an increase in planned aggregate expenditure.
    D. increase in the consumption function and an increase in planned aggregate expenditure.
    E. decrease in the consumption function and a decrease in planned aggregate expenditure.

7. If autonomous consumption equals $250 billion, the marginal propensity to consume (mpc) is .6, investment equals $180 billion, government purchases equal $75 billion, taxes equal $200, and net exports equal minus $40 billion, the planned aggregate expenditure equation is
    A. PAE = $250 billion + .6Y
    B. PAE = $585 billion + .6Y
    C. PAE = $505 billion + .6Y
    D. PAE = $625 billion + .6Y

E. PAE = $345 billion + .6Y

8. If, in the short run, real output is less than the equilibrium level of output, firms will respond by
    A. increasing the price of their products.
    B. decreasing the price of their products.
    C. increasing their production.
    D. decreasing their production.
    E. producing the same amount of output.

9. If the consumption function is C= $400 + .75Y, then the mpc equals
    A. $400.
    B. .25.
    C. $400 + .75.
    D. .75.
    E. 4.

10. John Maynard Keynes believed that the most effective stabilization policy was
    A. changes in government spending to reduce or eliminate output gaps.
    B. monetary policy to reduce or eliminate expansionary gaps.
    C. changes in government spending to reduce or eliminate recessionary gaps, but monetary policy to reduce or eliminate expansionary gaps.
    D. changes in taxes to reduce or eliminate output gaps.
    E. the self-correcting process of the market to reduce or eliminate output gaps.

11. The largest single component of planned aggregate expenditures is
    A. government spending
    B. consumption spending
    C. investment spending
    D. export spending
    E. import spending

12. The use of fiscal policy to eliminate output gaps is complicated by the fact that fiscal policy
    A. is more flexible than monetary policy.
    B. only affects planned aggregate expenditure, but has no effect on potential output.
    C. affects both planned aggregate expenditure and potential output.
    D. does not take into account the effects that automatic stabilizers have on potential output.
    E. includes not only government purchases, but also transfer payments and taxation.

13. If the marginal propensity to consume increases, the income-expenditure multiplier
    A. increases.
    B. decreases.
    C. remains unchanged.
    D. decreases by a smaller amount.
    E. increases by a larger amount.

14. Planned spending equals actual spending for households, governments, and foreigners in the basic Keynesian model, but for businesses
    A. planned spending equals actual inventories.
    B. planned spending equals planned inventories.
    C. actual investment may differ from planned investment.
    D. actual investment is always greater than planned investment.
    E. actual investment is always less than planned investment

15. The portion of planned aggregate expenditure that is determined within the model is called induced expenditure and includes
    A. that part of household consumption that is dependent upon income.
    B. all of household consumption.
    C. household consumption and investment spending.
    D. household consumption, investment spending, and government purchases.
    E. household consumption, investment spending, government purchases, and net exports.

16. The short-run equilibrium in the basic Keynesian model occurs where
    A. actual inventories are greater than the level planned by businesses.
    B. actual inventories are less than the level planned by businesses.
    C. planned aggregate expenditure equals the potential output.
    D. planned aggregate expenditure equals output.
    E. planned aggregate expenditure is greater than output.

17. In the basic Keynesian model, when planned aggregate expenditure equals output
    A. inventories are zero.
    B. consumption equals investment.
    C. unplanned changes in inventories are positive.
    D. unplanned changes in inventories equal zero.
    E. unplanned changes in inventories are negative.

18. If, in the short run, output is greater than the equilibrium level of output, firms will respond by
    A. increasing the price of their products.
    B. decreasing the price of their products.
    C. producing the same amount of output.
    D. increasing their production.
    E. decreasing their production.

19. A $100 increase in transfer payments or a $100 decrease in taxes will cause
    A. a smaller increase in planned aggregate expenditure than a $100 increase in government purchases.
    B. a larger increase in planned aggregate expenditure than a $100 increase in government purchases.
    C. the same increase in planned aggregate expenditure as would a $100 increase in government purchases.

D. a smaller decrease in planned aggregate expenditure than a $100 increase in government purchases.
E. a larger decrease in planned aggregate expenditure than a $100 increase in government purchases.

20. Fiscal policy is not always flexible enough to be useful for economic stabilization because
A. automatic stabilizers counteract the stabilizing features of government spending and taxation.
B. budget deficits are unconstitutional.
C. the legislative process allows policymakers inadequate time to determine the appropriate level of government spending and taxation.
D. it affects both planned aggregate expenditure and potential output.
E. the only effects of fiscal policy that matter are its effects on potential output.

Short Answer Problems
(Answers and solutions are given at the end of the chapter.)

1. The Consumption Function and Planned Aggregate Expenditure
This problem is designed to help you understand the relationship between the consumption function and planned aggregate expenditure. You will be asked to graph the consumption function, write the algebraic equation for planned aggregate expenditure, and differentiate between autonomous and induced expenditure.

A. On the graph below, plot the consumption function curve (label it C) for disposable income levels $0 to $700, assuming C = $175 billion, the marginal propensity to consume (mpc) equals .75, and taxes equal $100 billion.

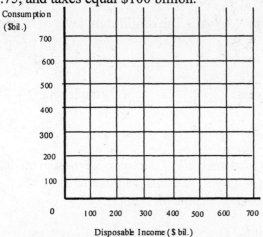

B. Assume that planned investment spending equals $50 billion, government purchases are $75 billion, and net exports equal –$75 billion. The algebraic equation for the planned aggregate expenditure curve would be PAE = $ _____ billion + _____ (Y - $ _____ billion) + $ _____ billion + $ _____ billion + $ _____ billion. Combining the autonomous portions of PAE would result in a simplified equation, PAE = $ _____ billion + _____ Y.
C. Plot the planned aggregate expenditure curve on the above graph and label it PAE.

D. Autonomous expenditure equals $_____ billion, and is graphically represented where the planned aggregate expenditure curve intersects the (vertical/ horizontal) _____ axis.

E. When disposable income equals $400 billion, the induced expenditure equals $_____ billion.

2. Numerical Determination of Short-run Equilibrium Output

The focus of this problem is the determination of the short-run equilibrium output within the framework of a numerical table.

(1) Output (Y)	(2) Planned aggregate expenditure	(3) Y– PAE	(4) Y = PAE?
$3,000			
3,500			
4,000			
4,500			
5,000			
5,500			
6,000			

A. Assume that planned aggregate expenditure is given by the equation PAE = $500 + .9 Y. Complete column 2 of the table by calculating the amount of planned aggregate expenditure when output equals $3,000 to $6,000.

B. Complete column 3 of the table by calculating the difference between output and planned aggregate expenditure when output equals $3,000 to $6,000.

C. Complete column 4 by determining whether or not Y = PAE. The equilibrium level of output equals $_____.

D. If output equals $ 3,500, firms will (increase/decrease) _____ the level of output.

E. If output equals $ 6,000, firms will (increase/decrease) _____ the level of output.

3. The Basic Keynesian Model

This problem is designed to help you understand the fundamentals of the basic Keynesian model. You will determine the equilibrium level of income (or output) and analyze the effects of changes in investment spending on the equilibrium level of income (or output).

A. Assume the consumption function is C = $200 billion + .8(Y-T), investment equals $ 150 billion, government purchases equal $200 billion, taxes equal $100 billion, and net exports equals minus $70 billion. Using this information, derive the aggregate expenditure function. PAE = $_____ billion + _____ Y.

B. On the graph below, plot the planned aggregate expenditure curve for level of output ranging from $0 billion to $5,000 billion (label the curve PAE).

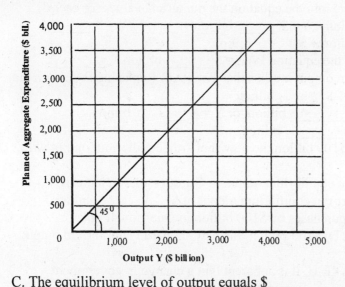

C. The equilibrium level of output equals $ _____ billion.

D. If the potential output (Y*) equals $2,500, there would now be a (recessionary/ expansionary) _____ gap in the economy.

E. If firms produce $3,000 billion of output, planned aggregate expenditure would equal $_____ billion. As a result, firms would have $_____ billion of goods they intended to sell but didn't. This would cause firms (increase / decrease) _____ their level of output.

Note: Question 3F – 3H are based on information in Appendix B of the textbook chapter.

F. The mpc equals _____ and the multiplier equals _____.

G. If investment spending decreases by $100 billion, the planned aggregate expenditure curve will shift (upward / downward) _____ and the equilibrium output will (increase / decrease) _____ by an amount equal to the change in planned aggregate expenditure times the multiplier.

H. On the graph above, draw the planned aggregate expenditure curve after a $100-billion decrease in investment spending (label it PAE_1). The new equilibrium output would equal $_____ billion.

4. Solving the Basic Keynesian Model Numerically
(Based on material in Appendix A of the textbook chapter.)

This problem uses algebraic equations to determine the short-run equilibrium output. You will derive the planned aggregate expenditure equation and, employing the equation for the short-run equilibrium condition, calculate the short-run equilibrium output, and determine the effect of changes in government purchases, taxes, and transfer payments of the short-run equilibrium output.

Use the following set of equations to answer the questions below:

C = $400 billion + .75(Y – T)
T = $200 billion
I^p = $250 billion
G = $300 billion
NX = $50 billion

A. Using the information above, substitute into the equation the numerical values for each component of planned aggregate expenditure. Y= $_____ billion + _____ (Y – $_____ billion) + $_____ billion + $_____ billion + $_____ billion.

B. After simplifying that equation yields the equation PAE = $_____ billion + _____Y.

C. The definition of short-run equilibrium output implies that Y = PAE. Replacing PAE with the equation found in Question 4B yields Y = $_____ billion + _____Y.

D. Now solve for Y in Y – _____ Y = $_____ billion, or Y = $_____ billion.

E. Thus, the equilibrium output equals $_____ billion.

F. If government purchases decrease by $100 billion the new short-run equilibrium output will equal $_____ billion.

G. Starting from the level of the short-run equilibrium output in Question 4E, an increase in taxation of $100 will result in a new short-run equilibrium output of $_____ billion.

H. If, instead of decreasing government purchases by $100 billion in Question 4F, the government decreased transfer payments by $100 billion, the new short-run equilibrium output would equal $_____ billion.

I. In comparing the answers to Questions 4F-H, it is apparent that a change in government purchases has a (greater/lesser/equal) _____ effect on the short-run equilibrium output than does an equal change in transfer payments or taxation.

IV. Becoming an Economic Naturalist: Case Study

The Economic Naturalist 13.3 discusses the impact of the Japanese recession on its neighboring countries of East Asia. The Japanese economy's slump during the 1990s resulted in less household and business spending on imports from these economies and, therefore, autonomous expenditures in the East Asian economies declined. The fall in autonomous expenditures subsequently led to a recessionary gap in those economies. Based on the textbook discussion of stabilization policy within the context of the basic Keynesian model, explain what the appropriate fiscal policy would have been to close the recessionary gap in the East Asian economies. Also, discuss the limitations of the use of fiscal policy to close the recessionary gap.

Answer:

V. Self-Test Solutions

Key Terms
1. m
2. f
3. b
4. l
5. k
6. d
7. i
8. g

9. j
10. c
11. h
12. a
13. e

Multiple-Choice Questions

1. B
2. D
3. C
4. A
5. B
6. E
7. E $250 billion + [.6(Y - $200 billion)] + $180 billion + $75 billion + (-$40 billion) = $345 billion + .6Y
8. C
9. D
10. A
11. B
12. C
13. A
14. C
15. A
16. D
17. D
18. E
19. A
20. C

Short Answer Problems

1.

A.

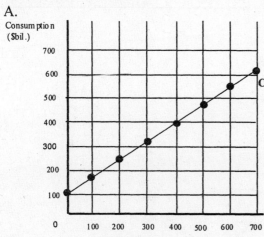

B. $175 billion + .75(Y - $100 billion) + $50 billion + $75 billion + (-$75) billion; $150 billion + .75Y

C.

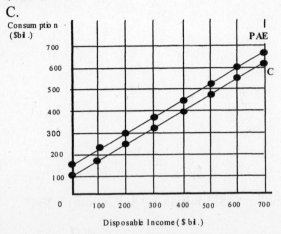

D. $150 billion (= $175 billion - $75 billion + $50 billion + 75 billion - $75 billion); vertical

E. $300 billion (= .75 x $400 billion)

2. A. B. C.

(1) Output (Y)	(2) Planned Aggregate Expenditure	(3) Y – PAE	(4) Y = PAE?
$3,000	$3,200	$-200	No
3,500	3,650	-150	No
4,000	4,100	-100	No
4,500	4,550	-50	No
5,000	5,000	0	Yes
5,500	5,450	50	No
6,000	5,900	100	No

C. $5,000

D. increase

E. decrease

3.

A. PAE = $400 billion + .8Y

B.

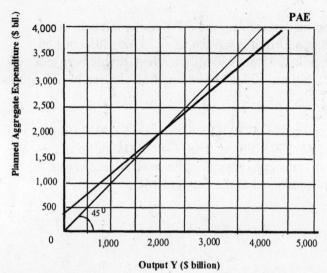

C. $2,000 billion

D. recesionary gap; $500

E. $2,800 billion (= $400 billion + .8($3,000 billion); $200 billion (Y – PAE, or $3,000 billion – $2,800 billion); decrease

F. .8 ; 5 $(= \dfrac{1}{1-.8} = \dfrac{1}{.2})$

G. downward; decrease

H.

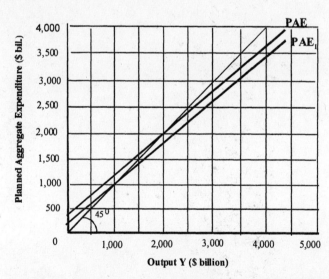

; $1,500 billion (The change in equilibrium output is – $100 billion x 5 = – $500 billion. Subtracting the change in equilibrium output from the initial equilibrium output, $2,000 billion - $500 billion, gives us the new equilibrium output of $1,500 billion.)

4.

A. $400 billion + .75 (Y - $200 billion) + $250 billion + $300 billion + $50 billion

B. AD = $850 billion + .75Y

C. Y = $850 billion + .75Y;

D. Y= $3,400 billion (The solution is found by first moving the .75 Y to the left side of the equation and subtracting it from Y. In equation form it is written, Y − .75 Y = $850 billion. Reducing the left-hand side yields the equation, .25Y = $850 billion. Next, divide both sides of the equation by .25. This gives us Y = $850 billion / .25, and dividing $850 billion by .25 equals $3,400 billion. Thus Y= $3,400 billion)

E. $3,400 billion

F. $3,000 billion (Y − .75Y =$750 billion, or .25Y = $750 billion, thus Y= $3,000 billion)

G. $3,100 billion (Y − .75 Y = $675, or .25Y = $775 billion, thus Y = $3,100 billion)

H. $3,100 billion (the effect of a decrease in transfer payments is the same as an increase in taxation, and thus the numerical derivation is identical to the answer to 4G).

I. greater

Chapter 14
Stabilizing the Economy:
The Role of the Fed

I. Pretest: What Do You Really Know?

Circle the letter that corresponds to the best answer. (Answers appear immediately after the final question).

1. Monetary policy is _____ flexible than fiscal policy because monetary policy changes are made by _____, while fiscal policy changes must be made by _____.
   A. more; the FOMC; legislative action
   B. more; legislative action; the FOMC
   C. more; the President; legislative action
   D. less; the FOMC; the President
   E. less; the President; legislative action

2. The benefit of holding money is _____, while the opportunity cost of holding money is
   _____.
   A. the nominal interest rate; the fees charged by banks
   B. the nominal interest rate; its usefulness in carrying out transactions
   C. increased income; lost purchasing power
   D. its usefulness in carrying out transactions; the nominal interest rate
   E. its usefulness in carrying out transactions; the price of wallets and billfolds

3. The following table shows Alex's estimated annual benefits of holding different amounts of money.

Average money holdings ($)	Total benefit ($)
300	30
400	39
500	46
600	51
700	54

   How much money will Alex hold if the nominal interest rate is 8 percent? (Assume she wants her money holdings to be in multiples of $100.)

A. 300
B. 400
C. 500
D. 600
E. 700

4. Lower real income ____ the demand for money and a lower price level ___ the demand for money.
   A. increases; increases
   B. increases; decreases
   C. increases; does not change
   D. decreases; decreases
   E. decreases; increases

5. Which of the following would be expected to increase the demand for money in the U.S.?
   A. Competition among brokers forces down the commission charge for selling bonds or stocks.
   B. The economy enters a recession.
   C. Political instability increases dramatically in developing nations.
   D. On-line banking allows customers to transfer funds between checking and stock mutual funds 24 hours a day.
   E. Financial investors become less concerned about the riskiness of stocks.

6. If the nominal interest rate is below the equilibrium value, then money demand is _____ than money supply, bond prices will ____, and the nominal interest rate will ____.
   A. greater; fall; increase
   B. greater; fall; decrease
   C. greater; rise; increase
   D. less; fall; increase
   E. less; rise; decrease

7. If the Fed wishes to increase nominal interest rates, it must engage in an open market ____ of bonds that ____ the money supply.
   A. sale; increases
   B. sale; decreases
   C. sale; does not change
   D. purchase; increases
   E. purchase; decreases

8. The Fed's control over real interest rates is;
   A. absolute
   B. greater than its control over nominal interest rates
   C. less than its control over nominal interest rate
   D. impossible
   E. unimportant

9. The interest rate that commercial banks charge each other for very short-term loans is called the:
   A. prime rate.
   B. federal funds rate.
   C. Federal Reserve discount rate.
   D. commercial paper rate.
   E. bank loan rate.

10. A lower real interest rate _____ investment spending and _____ consumption spending.
   A. increases; increases
   B. increases; decreases
   C. does not change; does not change
   D. decreases; increases
   E. decreases; decreases

Solutions and Feedback to Pretest
For each question you incorrectly answered, we strongly recommend taking the time to review the appropriate material before continuing. In the table below are listed for each question the pertinent Learning Objective from the following Key Point Review.

Correct Answer	Learning Objective
1. A	5
2. D	2
3. B	2
4. D	3
5. C	3
6. A	4
7. B	5
8. C	7
9. B	6
10. A	8

II. Key Point Review
The Forest

This chapter focuses on an examination of the workings of monetary policy, one of the two major types of stabilization policy. The central questions you need to be able to answer are:

- What factors affect the demand for money?
- What determines the money market equilibrium interest rate?
- How does the Fed uses its ability to control the money supply to influence nominal and real interest rates?
- How do interest rates affect planned aggregate expenditures and the short-run equilibrium output?

The Trees

Learning Objective 1: Define demand for money

As explained in an earlier chapter, the Fed uses three tools to control the money supply. This chapter shows that the Fed's control of the money supply is tantamount to controlling nominal interest rates. The nominal interest rate is the price of money and is determined by the supply and demand for money. The **demand for money** is the result of choices made by households and businesses. The demand for money is the amount of wealth an individual chooses to hold in the form of money. Households and businesses demand money to carry out transactions (i.e., use it as a medium of exchange) and as a way of holding wealth (i.e., the store of value function of money).

> **Hint:** When economists talk about household and business demand for money they are **not** asking how much money do you want. The answer to that question is always "more." The demand for money refers to how much of your wealth you want to hold in the form of money (and, by implication, how much of your wealth will be held in non-money forms).

Learning Objective 2: Define portfolio allocation decision and explain how it relates to the demand for money

There are almost an infinite number of forms in which wealth can be held. The decision about the forms in which to hold one's wealth is called the **portfolio allocation decision**. How much money one chooses to hold is based on the costs and benefits of holding money. The opportunity cost of holding money is the interest that could have been earned if the person had chosen to hold interest-bearing assets instead of money. The higher the prevailing interest rate, the greater the opportunity cost of holding money, and hence the less money individuals and businesses will demand. The principle benefit of holding money is its usefulness in carrying out transactions. The amount of money demanded to carry out transactions is affected at the macroeconomic level by real output and the price level. An increase in aggregate real output or income raises the quantity of goods and services that people and businesses want to buy and, thus, raises the demand for money. The higher the price of goods and services, the more dollars needed to make a given set of transactions and, therefore, a higher demand for money.

Learning Objective 3: Discuss macroeconomic factors that affect the demand for money and the effects of changes on the money demand curve

Macroeconomists are primarily interested in the aggregate, or economy-wide, demand for money, represented by the money demand curve. The **money demand curve** relates the aggregate quantity of money demand, M, to the nominal interest rate, i. Because an increase in the nominal interest rate increases the opportunity cost of holding money, which reduces the quantity of money demanded, the money demand curve slopes down. An increase in real output or the price level will cause the money demand curve to increase (shift to the right), while a fall in either will cause it to decrease (shift to the left). Other factors, such as technological and financial advances, also cause the money demand curve to shift.

Learning Objective 4: Identify the money market equilibrium

The supply of money is controlled by the Fed (the central bank of the United States). Its primary tool for controlling the money supply is open-market operations. The Fed has two additional tools to control the money supply: **discount window lending** and changing **reserve requirements**. When a bank has insufficient reserves, it may choose to borrow reserves from the Fed to increase its reserves. The interest rate the Fed charges banks on borrowed reserves is called the **discount rate**. By raising the discount rate the Fed discourages banks from increasing their reserves via discount window lending; lowering the discount rate has the opposite objective. The Fed is also responsible for setting the minimum reserve requirement. Although the Fed seldom uses this tool for the purpose of affecting the money supply, it can expand the money supply by lowering the minimum reserve requirement, or reduce the money supply by raising the minimum reserve requirement. Because the Fed can control the supply of money, the money supply curve is a vertical line that intercepts the horizontal axis at the quantity of money chosen by the Fed. The equilibrium in the market for money occurs at the intersection of the supply and demand for money curves. The equilibrium amount of money in circulation is the amount of money the Fed chooses to supply. The equilibrium nominal interest rate is the interest rate at which the quantity of money demanded by the public equals the fixed supply of money made available by the Fed.

Note: Money is a commodity and can be exchanged in the market. Like any other goods, it can satisfy wants and, therefore, households and businesses demand money. Unlike most other goods, the supply of money is controlled by the Fed to achieve public goals rather than to maximize profits. The money market, thus, behaves much like any other commodity market, but also has some unique features.

Learning Objective 5: Explain how monetary policy is used to control nominal interest rates

When the Fed increases the money supply by purchasing government bonds from the public, it drives up the price of bonds and, thus, lowers the equilibrium nominal interest rate. Similarly, if the banks borrow reserves via the discount window or the Fed lowers the minimum reserve requirements, the money supply increases and the equilibrium nominal interest rate decreases. When the Fed decreases the money supply through open-market sales of government bonds to the public, the price of bonds is driven down and, therefore, the equilibrium nominal interest rate must rise. Likewise, if the banks borrow fewer reserves via the discount window or the Fed raises the minimum reserve requirements, the money supply decreases and the equilibrium nominal interest rate increases.

Note: Recall from our earlier discussion, there is an inverse relationship between bond prices and interest rates, i.e., when the price of bonds rise, market interest rates will go down.

Learning Objective 6: Define the federal funds rate and explain why the Fed has focused on it

Although there are thousands of different interest rates determined in the financial markets, the textbook authors use the phrase *the nominal interest rate* to refer to an average measure of these interest rates because they tend to rise and fall together. Of all the market interest rates, the one that is most closely watched by the public, politicians, and the media, however, is the federal funds rate. The **federal funds rate** is the interest rate commercial banks charge each other for very short-term (usually overnight) loans. It is closely watched because for the past 35 years, the Fed has expressed its policies in terms of a target value for the federal funds rate. Because interest rates tend to move together, an action by the Fed to change the federal funds rate generally causes other interest rates to change in the same direction. The tendency of interest rates to move together, however, is not an exact relationship. This means that the Fed's control over other interest rates is somewhat less precise than its control over the federal funds rate.

Learning Objective 7: Discuss the Fed's ability to control the real rate of interest

Similarly, the Fed's control over real interest rates is less complete than its control over nominal interest rates. The real interest rate equals the nominal interest rate minus the rate of inflation. Because inflation tends to change relatively slowly in response to changes in policy or economic conditions, actions by the Fed to change nominal interest rates allows it to control real interest rates in the short run. In the long run, however, the inflation rate and other variables will adjust, and the balance of saving and investment will determine the real interest.

Note: The reason it is important that the Fed be able to influence (if not control) changes in real (not nominal) interest rates cause changes in economic behavior. Therefore, if the Fed is to be effective in formulating and implementing monetary policy it must be able to influence real interest rates.

Learning Objective 8: Explain how interest rates affect consumption and investment spending, aggregate demand, and short-run equilibrium output

Because the Fed can control the money supply and interest rates (at least, in the short run), monetary policy can be used to eliminate output gaps and stabilize the economy. Consumption and planned investment spending are inversely related to real interest rates, that is, a decrease in real interest rates will cause consumption and planned investment spending to increase. Because consumption and planned investment spending are components of planned aggregate expenditures, changes in real interest rates cause changes in planned aggregate expenditures. By adjusting real interest rates, the Fed can move planned aggregate expenditures in the desired direction. For example, an expansionary monetary policy, or monetary easing, is a reduction in interest rates by the Fed, made with the intention of reducing a recessionary gap. If the economy faces a recessionary gap, the Fed could reduce real interest rates to stimulate consumption and investment spending. This will increase planned aggregate expenditures and, as a result, output will rise and the recessionary gap will be reduce or eliminated. When the economy experiences inflationary pressures, the Fed may implement a contractionary monetary policy, or monetary tightening, by increasing interest rates with the intention of reducing an expansionary gap.

Learning Objective 9: Define and discuss the Fed's policy reaction function
Economists often try to summarize the behavior of the Fed in terms of a **policy reaction function,** describing how the action a policymaker takes depends on the state of the economy. An example of a monetary policy reaction function that will be used in the next few chapters is: $r = r^* + g(\pi - \pi^*)$, where r = the actual real interest rate set by the Fed, r^* = the Fed's long-run target for the real interest rate, π = the actual inflation rate, π^* = the Fed's long-run target for the inflation rate, and g = a positive number chosen by the Fed. The policy reaction function indicates that when actual inflation is greater than the Fed's long-run target inflation rate, the Fed will push up the real interest rate; conversely, when actual inflation is less than the Fed's long-run target inflation rate, the Fed will lower the real interest rate. The policy reaction function can be represented in a graph showing the Fed's target real interest rate on the vertical axis and the target rate of inflation on the horizontal axis. An upward sloping curve represents the policy reaction function with the slope of the curve equal to g (in the above equation). The more aggressive the Fed's monetary policy the steeper the slope of the curve while a flatter slope represents a more conservative monetary policy. It is up to the Fed to determine how aggressive or conservative its policy reaction function will be at any point in time. Doing so is a complex process, involving a combination of statistical analysis of the economy and human judgment.

III. Self-Test

Key Terms
Match the term in the right-hand column with the appropriate definition in the left-hand column by placing the letter of the term in the blank in front of its' definition. (Answers are given at the end of the chapter.)

1. ____ The choice about which forms to hold one's wealth.

2. ____ The interest rate that commercial banks charge each other for very short-term (usually overnight) loans.

3. ____ Shows the relationship between the aggregate quantity of money demanded and the nominal interest rate.

4. ____ Describes how the action a policymaker takes depends on the state of the economy.

5. ____ The amount of wealth an individual chooses to hold in the form of money.

6. ____ The lending of reserves by the Federal Reserve to commercial banks.

7. ____ The Fed's long-run target for the real interest rate.

8. ____ The interest rate that the Fed charges commercial banks to borrow reserves.

9. ____ The Fed's long-run target for the inflation rate.

10.____ The minimum values of the ratio of bank reserves to bank deposits that commercial banks are allowed to maintain.__

a. demand for money

b. discount rate

c. discount window lending

d. federal funds rate

e. money demand curve

f. policy reaction function

g. portfolio allocation decision

h. reserve requirements

i. target inflation rate

j. target real interest rate

Multiple-Choice Questions
Circle the letter that corresponds to the best answer. (Answers are given at the end of the chapter.)

1. The portfolio allocation decision is related to the demand for money because
    A. money can be used to buy a portfolio.
    B. money is one of the many forms in which wealth can be held and is a part of most asset portfolios.
    C. the portfolio allocation decision determines how much of an individual's money is going to be held in the form of currency and how much in the form of balances in a checking account.
    D. money is the main form of wealth for most people.
    E. portfolio allocation explains why the amount of money people hold is directly related to interest rates.

2. E-Buy, a web-based auction firm receives an average of $25,000 in payments for its services each day that it deposits in its bank account at the end of each day. E-Commerce Management Systems, Inc. proposed a computerized cash management system to track E-Buys' inflows and outflows of payments and electronically transfer the funds to an interest-bearing bank account. The cost of the system is $500 per year and E-Buys estimates that it would reduce its cash holding by approximately $10,000 per day. E-Buy should
    A. accept the proposal.
    B. reject the proposal.
    C. accept the proposal if the average interest rate they can earn on the funds is at least 10 percent.
    D. reject the proposal if the average interest rate they can earn on the funds is less than 10 percent.
    E. accept the proposal if the average interest rate they can earn on the funds is greater than 5 percent.

3. As the number of ATM machines increases in a country
    A. the supply of money will increase.
    B. the supply of money will decrease.
    C. people will hold more of their wealth in the form of money. (i.e., the demand for money will increase).
    D. people will hold less of their wealth in the form of money (i.e., the demand for money will decrease).
    E. interest rates will increase.

4. When the Fed buys government bonds, bond prices
    A. increase and interest rates fall.
    B. decrease and interest rates fall.
    C. increase and interest rates rise.
    D. decrease and interest rates rise.
    E. and interest rates fall.

5. The Fed communicates its monetary policy to the public in terms of targets for the federal funds rate because it is
    A. the only interest rate that they can control.
    B. the interest rate that most individuals pay when they borrow money to buy a car, a household appliance, or a house.
    C. the interest rate that the Fed has the greatest control over.
    D. one of the tools of monetary policy.
    E. the most important of all the interest rates that are determined in the various financial markets.

6. The real interest rate
    A. cannot be controlled by the Fed because monetary policy only affects nominal interest rates.
    B. can be controlled by the Fed in the short run, but not in the long run.
    C. can be controlled by the Fed in the long run, but not in the short run.
    D. equals the nominal interest rate plus the inflation rate.
    E. equals the inflation rate minus the nominal interest rate.

7. If the Fed implements an open-market sale of government bonds, the
    A. money market equilibrium interest rate will rise.
    B. money market equilibrium interest rate will fall.
    C. price of bonds will rise.
    D. supply of money will increase.
    E. demand for bonds will decrease

8. If the Fed implements an open-market purchase of government bonds, this will cause a(n)
    A. decrease in consumption spending, an increase in investment spending, and an increase in planned aggregate expenditures.
    B. increase in consumption and investment spending, and an increase in planned aggregate expenditures.
    C. decrease in consumption and investment spending, and an increase in planned aggregate expenditures.
    D. decrease in consumption spending, a decrease in investment spending, and an increase in planned aggregate expenditures.
    E. increase in consumption spending, a decrease in investment spending, and a decrease in planned aggregate expenditures.

9. To close a recessionary gap the Fed should
    A. sell government bonds to increase bond prices and lower interest rates, causing consumption, investment spending, and planned aggregate expenditures to increase.
    B. sell government bonds to decrease bond prices and lower interest rates, causing consumption, investment spending, and planned aggregate expenditures to increase.
    C. buy government bonds to increase bond prices and lower interest rates, causing consumption, investment spending, and planned aggregate expenditures to increase.
    D. buy government bonds to decreases bond prices and increase interest rates, causing consumption, investment spending, and planned aggregate expenditures to decrease.

E. buy government bonds to decreases bond prices and lower interest rates, causing consumption, investment spending, and planned aggregate expenditures to increase.

10. An expansionary monetary policy will cause a(n)
   A. decrease in interest rates, an increase in planned aggregate expenditures, and is designed to reduce an expansionary gap.
   B. increase in interest rates, a decrease in planned aggregate expenditures, and is designed to reduce an expansionary gap.
   C. decrease in interest rates, a decrease in planned aggregate expenditures, and is designed to reduce a recessionary gap.
   D. decrease in interest rates, an increase in planned aggregate expenditures, and is designed to reduce a recessionary gap.
   E. increase in interest rates, increase in planned aggregate expenditures, and is designed to reduce a recessionary gap.

11. The Fed's policy reaction function
   A. is mandated by law.
   B. is a model of the behavior of the Fed.
   C. can be determined by statistical analysis of the economy.
   D. is determined by its short-run target rate of inflation.
   E. only provides information about the central bank's inflation target.

12. The more aggressive the Fed's monetary policy
   A. the higher the value of g in the policy reaction function and the flatter the slope of the policy reaction curve.
   B. the lower the value of g in the policy reaction function and the flatter the slope of the policy reaction curve.
   C. The higher the value of g in the policy reaction function and the steeper the slope of the policy reaction curve.
   D. the lower the value of g in the policy reaction function and the steeper the slope of the policy reaction curve.
   E. the lower the real interest rate will be for a given rate of inflation.

13. The higher the price of bonds, with no change in the cost of transferring funds between bonds and checkable deposits, the
   A. more likely people are to hold their wealth in the form of bonds than money.
   B. more likely people are to hold their wealth in the form of money than bonds.
   C. the greater the differential between nominal and real interest rates.
   D. the smaller the quantity of money demanded.
   E. the greater the demand for money.

14. A decrease in aggregate real output or income will
   A. decrease the quantity of goods and services that people and businesses want to buy and sell and, thus, decrease the demand for money.
   B. decrease the quantity of goods and services that people and businesses want to buy and sell and, thus, increase the demand for money.

C. increase the quantity of goods and services that people and businesses want to buy and sell and, thus, decrease the demand for money.

D. increase the quantity of goods and services that people and businesses want to buy and sell and, thus, increase the demand for money.

E. decrease the quantity of goods and services that people and businesses want to buy and sell, but have no effect on the demand for money.

15. A contractionary monetary policy
  A. is achieved if the Fed implements an open-market purchase of government bonds.
  B. will decrease the money market equilibrium interest rate.
  C. will increase the money market equilibrium interest rate.
  D. will raise the price of bonds.
  E. will shift the money supply curve to the right.

16. The Fed can control real interest rates only in the short run because
  A. the U.S. Congress has not given it the legal authority to control interest rates in the long run.
  B. nominal interest rates only adjust slowly to changing economic conditions and policy.
  C. saving and investment are not relevant to short-run real interest rates.
  D. saving and investment are not relevant to long-run real interest rates.
  E. the inflation rate only adjusts slowly to changing economic conditions and policy.

17. If the Fed wants to lower the money market equilibrium interest rate, it should
  A. decrease the supply of money.
  B. shift the supply of money to the left.
  C. sell government bonds.
  D. purchase government bonds.
  E. decrease the price of bonds.

18. A contractionary monetary policy is designed to produce a(n)
  A. increase in planned aggregate expenditures, and reduce an expansionary gap.
  B. decrease in planned aggregate expenditures, and reduce an expansionary gap.
  C. increase in planned aggregate expenditures, and reduce a recessionary gap.
  D. decrease in planned aggregate expenditures, and reduce a recessionary gap.
  E. increase in planned aggregate expenditures, and increase an expansionary gap.

19. If the Fed purchases government bonds, this will cause a(n)
  A. increase in planned aggregate expenditures and output and reduce a recessionary gap.
  B. increase in planned aggregate expenditures and output and reduce an expansionary gap.
  C. decrease in planned aggregate expenditures and output and reduce a recessionary gap.
  D. decrease in planned aggregate expenditures and output and reduce an expansionary gap.
  E. increase in planned aggregate expenditures, decrease output, and reduce an expansionary gap.

20. If the Fed wants to increase the money market equilibrium interest rate, it should
    A. lower the reserve requirement.
    B. decrease the discount rate.
    C. increase the discount rate.
    D. buy government bonds.
    E. tell banks to increase the federal funds rate.

Short Answer Problems
(Answers and solutions are given at the end of the chapter.)

1. Cost and Benefit of Holding Money
The following table shows the estimated annual benefits to Siam of holding different amounts of money.

Average Money Holdings	Total Annual Benefit	Marginal Annual Benefit
$1,000	$60	XXXXXXXX
1,100	72	
1,200	82	
1,300	90	
1,400	96	
1,500	100	
1,600	102	
1,700	102	

A. Complete column 3 by calculating the extra benefit of each additional $100 in money holdings greater than $100.
B. How much money will Siam hold if the nominal interest rates is 10 percent? $_____; if the nominal interest rates is 8 percent? $_____; if the nominal interest rates is 6 percent? $_____; if the nominal interest rate is 4 percent $_____; if the nominal interest rate is 2 percent $_____?
C. On the graph below plot Siam's money demand curve for nominal interest rates between 2 and 12 percent.

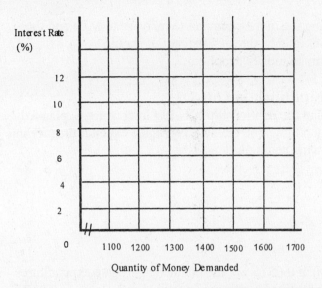

Quantity of Money Demanded

D. If Siam won a million-dollar lottery, his money demand curve shift to the (right/left) _____ representing a(n) (increase/decrease) _____ in the demand for money.

2. Money Market and Equilibrium Interest Rate

This problem focuses on the Fed's control of the money supply to achieve targeted nominal interest rates. Assume that the price level and real GDP are at levels such that the money demand is initially at MD1.

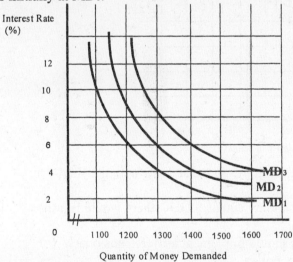

Quantity of Money Demanded

A. If the Fed wants to set the nominal equilibrium interest rate at 4 percent, it should set the money supply at $ _____.

B. If real GDP increases so that the money demand rises to MD2 and the Fed wants to keep the nominal equilibrium interest rate at 4 percent, it should (increase/decrease) _____ the nominal money supply to $ _____.

C. If the Fed now decides to raise the nominal equilibrium interest rate to 6 percent, it should (increase/decrease) _____ the nominal money supply to $ _____.

D. If the price level subsequently rises causing the money demand to increase to MD3 and the
    Fed wants to keep the nominal equilibrium interest rate at 6 percent, it should
    (increase/decrease) _____ the nominal money supply to $_____.

3. Monetary Policy and Short-Run Equilibrium Output

This problem will help you to better understand the relationship between interest rates, planned
aggregate expenditures, output, and monetary policy. The planned aggregate expenditures for the
economy of Hinderland is given by the following equations:

$C = \$750 + 0.75(Y - T) - 300r$

$I^P = \$400 - 600r$

$G = \$500$

$T = \$400$

$NX = -\$55$

A. If the Fed sets the nominal interest rate (r) at 0.05 (5 %), the planned aggregate expenditures
    for the Hinderland economy would be represented by the equation $PAE = \$$_____ +
    .75Y.

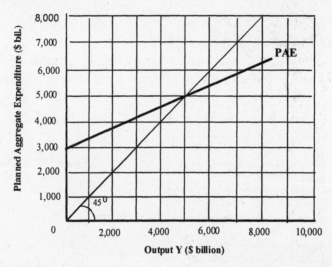

B. Given the Hinderland planned aggregate expenditures in the above graph, the short-run
    equilibrium output would equal $_____ .
C. If potential output (Y^*) in the Hinderland economy equals $5,050, there would be a(n)
    _____ gap of $_____ .
D. If the Fed wanted to close the output gap, it should implement a(n) (expansionary/
    contractionary) _____ monetary policy.

**Note: Questions 3E – 3F require an algebraic solution using the PAE equation from
question 3A. The use of algebraic equations to determine monetary policy is discussed in
Appendix A of the textbook chapter.**

E. To close the gap, the Fed would need to (decrease/ increase) _____ nominal
    interest rates to _____ percent.

F. Following the expansionary monetary policy, assume the recessionary gap is closed at $Y =$ $5,050, and the Fed determines that the inflation rate is 1.5%. Applying the Taylor rule, this would suggest that the real interest rate in the economy would equal_____ %.

IV. Becoming an Economic Naturalist: Case Study

In the Economic Naturalist 14.4, the Fed's role in responding to the economic expansion of 2002-04 and its "pre-emptive strike against inflation" that began in June 2004 are discussed. During the latter half of 2004 and first half of 2005, the Fed has continued to raise the discount rate and the market determined federal funds rate has also risen. How would an economist characterize the monetary policy (expansionary or contractionary) during the latter half of 2004 and first half of 2005? Looking at the discount rate and federal funds rate since July 2005, has the Fed maintained the same direction in its monetary policy? Explain your answer.

Answer:

V. Self-Test Solutions

Key Terms
1. g
2. d
3. e
4. f
5. a
6. c
7. j
8. b
9. i
10. h

Multiple-Choice Questions
1. B
2. E $10,000 x 0.05 = $500. Therefore, an interest rate of greater than 5% would imply that the benefit would be greater than the cost.
3. D
4. A
5. C
6. B
7. A
8. B
9. C
10. D
11. B
12. C
13. B

14. A
15. C
16. E
17. D
18. B
19. A
20. C

Short Answer Problems

1.

A.

Average Money Holdings	Total Annual Benefit	Marginal Annual Benefit
$1,000	$60	XXXXXXXX
1,100	72	12
1,200	82	10
1,300	90	8
1,400	96	6
1,500	100	4
1,600	102	2
1,700	102	0

B. $1,200; $1,300; $1,400; $1,500; $1,600

C.

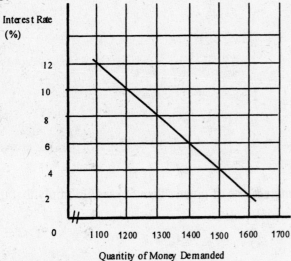

D. right; increase

2.

A. $1300

B. increase; $1,400

C. decrease; $1,300

D. increase; $1,400

3.

A. $1,250 ($750 + .75(Y – $400) – $300(.05) + $400 – $600(.05) + $500 + (–$55)

B. $5,000

C. recessionary gap; $50 (Y* – Y = output gap)

D. expansionary

E. decrease; 3.6 ($5,050 = $1,295 + .75($5,050) – 900i, or $5,050 = $1,295 + $3,787.5 – 900$i$.
Combining the constant values gives us –$32.5 = – 900$i$., or 3.6 = i)

F. 1.75 [r = 0.01 – 0.5 ($\frac{\$5,050 - \$5,050}{\$5,050}$) + 0.5(.015)]

Chapter 15
Inflation, Aggregate Supply, and Aggregate Demand

I. Pretest: What Do You Really Know?

Circle the letter that corresponds to the best answer. (Answers appear immediately after the final question).

1. All else equal, an increase in the rate of inflation _____ aggregate demand and _____ short-run equilibrium output.
    A. increases; increases
    B. increases; decreases
    C. does not change; does not change
    D. decreases; increases
    E. decreases; decreases

2. Suppose in an economy PAE = $5,000 + .75 Y - 10,000r and the central bank acts according to the following policy reaction function:

Rate of inflation (π)	Real interest rate set by central bank (r)
0.00 (=0%)	0.03 (=3%)
0.01	0.04
0.02	0.05
0.03	0.06
0.04	0.07

    If inflation is 1%, the central bank will set a real interest rate of _____ percent and short-run equilibrium output will equal _____.
    A. 3; 18,400
    B. 4; 18,400
    C. 6; 18,400
    D. 6; 17,600
    E. 6; 15,000

3. High levels of inflation ___ the real value of money and, hence, _____ aggregate demand.
    A. reduce; increase
    B. reduce; decrease

    C. have no impact on; have no impact on
    D. increase; decrease
    E. increase; increase

4. Which of the following will shift the aggregate demand curve to the left?
    A. Income taxes are lowered.
    B. The government increases spending on education.
    C. Consumers become optimistic about the future.
    D. A new technology is developed that will increase profits.
    E. Foreign economies fall into recession, reducing their demand for domestic exports.

5. If for any given inflation rate, the Fed raises interest rates more than normal, this is called a monetary _____ and the aggregate demand curve shifts to the _____.
    A. tightening; right
    B. tightening; left
    C. gap; right
    D. easing; right
    E. easing; left

6. An upward shift in the Fed's policy reaction function is a monetary _____ and the aggregate demand curve _____.
    A. tightening; shifts right
    B. tightening; shifts left
    C. tightening; does not shift
    D. easing; shifts right
    E. easing; shifts left

7. An increase in interest rates by the Fed based on a given policy reaction function represents a _____ the aggregate demand curve, but higher than normal interest rates resulting from an upward shift in the Fed's policy reaction function represents a _____ the aggregate demand curve.
    A. shift left of; movement up
    B. shift left of ; shift right of
    C. movement up; movement down
    D. movement up; shift left of
    E. movement down; shift left of

8. The tendency for inflation to change relatively slowly from year to year in industrial countries is called:
    A. the inflation gap
    B. inflation expectations.
    C. inflation inertia.
    D. potential inflation.
    E. autonomous inflation.

9. When actual output is less than potential output there is ____ output gap and the rate of inflation will tend to ____.
   A. an expansionary; increase
   B. an expansionary; decrease
   C. no; remain the same
   D. a recessionary; increase
   E. a recessionary; decrease

10. Within the context of the Aggregate Demand-Aggregate Supply Diagram, the long-run equilibrium occurs where the:
   A. long-run aggregate supply and short-run aggregate supply curves intersect.
   B. short-run aggregate supply and aggregate demand curves intersect.
   C. short-run aggregate supply, long-run aggregate supply and aggregate demand curves intersect.
   D. actual output is less than potential output.
   E. actual output is greater than potential output.

Solutions and Feedback to Pretest
For each question you incorrectly answered, we strongly recommend taking the time to review the appropriate material before continuing. In the table below are listed for each question the pertinent Learning Objective from the following Key Point Review.

Correct Answer	Learning Objective
1. E	2
2. B	5
3. B	1
4. E	2
5. B	2
6. B	2
7. D	2
8. C	3
9. E	6
10. C	6

II. Key Point Review
The Forest

This chapter focuses on the development of the aggregate demand/aggregate supply diagram to analyze how macroeconomic policies affect inflation and discusses the sources of inflation. The central questions you need to be able to answer are:
- What factors determine the aggregate demand in the macroeconomy?
- What factors determine the short-run and long-run aggregate supply ?
- Where do the short-run and long-run equilibria occur on the aggregate demand-aggregate supply diagram?
- How does the economy self-correct when the short-run equilibrium does not equal potential output?

- What are the sources of inflation?
- How does fiscal policy affect the aggregate supply?

The Trees

Learning Objective 1: Define aggregate demand curve and explain why it is downward sloping

To incorporate inflation into the model, a new relationship is introduced between aggregate demand (AD) and the rate of inflation (π). Graphically, this relationship is called the aggregate demand curve. Because short-run equilibrium output equals aggregate demand, the **aggregate demand curve** not only shows the relationship between AD and inflation, but also shows the relationship between short-run equilibrium output and inflation. When the Fed raises real interest rates in response to higher inflation rates, aggregate demand and the short-run equilibrium output decrease. The aggregate demand curve is, therefore, downward sloping. In addition to the effect of inflation on monetary policy, there are three other reasons why inflation reduces aggregate demand. First, higher inflation reduces the real value of money held by households and businesses causing them to restrain spending and, thus, reduces aggregate demand. Second, higher inflation affects income distribution as it redistributes resources from relatively high-spending, less-affluent households to relatively high-saving, more-affluent households, causing overall spending to decline. Third, as domestic goods become relatively more expensive to prospective foreign purchasers, export sales decline, reducing aggregate demand. To summarize, changes in the Fed's response to higher inflation, and the effects of inflation on the real value of money, income distribution, and net exports, cause a movement along the aggregate demand curve.

Learning Objective 2: Identify the factors that cause the AD curve to shift

In addition to the above factors that cause movements along the aggregate demand curve, there are also factors that cause the aggregate demand curve to shift. For a given level of inflation, any change in the economy that affects the aggregate demand and short-run equilibrium will cause the AD curve to shift. This chapter focuses on two sorts of changes in the economy that shift the aggregate demand curve: changes in spending cause by factors other than output or interest rates (refer to as exogenous changes in spending) and changes in the Fed's policy reaction function. The components of planned aggregate expenditures include consumption, investment spending, government purchases, and net exports. A change in any other these components that is caused by something other than a change in output or interest rates is called a change in exogenous spending. An increase in exogenous spending will cause the AD curve to shift to the right, while a decrease in exogenous spending will cause the AD curve to shift to the left. If the Fed's policy reaction function shifts upward, (i.e., the Fed chooses a "tighter" monetary policy by setting the real interest rate higher than normal for a given rate of inflation), the aggregate demand curve will shift to the left. An easing of monetary policy (the Fed's policy reaction function shifts downward) causes the AD curve to shift to the right.

Learning Objective 3: Explain the importance of inflation inertia in determining the short-run aggregate supply (SRAS)

The rate of inflation in low-inflation industrial economies tends to change relatively slowly from year to year (**inflation inertia**). Inflation inertia is due to (1) the public's inflation expectations for the next few years, which are highly influenced by the recent inflation experience, and (2) long-term wage and price contracts, which tend to build the effects of people's inflation expectations into current price level. Although the rate of inflation is inertial, it does change over time.

Hint: You can think of inflation inertia as a virtuous cycle, in which low inflation begets successive periods of low inflation. If inflation begins to rise, however, a vicious cycle can set in, with high inflation creating inflationary expectations that will lead to successive period of high inflation.

Learning Objective 4: Explain the relationship between output gaps and changes in inflation

One factor that can cause inflation to change is the output gap. If the output gap is zero, the rate of inflation will tend to remain the same. When an expansionary gap exists, the rate of inflation will tend to increase; and a recessionary gap tends to cause the rate of inflation to decrease. For example, if a recessionary gap exists, firms will be selling less than their capacity to produce, and they will have an incentive to reduce the *relative* price of their product in order to sell more of it. Cutting the *relative* price means that firms will raise their prices by less than the increase in their costs, as determined by the current inflation rate. As a result, the rate of inflation will tend to fall when a recessionary gap exists. On the other hand, if an expansionary gap exists, firms will be selling more than their normal production and they will ultimately increase the relative price of their product. Doing so will mean that they raise prices by an amount greater than the increase in their costs. In this manner, inflation will tend to rise when an expansionary gap exists.

Learning Objective 5: Define long-run and short-run aggregate supply lines, and short-run and long-run equilibrium

The adjustment of inflation in response to output gaps can be conveniently shown using the AD/AS diagram. The AD/AS diagram is a tool economists use to determine the level of output prevailing at any particular time. The aggregate supply component of the AD/AS diagram is represented by two curves called the long-run aggregate supply line and the short-run aggregate supply line. The **short-run aggregate supply line**, or SRAS line, is a horizontal line showing the current rate of inflation, as determined by past expectations and pricing decisions. The AD/AS diagram can be used to determine the level of output prevailing at any particular time, called the **short-run equilibrium** output. The short-run equilibrium occurs when inflation equals the value determined by past expectations and pricing decisions and output equals the level of short-run equilibrium output that is consistent with that inflation rate. Graphically, the short-run equilibrium occurs at the intersection of the AD curve and the SRAS line. The **long-run aggregate supply line**, or LRAS line, is a vertical line at the economy's potential output (Y*). This point is referred to as the long-run equilibrium of the economy. The **long-run equilibrium** occurs where actual output equals potential output and the inflation rate is stable. Graphically, long-run equilibrium occurs when the AD curve, the SRAS line and the LRAS line all intersect

236   Chapter 15

at a single point. An expansionary gap at the short-run equilibrium output would set in motion a similar adjustment process, but in the opposite direction (e.g., inflation rate would rise, SRAS line shifts upward).

Learning Objective 6: Discuss the self-correcting tendency of the economy
The AD/AS diagram makes the important general point that the economy tends to be self-correcting. That is, given enough time, output gaps tend to disappear without changes in monetary or fiscal policy. This view contrasts with the basic Keynesian model, which does not include a self-correcting mechanism. This difference derives from the fact that the basic Keynesian model concentrates on the short-run period, during which prices do not adjust, while the extended AD/AS model focuses on the changes in prices and inflation over the long-run period. Whether monetary and fiscal policies are needed to stabilize output then depends crucially on the speed with which the self-correction process takes place. If self-correction takes place slowly, active use of monetary and fiscal policy can help to stabilize output. If it takes place rapidly, however, an active stabilization policy is not only unnecessary, but is probably harmful. The speed with which a particular economy corrects itself depends upon the prevalence of long-term contracts and the efficiency and flexibility of product and labor markets. In addition, the larger the size of the output gap, the longer the self-correction will take. The self-correcting tendency of the economy also explains why the income-expenditure multiplier is smaller in practice than the basic Keynesian model suggests.

> **Note:** How long is the long-run period? The long run is not defined in concrete measures, such as months or years. It is conceptually defined as a period sufficiently long to allow the economy to fully adjust prices and output. In concrete terms, the long run can vary depending upon a variety of factors that impact the economy's ability to adjust. Some economies may adjust faster than others, and a given economy can adjust faster to some circumstances, but more slowly under other circumstances.

Learning Objective 7: Show the effects of excessive aggregate demand and supply shocks on inflation
The analysis of the AD/AS diagram indicates that inflation rises and falls in response to output gaps. But, what causes output gaps? An expansionary output gap may result from excessive aggregate spending that puts upward pressure on prices ("too much money chasing too few goods"). Wars and military buildups have historically been one reason for excessive aggregate spending. Inflation may also arise from an **aggregate supply shock**, either an inflation shock or a shock to potential output. An **inflation shock** is a sudden change in the normal behavior of inflation, unrelated to the nation's output gap. For example, a large increase in energy or food prices (an adverse inflation shock) shifts the SRAS line upward. An adverse inflation shock creates stagflation, a combination of recession and higher inflation, creating a difficult dilemma for policymakers. If they take no action, eventually inflation will subside and output will recover, but in the interim the economy may suffer a protracted period of recession. Monetary or fiscal policy, on the other hand, can be used to shorten the recession, but will lock in higher inflation. A **shock to potential output** is a sharp change in potential output, shifting the LRAS line. Like an inflation shock, an adverse shock to potential output results in stagflation. The adverse shock

to potential output, however, implies that productive capacity has fallen and, therefore, output does not recover as it does following an inflation shock.

Learning Objective 8: Explain how fiscal policy may have supply-side impacts.
Fiscal policy, government spending and taxation such as public capital expenditures (for roads, airports, or schools), not only affects aggregate expenditures but also may increase potential output if it changes firms' costs of production. Government tax and transfer programs affect incentives, and, thus, the economic behavior of households and businesses. Households and business may respond to changes in their marginal tax rates by working more or less, investing more or less, and taking more or less risk. These changes may cause the aggregate supply curves to shift.

III. Self-Test

Key Terms
Match the term in the right-hand column with the appropriate definition in the left-hand column by placing the letter of the term in the blank in front of its' definition. (Answers are given at the end of the chapter.)

1. _____ Either an inflation shock or a shock to potential output.

2. _____ A horizontal line showing the current rate of inflation, as determined by past expectations and pricing decisions.

3. _____ Shows the relationship between short-run equilibrium output and inflation.

4. _____ A situation in which actual output equals potential output and the inflation rate is stable.

5. _____ A substantial reduction in the rate of inflation.

6. _____ A sudden change in the normal behavior of inflation, unrelated to the nation's output gap

7. _____ A vertical line showing the economy's potential output (Y^*).

8. _____ A situation in which inflation equals the value determined by past expectations and pricing decisions, and output equals the level of short-run equilibrium output that is consistent with that inflation.

9. _____ A policy that affects potential output.

10. _____ The amount by which taxes rise when before-tax income rises by one dollar.

11. _____ Total taxes divided by total before-taxes income.

a. aggregate demand (AD) curve

b. aggregate supply shock

c. average tax rate

d. disinflation

e. inflation shock

f. long-run aggregate supply (LRAS) line

g. long-run equilibrium

h. marginal tax rate

i. short-run aggregate supply (SRAS) line

j. short-run equilibrium

k. supply-side policy

Multiple-Choice Questions
Circle the letter that corresponds to the best answer. (Answers are given at the end of the chapter.)

1. When the Fed responds to higher inflation by raising real interest rates
    A. consumption and investment spending rise and, thus, total spending increases.
    B. consumption and investment spending fall and, thus, total spending increases.
    C. consumption and investment spending rise and, thus, total spending decreases.
    D. consumption and investment spending fall and, thus, total spending decreases.
    E. the Fed changes its policy reaction function.

2. A decrease in taxes will cause a
    A. movement downward along the AD curve.
    B. movement upward along the AD curve.
    C. rightward shift in the AD curve.
    D. leftward shift in the AD curve.
    E. decrease in AD.

3. Inflation inertia is attributable to
    A. inflation shocks and shocks to potential output.
    B. output gaps and inflation shock.
    C. disinflation and inflation shock.
    D. output gaps and disinflation.
    E. inflation expectations and long-term wage and price contracts.

4. When an expansionary gap exists, the rate of inflation will
    A. tend to rise.
    B. tend to fall.
    C. remain unchanged.
    D. become disinflation.
    E. shift the SRAS line downward.

5. If, at the short-run equilibrium output, a recessionary gap exists, the
    A. SRAS line will move upward until actual output equals potential output.
    B. SRAS line will move downward until actual output equals potential output.
    C. LRAS line will move upward until actual output equals potential output.
    D. LRAS line will move downward until actual output equals potential output.
    E. LRAS line and SRAS line will move upward until actual output equals potential output.

6. The tendency for the economy to be self-correcting
    A. is highlighted by the AD/AS diagram.
    B. is highlighted by the basic Keynesian model.
    C. is an underlying assumption of all macroeconomic models.
    D. implies that fiscal and monetary policies are not needed to stabilize output.
    E. has been called into question by the analysis of the AD/AS diagram.

7. Excessive aggregate demand can result in
   A. a recessionary gap and a rising inflation rate.
   B. too many goods chasing too little spending.
   C. an expansionary gap and an increasing inflation rate.
   D. an expansionary gap and an increasing unemployment rate.
   E. a recessionary gap and a rising unemployment rate.

8. If the inflation rate has risen to a level inconsistent with economic efficiency and long-term growth, and the Fed tightens monetary policy, the
   A. the monetary policy reaction function shifts upward and the SRAS curve will shift downward.
   B. the monetary policy reaction function shifts downward and the AD curve will shift to the left.
   C. the monetary policy reaction function shifts upward and the AD curve will shift to the right.
   D. the monetary policy reaction function shifts upward AD curve shifts to the left.
   E. the monetary policy reaction function shifts downward and the AD curve shifts to the right.

9. The distributional effects of inflation contribute to a downward-sloping AD curve because inflation redistributes income from
   A. less affluent, lower-spending families to more affluent families who spend more, causing overall spending to decline.
   B. relatively higher-spending, less-affluent families to relatively higher-saving, more-affluent families, causing overall spending to decline.
   C. relatively lower-spending, more-affluent families to relatively higher spending, less-affluent families, causing overall spending to decline.
   D. relatively lower-spending, less-affluent families to relatively higher spending, more-affluent families, causing overall spending to decline.
   E. relatively higher-spending, more-affluent families to relatively lower saving, less-affluent families, causing overall spending to decline.

10. If the Fed were to shift its policy reaction function downward (i.e., an easing of monetary policy), the
    A. SRAS line would shift upward.
    B. LRAS line would shift upward.
    C. SRAS line would shift downward.
    D. AD curve would shift to the left.
    E. AD curve would shift to the right.

11. A current high rate of inflation will tend to promote a
    A. virtuous circle of high expected inflation and a high rate of actual inflation.
    B. virtuous circle of low expected inflation and a low rate of actual inflation.
    C. vicious circle of high expected inflation and a high rate of actual inflation.
    D. vicious circle of low expected inflation and a low rate of actual inflation.
    E. built-in expectation of low inflation in the future.

12. A short-run equilibrium with an output gap of zero implies
    A. zero inflation in the near future.
    B. the rate of inflation will remain the same.
    C. the rate of inflation will rise.
    D. the rate of inflation will fall.
    E. firms have no incentive to raise the prices of their goods and services.

13. If an expansionary gap exists at the short-run equilibrium output, the
    A. SRAS line will move upward until actual output equals potential output.
    B. SRAS line will move downward until actual output equals potential output.
    C. LRAS line will move upward until actual output equals potential output.
    D. LRAS line will move downward until actual output equals potential output.
    E. LRAS line and SRAS line will move downward until actual output equals potential output.

14. If the self-correction process of the economy takes place very slowly, so that actual output differs from potential output for protracted periods of time, then active
    A. stabilization policies are probably not justified.
    B. stabilization policies may end up doing more harm than good.
    C. use of monetary and fiscal policy can cause actual output to overshoot potential output.
    D. use of monetary and fiscal policy can help to stabilize output.
    E. stabilization policy can cause the output gap to become larger.

15. Inflation escalated to the double-digit level in the United States during the 1970s because of
    A. excessive aggregate demand due to the military buildup under President Reagan.
    B. an adverse inflation shock caused by the military buildup under President Reagan.
    C. adverse inflation shocks caused by two oil crises that significantly raised world oil prices.
    D. a positive inflation shock that resulted in high inflation and a recessionary gap.
    E. a positive inflation shock that resulted in two periods of stagflation.

16. At high rates of inflation, the purchasing power of money
    A. declines and households restrain their spending, causing aggregate demand to decline.
    B. rises and household increase their spending, causing aggregate demand to rise.
    C. rises and households restrain their spending, causing aggregate demand to decline.
    D. declines and households restrain their spending, causing aggregate demand to increase.
    E. declines and households increase their spending, causing aggregate demand to decline.

17. The development of new cost-saving technology would
    A. increase exogenous spending and, thus, cause a movement down along the AD curve.
    B. increase exogenous spending and, thus, cause a movement up along the AD curve to the left.
    C. increase exogenous spending and, thus, shift the AD curve to the right.
    D. increase exogenous spending and, thus, shift the AD curve to the left.
    E. decrease exogenous spending and, thus, shifts the AD curve to the right.

18. A short-run equilibrium with an recessionary gap implies that
  A. firms will raise the prices of their goods and services more than needed to fully cover their increases in costs.
  B. firms will raise the prices of their goods and services as much as needed to fully cover their increases in costs.
  C. negative inflation.
  D. firms have incentives to lower the relative prices of their goods and services..
  E. firms have incentives to raise the relative prices of their goods and services.

19. Unlike an adverse inflation shock, a shock to potential output causes
  A. lower output and higher inflation.
  B. higher output and lower inflation.
  C. no output losses.
  D. only temporary output losses.
  E. permanent output losses.

20. A cut in marginal tax rates will
  A. increase aggregate demand and decrease aggregate supply.
  B. decrease aggregate demand and decrease aggregate supply.
  C. increase aggregate demand and increase aggregate supply.
  D. decrease aggregate demand and decrease aggregate supply.
  E. decrease aggregate demand and increase aggregate supply.

Short Answer Problems
(Answers and solutions are given at the end of the chapter.)

1. Aggregate Demand Curve
This problem is designed to help you better understand why the AD curve is downward sloping and the factors that can cause the AD curve to shift. Assume the planned aggregate expenditures is given by the equation, $PAE = \$950 + .75Y - 900r$

A. The inflation rates and interest rates in the table below show the Fed's policy reaction function. Complete the table by calculating the level of aggregate demand for each combination of inflation rate and interest rate.

Inflation rate, π	Interest rate, r	aggregate demand, AD
0.00	0.03	
0.01	0.04	
0.02	0.05	
0.03	0.06	
0.04	0.07	
0.05	0.08	
0.06	0.09	

B. On the graph below, draw the AD curve that is shown in the above table, label it AD.

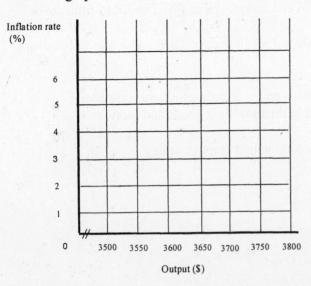

C. Assume that the Fed shifts its policy reaction function downward by reducing the nominal interest rates 1% at each rate of inflation. Complete column 2 of the following table, by indicating the new interest rates for rates of inflation from 0 to 6 percent.

Inflation Rate, π	Interest Rate, r	Aggregate Demand, AD
0.00		
0.01		
0.02		
0.03		
0.04		
0.05		
0.06		

D. Complete column 3 of the above table, by calculating the new levels of aggregate demand for rates of inflation from 0 to 6 percent.

E. On the graph above, draw the new AD curve shown in the above table and label it AD_1.

F. If new technological innovations caused the autonomous investment spending to increase by $20, in the table below calculate the new levels of aggregate demand for rates of inflation from 0 to 6 percent.

Inflation Rate, π	Interest Rate, r	Aggregate Demand, AD
0.00	0.02	
0.01	0.03	
0.02	0.04	

0.03	0.05	
0.04	0.06	
0.05	0.07	
0.06	0.08	

G. On the graph above, plot the new AD curve shown in the last table and label it AD$_2$.

2. AD/AS Diagram

This problem will give you practice drawing the SRAS and LRAS lines, determining the short-run and long-run equilibria, analyzing output gaps, and analyzing the economic adjustments to output gaps.

A. Assuming the current inflation rate in the economy is 3 percent, draw the short-run aggregate supply (SRAS) line on the graph below.

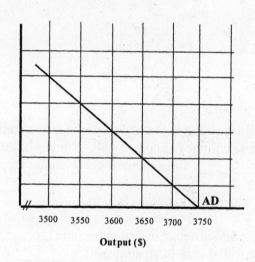

3500   3550   3600   3650   3700   3750

Output ($)

B. Given the AD curve and SRAS line on the graph above, the short-run equilibrium output is $_____ .

C. Assuming the potential output in the economy is $3,650 billion, insert the long-run aggregate supply (LRAS) line on the graph above.

D. Given the short-run equilibrium output and the potential output, the graph indicates that a(n) _____ gap exists.

E. The output gap will cause the inflation rate to (increase/decrease/ remain unchanged) _____ .

F. As the inflation rate adjusts to the output gap, the (SRAS / LRAS) _____ line will shift (upward/downward) _____ until the actual output equals the potential output.

G. When the actual output equals potential output, the economy will settle into its ______________________ equilibrium at $____________.

3. Sources of Inflation

This problem focuses on the effects of excessive aggregate demand on the economy in the short run and long run. Assume the economy is initially in long-run equilibrium at the point where the AD curve, and the SRAS and LRAS lines intersect on the graph below.

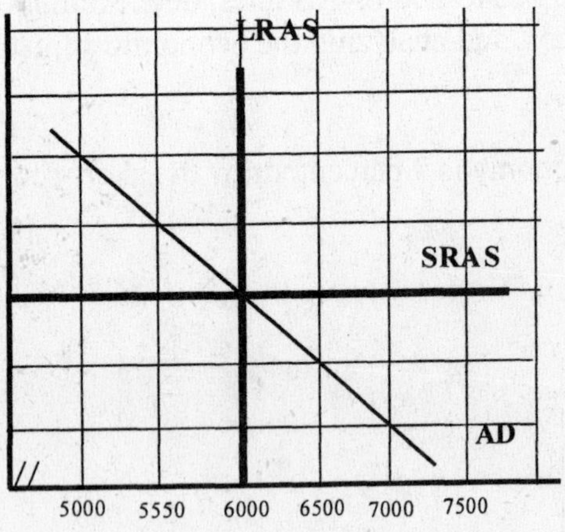

A. Suppose government purchases due to a military buildup in anticipation of a potential war cause the AD to increase by $500 billion. As a result, the (AD curve / SRAS line / LRAS line) ________________ will shift ____________________. Draw the new curve on the graph above.

B. The new short-run equilibrium output will equal $ __________ billion.

C. In the short run, the military buildup has caused the actual output to become (greater than / less than / equal to) ________________ the potential output, creating a(n) ________________ gap.

D. The output gap eventually will cause the inflation rate to (rise / fall) ______________ and the (AD curve / SRAS line / LRAS line) __________________ will shift ________________.

E. Draw the new curve on the above graph showing its location after the self-correcting process is complete.

F. The economy will achieve its long-run equilibrium output at $ ________ billion and the inflation rate will equal __________ percent.

G. The long-run equilibrium output after the military buildup is (greater than / less than / equal to) ______________________ the initial long-run equilibrium output, and the inflation rate is (greater than / less than / equal to) ______________________ the initial long-run equilibrium inflation rate.

H. If the policymakers decided that the inflation rate had risen to a level incompatible with long run economic growth, the Fed might implement a(n) (tight / easy) _____ monetary policy that would shift the (AD curve / SRAS line / LRAS line) _____ to the

_____.

I. In comparison to a "do nothing policy," in the short run such a monetary policy would cause a(n) _____, with output (increasing/decreasing / remaining unchanged) _____, and the rate of inflation (increased/decreased/ unchanged) _____.

J. In the long run, such a monetary policy would leave output (greater than / less than / equal to) _____ a "do nothing policy," and the rate of inflation would be (greater than / less than / equal to) _____ a "do nothing policy."

4. Aggregate Supply Shocks

This problem focuses on the effects of aggregate supply shocks on the economy in the short run and long run. Assume the economy is initially in long-run equilibrium at the point where the AD curve and that the SRAS and LRAS lines intersect on the graph below.

Output ($bil)

A. Because of a disruption in the worldwide supply of crude oil, the price of energy rises and drives the inflation rate to 4%. As a result, the (AD curve / SRAS line / LRAS line) _____ will shift _____. Draw the new curve on the graph above.

B. The new short-run equilibrium output will equal $ _____ billion.

C. The adverse supply shock has created a(n) _____, combined with a (higher / lower) _____ rate of inflation. This combination is referred to as

_____.

D. The output gap eventually will cause the inflation rate to (rise / fall) _____ and the (AD curve / SRAS line / LRAS line) _____ will shift _____.

E. When the self-correcting process is complete, the economy will achieve its long-run equilibrium output at $ _____ billion, and the inflation rate will equal _____ percent.

F. The long-run equilibrium output after the adverse supply shock is (greater than / less than / equal to) _____ the initial long-run equilibrium, and the inflation rate is (greater / less / equal) _____ the initial long-run equilibrium.

G. If the policy makers chose to eliminate the output gap more quickly than the self-correcting process, the Fed might implement a(n) (tight / easy) _____ monetary policy that would shift the (AD curve / SRAS line / LRAS line) _____ to the _____.

H. If the policymakers chose to eliminate the output gap more quickly, the long-run equilibrium output would be (greater than / less than / equal to) _____ a "do nothing policy," and the inflation rate would be (greater than / less than / equal to) _____ a "do nothing policy".

IV. Becoming an Economic Naturalist: Case Study

The Economic Naturalist 15.2 discusses the affects of the OPEC oil embargo and the Iranian Revolution on the oil prices and the U.S. economy. Both constituted an adverse inflation shock that resulted in higher inflation and recession in the U.S. during much of the 1970s. Explain the economic consequences for the U. S. economy if significantly greater production of energy supplies (either through new discoveries of oil, or new technologies such as hydrogen produced energy) were to be achieved during the second decade of the 21st century.

Answer:

V. Self-Test Solutions

Key Terms
1. b
2. i
3. a
4. g
5. d
6. e
7. f
8. j
9. k
10. h
11. c

Multiple-Choice Questions

1. D
2. C Taxes are a component of autonomous aggregate demand and a decrease in taxation, therefore, cause the AD curve to shift to the right.
3. E
4. A
5. B
6. A
7. C
8. D
9. B
10. E
11. C
12. B
13. A
14. D
15. C
16. A
17. C
18. D
19. E
20. C

Short Answer Problems

1.

A.

Inflation Rate, π	Interest Rate, r	Aggregate Demand, AD
0.00	0.03	$3,692
0.01	0.04	3,656
0.02	0.05	3,620
0.03	0.06	3,584
0.04	0.07	3,548
0.05	0.08	3,512
0.06	0.09	3,476

B.

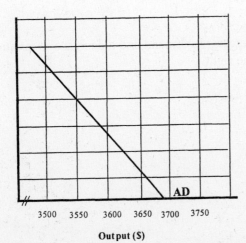

Output ($)

C., D.

Inflation Rate, π	Interest Rate, r	Aggregate Demand, AD
0.00	0.02	$3,728
0.01	0.03	3,692
0.02	0.04	3,656
0.03	0.05	3,620
0.04	0.06	3,584
0.05	0.07	3,548
0.06	0.08	3,512

E.

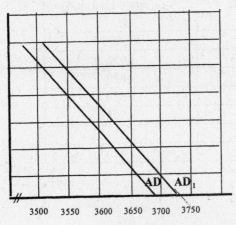

Output ($)

F.

Inflation Rate, π	Interest Rate, r	Aggregate Demand, AD
0.00	0.02	$3,808
0.01	0.03	3,772
0.02	0.04	3,736
0.03	0.05	3,700
0.04	0.06	3,664
0.05	0.07	3,628
0.06	0.08	3,592

G.

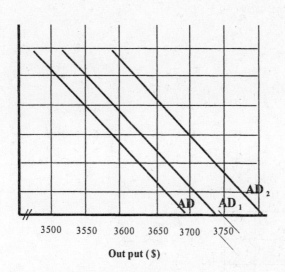

2.

A.

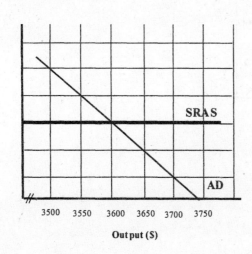

B. $3,600

C.

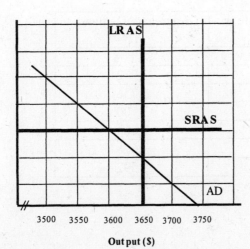

Output ($)

D. recessionary
E. decrease
F. SRAS; downward
G. long-run; $3,650

3.
A. AD curve; rightward;

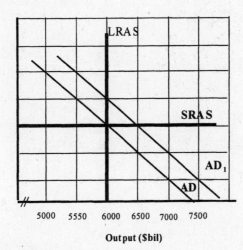

Output ($bil)

B. $6,500 billion
C. greater than; expansionary gap
D. rise; SRAS line; upward

E.

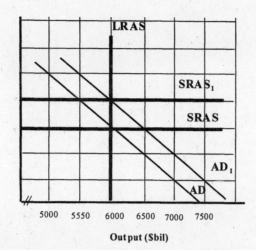

Output ($bil)

F. $6,000 billion; 4 percent
G. equal; greater
H. tight; AD curve; left
I. recessionary gap; decreasing; unchanged;
J. equal; less

4.
A. SRAS line; upward;

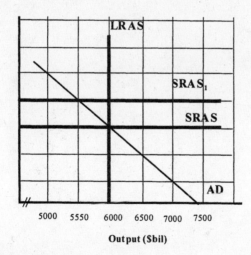

Output ($bil)

B. $5,500 billion
C. recessionary gap; higher; stagflation
D. fall; SRAS line; downward
E. $6,000 billion; 3
F. equal; equal
G. easy; AD curve; right
H. equal; greater

Chapter 16
The Practice and Pitfalls of
Macroeconomic Policy

I. PreTest: What Do You Really Know?

Circle the letter that corresponds to the best answer. (Answers appear immediately after the final question).

1. The monetary policy reaction function indicates a
   A. positive relationship between nominal interest rates and the inflation rate.
   B. negative relationship between nominal interest rates and the inflation rate.
   C. positive relationship between real interest rates and the inflation rate.
   D. negative relationship between real interest rates and the inflation rate.
   E. positive relationship between nominal interest rates and the real interest rates.

2. The effect of the Fed implementing a tighter monetary policy by reducing the target inflation rate is to
   A. shift the monetary policy reaction function up (to the left).
   B. shift the monetary policy reaction function down (to the right).
   C. move down the monetary policy reaction function.
   D. move up the monetary policy reaction function.
   E. move up or down the monetary policy reaction function depending upon whether people have anchored expectations.

3. If the Fed determines that the current inflation target is impeding long-run economic growth and lowers the target inflation rate
   A. the SRAS curve will shift down causing the AD curve to shift to the left and reduce the short-run equilibrium output.
   B. the SRAS curve will shift up causing the AD curve to shift to the right and increase the short-run equilibrium output.
   C. the AD curve to shift to the left causing the short-run equilibrium output to increase and ultimately the SRAS curve will shift down.
   D. the AD curve to shift to the right causing the short-run equilibrium output to increase and ultimately the SRAS curve will shift up.
   E. the AD curve to shift to the left causing the short-run equilibrium output to decline and

ultimately the SRAS curve will shift down.

4. At the long-run equilibrium with a stable monetary policy,
   A. the target inflation rate equals the target interest rate equals actual interest rate and potential output.
   B. the target inflation rate equals the target interest rate equals actual interest rate, and equilibrium output equals potential output.
   C. the target inflation rate equals the target interest rate equals actual interest rate, and equilibrium output equals natural rate of unemployment.
   D. the target inflation rate equals the actual inflation, target interest rate equals actual interest rate, and output equals potential output.
   E. the target inflation rate equals the target interest rate equals actual interest rate and the natural rate of unemployment.

5. The double-digit inflation of the late 1970s was conquered
   A. through tighter monetary policy, but at the expense of lower output and higher unemployment during the early 1980s.
   B. through tighter monetary policy, but at the expense of lower output and higher unemployment throughout 1980s.
   C. through tighter monetary policy without suffering lower output and higher unemployment during the 1980s.
   D. through tighter fiscal policy, but at the expense of lower output and higher unemployment during the early 1980s.
   E. through easier monetary policy, but at the expense of lower output and higher unemployment during the early 1980s.

6. When responding to shocks in aggregate spending, the Fed
   A. must choose between inflation and output stability, but does not face this dilemma when responding to shocks in aggregate supply.
   B. does not face the dilemma of choosing between inflation and output stability as it does when responding to shocks in aggregate supply.
   C. must choose between inflation and output stability, just as it does when responding to shocks in aggregate supply.
   D. must choose between adjusting its inflation targets or adjusting its interest rate targets, but does not face this dilemma when responding to shocks in aggregate supply.
   E. does not face the dilemma of choosing between adjusting its inflation targets or adjusting its interest rate targets as it does when responding to shocks in aggregate supply.

7. When people have anchored inflationary expectations
   A. the SRAS curve will shift down more slowly when an adverse inflation shock creates a recession.
   B. the SRAS curve will shift up more slowly when an adverse inflation shock creates a recession.
   C. the SRAS curve will shift down faster when an adverse inflation shock creates a recession.
   D. the SRAS curve will shift up more slowly when an adverse inflation shock creates a

recession.

    E. the Fed is more likely to accommodate higher inflation rates.

8. The core rate of inflation includes rate of increase in
    A. all prices in the economy.
    B. the price of energy and food.
    C. all prices except energy, food and transportation.
    D. all prices except energy and food.
    E. all prices except basic commodities.

9. The credibility of monetary policy
    A. is determined by people's anchored inflationary expectations.
    B. is the degree to which the public believe the central bank's promises to keep inflation low without imposing short-run economic costs.
    C. is less important in advanced economies like the U.S. and Europe and then it is in developing economies such as Mexico and Thailand.
    D. is enhanced if central bankers are insulated from short-term political considerations, announce numerical inflation targets and are inflation doves.
    E. determines whether inflationary expectation are anchored and is largely determined by the characteristics of the central bank.

10. Macroeconomic policymaking is
    A. an exact science.
    B. as much art as science.
    C. the equivalent of operating a car with the policymaker as driver.
    D. all art and no science.
    E. all science and no art.

Solutions and Feedback to PreTest
For each question you incorrectly answered, we strongly recommend taking the time to review the appropriate material before continuing. In the table below are listed for each question the pertinent Learning Objective from the following Key Point Review.

Correct Answer	Learning Objective
1. C	1
2. A	1
3. E	1
4. D	1
5. A	2
6. B	2
7. C	3
8. D	3
9. E	4
10. B	5

II. Key Point Review
<u>The Forest</u>

This chapter focuses on the use of monetary policy to reduce inflation and to maintain low inflation when the economy is hit by shocks to aggregate demand and aggregate supply. The central questions you need to be able to answer are

- What are the short-run and long-run economic effects of an anti-inflationary monetary policy?
- What policy options are available to the Fed in response to a shock in aggregate demand?
- What policy options are available to the Fed in response to a shock in aggregate supply?
- What institutional characteristics determine the credibility of monetary policy?
- Why is macroeconomic policymaking an inexact science?

<u>The Trees</u>

Learning Objective 1: Explain the short-run and long-run effects of an anti-inflationary monetary policy.
When the Fed adopts a tighter monetary policy, i.e., reducing its target inflation rate, the monetary policy reaction function shifts to the left (or upwards).The Fed actions will cause market interest rates to increase and, thus, consumption and investment spending will decline causing aggregate demand to decrease at every inflation rate (AD curve shifts to the left). The leftward shift in the AD curve will now intersect the short-run aggregate supply (SRAS) curve at a lower output level, indicating a decrease in the short-run equilibrium output. The new equilibrium output will also be less than the potential output, indicating that the Fed's action has allowed a recessionary gap to develop, with the unemployment rate greater than the natural rate of unemployment. Because of inflation inertia there will be no immediate impact on inflation, but eventually the recessionary gap will cause inflation to fall and the SRAS curve will gradually decline. As the inflation rate falls the Fed can begin to lower interest rates, spurring new investment spending. The new investment spending will help the economy to recover from the recession and output will move back toward the level of potential output. The long-run equilibrium will be achieved when the output returns to the level of potential output, but it will now be combined with a lower level of inflation (than when the tighter monetary policy was initiated).

Learning Objective 2: Discuss the Fed's policy options when faced with a rising inflation rate due to increased aggregate demand.
When the economy has reached a long-run equilibrium (at the level of potential output), an increase in aggregate demand will initially cause output to rise (without any impact on inflation in the short run) creating an expansionary gap. The expansionary gap will eventually put upward pressure on prices and the inflation rate will increase. At this point, the Fed has a choice. If the Fed acts to implement an **accommodating policy** that allows inflation to rise about its target inflation rate, the inflation rate will rise. The higher inflation rate will eventually cause the SRAS curve to shift upward and the output will move back to the potential output level at a permanently higher inflation rate (with both inflation and real interest rates above the Fed's targets). The alternative is for the Fed to prevent inflation from rising by raising its target for the real interest rate. An increase in the Fed's target real interest rate will shift the Fed's monetary

policy reaction function up (to the left), raising real interest rates in the economy. The higher real interest rates will shift the AD curve to the back to the left and output will remain at the level of potential output, but unlike the results of the accommodating policy, inflation will remain at the initial level.

Learning Objective 3: Discuss the Fed's policy options when faced with a rising inflation rate due to adverse shocks in aggregate supply.
When faced with rising inflation due to shocks in aggregate demand the Fed can potentially choose inflation and output stability, but shocks to aggregate supply create a dilemma of stabilizing inflation **or** output, but not both simultaneously. When faced with an aggregate supply shock, if the Fed wants to maintain its initial target inflation rate, the economy may face a protracted recessionary or expansionary gap. For example, if an adverse aggregate supply shock shifts the SRAS curve upward, the economy would experience higher inflation and a recessionary gap in the short run. At this point the Fed faces a dilemma. If the Fed maintains its target inflation rate (i.e., no change in the monetary policy reaction function), the recessionary gap will eventually induce firms to lower prices and the SRAS will gradually shift back down as the inflation rate returns to the initial level. In the long run, thus, inflation returns to the initial rate and output returns to its potential level, but in the interim the economy experiences a recession. Alternatively, the Fed may choose to avoid the recession by adjusting its target inflation rate upward (i.e., shifting the monetary policy reaction function down – to the right) causing the AD curve to shift to the right. This will quickly alleviate the recession as output returns to the potential, but the inflation rate will be permanently higher. In making such a choice the Fed might like to know how long it would take the economy to return to its long-run equilibrium if it did not change monetary policy. In part, this depends on whether or not people have **anchored inflationary expectations**. That is, if people's expectations of future inflation do not change when inflation temporarily rises, the economy will more quickly return to it long-run equilibrium. In general, inflationary expectations tend to be less anchored when the Fed has more frequently implemented accommodating policies. Thus, the Fed has a stake in convincing the public that it will maintain its original inflation target. Many economists believe that a bulge in inflation is not inevitable when there is an adverse supply shock if the Fed can prevent a change in inflationary expectations. To allow a temporary increase in inflation but keep long-term inflationary expectations from rising, the Fed can focus on the **core rate of inflation**. The core rate of inflation is the rate of increase of all prices except energy and food, the two items most frequently responsible for aggregate supply shocks. A focus on the core rate of inflation means that the Fed would only adopt a tighter monetary policy if the core rate of inflation exceeds its target inflation rate.

Learning Objective 4: Identify the institutional characteristics that determine whether inflationary expectations are anchored.
Most economists believe that the credibility of monetary policy determines whether inflationary expectations are anchored. The credibility of monetary policy, in turn, is determined by a number of institutional characteristics, including central bank independence, announcement of a numerical inflation target, the central banks reputation as an inflation fighter. The credibility of monetary policy may be enhanced if the central bank is insulated from short-term political considerations. Independence can allow the central bank to take a long-term view of the economy and, for example, pursue anti-inflationary policy even if it leads to a temporary

recession. Four of the many factors that can contribute to a central bank's independence are: the length of appointments to the central bank; whether the central bank's actions are subject to frequent interference, review or veto by the legislative branch; whether the central bank has an obligation to finance the national deficit by buying newly issued government bonds; and the degree to which the central bank's budget is controlled by the legislative or executive branches of government. A second institutional characteristic that affects the credibility of monetary policy is whether the central bank announces its target inflation rate to the public. By announcing the target, the central bank provides more information, reduces uncertainty in the financial markets and allows people to plan more effectively. Not all economists believe a public announcement of a specific inflation target is necessary. Some argue that such a system is too rigid and may reduce the central bank's flexibility to deal with unexpected circumstances. Ultimately, monetary credibility is won and maintained by the central bank's performance. A central bank's performance will depend partly on its reputation as being an **inflation hawk** (someone committed to achieving and maintaining low inflation even at the cost of reduced output and employment in the short run) or an **inflation dove** (someone not strongly committed to achieving and maintaining low inflation).

Learning Objective 5: Explain why is macroeconomic policymaking an inexact science.
Monetary policy is an inexact science because we lack perfect information about the current state of the economy, the future path of the economy, the precise value of potential output, and how the economy will respond to changes in fiscal and monetary policy. A lack of information about the current state of the economy may prevent policy makers from acting in a timely manner, while imperfect information about the future path of the economy may cause policymakers to take unnecessary and unwise actions. The inability to precisely measure potential output means that we can't determine the existence of an output gap, or how large it may be, at any point in time. This obviously hinders our ability to formulate macroeconomic policy. Even if we were able to formulate appropriate macroeconomic policies, the timing of its implementation and impact will affect the outcome. Because policymakers often take a long time to implement appropriate policy there is an **inside lag**, the delay between the date the policy change is needed and the date it is implemented, that hinders the effectiveness of macroeconomic policy. In addition, the **outside lag** of macroeconomic policy, the delay between the date a policy change is implemented and the date by which most of its effects on the economy have occurred, further hinders the timeliness and effectiveness of macroeconomic policy. In sum, macroeconomic policy is both an art as well as a science.

Note: The inside lag is substantially shorter for monetary policy than for fiscal policy, because the Federal Open Market Committee meets eight times per year to formulate monetary policy. Fiscal policy, on the other hand, is the responsibility of both houses of Congress and the President. Even after Congress has approved a policy change and the President has signed the bill into law, it may take a long time to implement tax changes or make additional expenditures.

III. Self-Test

Key Terms
Match the term in the right-hand column with the appropriate definitions in the left-hand column by placing the letter of the term in the blank in front of its' definition. (Answers are given at the end of the chapter.)

1. ____ A substantial reduction in the rate of inflation.
2. ____ A policy that allows the effects of a shock to occur.
3. ____ The delay between the date a policy change is implemented and the date by which most of its effects on the economy have occurred.
4. ____ The rate of increase of all prices except energy and food.
5. ____ Someone who is committed to achieving and maintaining low inflation, even at some short-run cost in reduced output and employment.
6. ____ When central bankers are insulated from short-term political considerations and are allowed to take a long-term view of the economy.
7. ____ The degree to which the public believes the central bank's promises to keep inflation low, even if doing so may impose short-run economic costs.
8. ____ Someone who is not strongly committed to achieving and maintaining low inflation.
9. ____ The delay between the date a policy change is needed and the date it is implemented.
10. ____ When people's expectations of future inflation do not change even if inflation rises temporarily.

a. accommodating policy
b. anchored expectations
c. central bank independence
d. core rate of inflation
e. credibility of monetary policy
f. disinflation
g. inflation dove
h. inflation hawk
i. inside lag
j. outside lag

Multiple-Choice Questions
Circle the letter that corresponds to the best answer. (Answers are given at the end of the chapter.)

1. With the economy initially in a long-run equilibrium, if the Fed reduces its target inflation rate, the
   A. monetary policy reaction function shifts left (upward) causing the aggregate demand curve to shift to the left.
   B. monetary policy reaction function shifts right (downward) causing the aggregate demand curve to shift to the left.
   C. monetary policy reaction function shifts left (upward) causing the aggregate demand curve to shift to the right.
   D. monetary policy reaction function shifts right (upward) causing the aggregate demand curve to shift to the right.
   E. monetary policy reaction function shifts left (upward) causing the SRAS curve to shift to the left.

2. With the economy initially in a long-run equilibrium, if the Fed reduces its target inflation rate, in the short-run the
   A. actual inflation rate will decrease and the target interest rate will decline.
   B. actual inflation rate will increase and the target interest rate will rise.
   C. economy will experience a recessionary gap as higher interest rates decrease aggregate expenditures.
   D. economy will experience a expansionary gap as lower interest rates increase aggregate expenditures.
   E. SRAS curve will shift downward and the equilibrium output will equal the potential output.

3. With the economy initially in a long-run equilibrium, if the Fed reduces its target inflation rate, in the long-run the
   A. inflation rate and interest rates will rise and the economy will experience a recessionary gap.
   B. inflation rate and interest rates will fall and the economy will experience a recessionary gap.
   C. inflation rate and interest rates will rise and the economy will experience a expansionary gap.
   D. inflation rate and interest rates will rise, SRAS curve will shift downward and the equilibrium output will equal the potential output.
   E. inflation rate and interest rates will fall, SRAS curve will shift downward and the equilibrium output will equal the potential output.

4. In the late 1970s, under the direction of Chairman Paul Volcker, the Fed implemented an anti-inflationary monetary policy. The U.S. macroeconomic data for the late 1970s to the mid-1980s
   A. does not support the theoretical analysis because the economy experienced recession during 1979-82 and disinflation and eventually a return to potential output by the mid-1980s.
   B. does not support the theoretical analysis as the economy experienced recession during 1979-82 and rising inflation and unemployment by the mid-1980s.
   C. supports the theoretical analysis as the economy experienced recession during 1979-82 and rising inflation and unemployment by the mid-1980s.
   D. supports the theoretical analysis as the economy experienced recession during 1979-82 and disinflation and eventually a return to potential output by the mid-1980s.
   E. partially supports the theoretical analysis as the economy experienced recession during 1979-82 and disinflation and eventually a return to potential output by the mid-1980s, but the higher interest rates throughout the period were not predicted by the theory.

5. When the economy is experiencing an expansionary gap caused by excessive growth in aggregate demand, if the Fed implements an accommodating policy,
   A. inflation will rise and output will gradually move back to the potential output level in the long run.
   B. inflation will fall and output will gradually move back to the potential output level in the long run.

   C. a recessionary gap will develop and gradually inflation will fall as the economy moves back to the potential output level in the long run.

   D. a recessionary gap will develop and gradually inflation will rise as the economy moves back to the potential output level in the long run.

   E. the SRAS curve will shift downward and gradually inflation will fall as the economy moves back to the potential output level in the long run.

6. When the economy is experiencing an expansionary gap caused by excessive growth in aggregate demand, if the Fed does NOT implement an accommodating policy,
   A. it must lower its target real interest rate which shifts its monetary policy reaction function up (to the left) and causes the AD curve to shift to the left.
   B. it must raise its target real interest rate which shifts its monetary policy reaction function up (to the left) and causes the AD curve to shift to the left.
   C. it must lower its target real interest rate which shifts its monetary policy reaction function down (to the right) and causes the AD curve to shift to the left.
   D. it must raise its target real interest rate which shifts its monetary policy reaction function up (to the left) and causes the AD curve to shift to the right.
   E. a recessionary gap will develop and gradually inflation will rise as the economy moves back to the potential output level in the long run.

7. If the economy is in a long-run equilibrium with $Y=Y^*$, $\pi=\pi^*$, and $r=r^*$, an adverse shock to aggregate supply will
   A. create a dilemma in which the Fed must choose between avoiding a higher interest rates and avoiding higher inflation.
   B. create a dilemma in which the Fed must choose between avoiding a recession and avoiding an expansionary gap.
   C. create a dilemma in which the Fed must choose between avoiding a recession and avoiding higher inflation.
   D. result in the AD curve shifting to the left if the Fed does not implement an accommodating policy.
   E. result in the AD curve shifting to the left if the Fed implements an accommodating policy.

8. If the economy is in a long-run equilibrium with $Y=Y^*$, $\pi=\pi^*$, and $r=r^*$, and the Fed responds to an adverse shock to aggregate supply by maintaining its target inflation rate
   A. the monetary policy reaction function will shift down (to the right), real interest rates will fall and inflation will be permanently higher.
   B. the monetary policy reaction function will shift up (to the left), real interest rates will rise and a recession will follow.
   C. the monetary policy reaction function will NOT shift, but real interest rates will fall and inflation will be permanently higher.
   D. real interest rates will rise and a recessionary gap will exist until the SRAS curve shifts downward to a long-run equilibrium at the initial inflation rate.
   E. real interest rates will remain unchanged, the AD curve will shift to the right, and output will quickly return to the potential level, but inflation will be permanently higher.

9. If the economy is in a long-run equilibrium with Y=Y*, π=π*, and r=r*, and the Fed
    responds to an adverse shock to aggregate supply by implementing an accommodating policy
    A. real interest rates will rise and a recessionary gap will exist until the SRAS curve shifts
        downward to a long-run equilibrium at the initial inflation rate.
    B. the inflation rate will rise and a recessionary gap will exist until the SRAS curve shifts
        downward to a long-run equilibrium at the initial inflation rate.
    C. the MPRF curve will shift down, the AD curve will shift to the right, and a recessionary
        gap will exist until the SRAS curve shifts downward to a long-run equilibrium at the
        initial inflation rate.
    D. the MPRF curve will shift up, the AD curve will shift to the right, and output will quickly
        return to the potential level, but inflation will be permanently higher.
    E. the MPRF curve will shift down, the AD curve will shift to the right, and output will
        quickly return to the potential level, but inflation will be permanently higher.

10. Assume the economy is in a long-run equilibrium with Y=Y*, π=π*, and r=r*, and the Fed
    responds to an adverse shock to aggregate supply by maintaining its target inflation rate. The
    SRAS curve will shift downward more quickly if
    A. workers ask for inflationary wage increases and firms rise prices.
    B. the Fed has a history of frequently accommodating higher inflation rates.
    C. people have anchored inflationary expectations.
    D. central bank's actions are frequently reviewed by the legislature.
    E. If the central bank has an obligation to finance the national debt by buying newly issued
        government bonds.

11. Since the mid-1980s, real GDP growth and inflation rates in the U.S. have become much less
    volatile (variability in real GDP declines by half and inflation by two-thirds) than previously.
    Monetary policy is one factor that has contributed to this trend because since the 1980s the
    Fed has
    A. more consistently implemented accommodating policies.
    B. more consistently maintained its target inflation rate.
    C. adopted new technologies that have improved the ability of the economy to absorb
        shocks.
    D. increased openness of the U.S. economy to trade and international capital flows.
    E. deregulated the U.S. economy.

12. Unlike the oil price increases of the 1970s, the run up in oil prices during 2002-05 has not led
    to a recession nor to substantial increases in inflation in the U.S. Which of the following
    factors has contributed to the different response during the more recent oil price increases?
    A. The real price of oil was higher in 2005, exceeding $60 per barrel, than it was in 1981
        ($35 per barrel).
    B. Even though the U.S. continues to be a manufacturing-oriented economy, increased
        energy efficiency since the 1970s has reduced the impact of higher oil prices on the
        economy.
    C. Inflationary expectations are less anchored than they were during the 1970s.
    D. Inflationary expectations are more anchored than they were during the 1970s.
    E. The Fed has acquired a reputation for implementing accommodating policy since the

1980s.

13. In order to allow a temporary bulge in inflation from a supply shock, but keep long-term inflationary expectations from rising, the Fed should
   A. focus on controlling the core rate of inflation.
   B. focus on controlling the price of energy and food.
   C. implement accommodating monetary policy.
   D. raise its target inflation rate.
   E. lower the real interest rate.

14. A central bank's independence and the credibility of monetary policy are enhanced when
   A. appointments to the central bank are shortened.
   B. its actions are subject to frequent reviews or veto by the legislative branch of government.
   C. The central bank is obliged to finance the national debt by buying newly issued government bonds.
   D. the central bank is allowed to set and control its own budget.
   E. the central bank's budget is set and control by the legislature.

15. Advocates of central banks announcing explicit numerical targets for inflation believe
   A. the inflation target should be zero.
   B. the experience of the U.S. since the 1980s confirms the benefits of such announcements.
   C. that inflation targets must be adhered to strictly in order to be effective.
   D. that the targets work well in industrialized economies such as the U.S. and Europe, but are less effective in developing countries like Brazil, Chile and Mexico.
   E. the targets reduce uncertainty in financial markets and allow people to plan more effectively.

16. In late 2002, the Fed had reduced the federal funds rate to 1.75% and with the inflation rate of 1.5% at the time, the
   A. real interest rate on federal funds was negative.
   B. Fed was concerned that the inflation rate in the U.S. was too low.
   C. Fed was concerned that the inflation rate in the U.S. was too high.
   D. Fed subsequently raised the federal funds rate to ensure that the real interest rate was positive.
   E. Fed subsequently raised the inflation rate to ensure that the real interest rate was positive.

17. Central banks that have acquired reputations as inflation hawks
   A. find it easier to anchor inflationary expectations.
   B. find it more difficult to anchor inflationary expectations.
   C. are more likely to implement accommodating monetary policy.
   D. are less likely to achieve credibility of their monetary policy.
   E. more often allow inflation to rise skyward.

18. A central bank can acquire a reputation as an inflation hawk by
   A. announcing numerical inflation targets

   B. appointing people to the central bank who have a professional or academic background.
   C. maintaining target inflation rates regardless of the short-term economic consequences.
   D. maintaining target real interest rates regardless of the short-term economic consequences.
   E. refusing to associate with inflation doves.

19. Macroeconomic policymaking is made more difficult by
   A. accurate knowledge of the current state of the economy.
   B. certainty about the future path of the economy.
   C. our inability to precisely measure potential output.
   D. anchored inflationary expectations
   E. our inability to precisely measure the unemployment rate.

20. When policy changes are needed, it can take a long time for policymakers to implement the
   appropriate policy changes. The policy making lags include
   A. the inside lag, or the delay between the date a policy change is implemented and the date
       by which most of its effects on the economy have occurred.
   B. the outside lag, or the delay between the date a policy change is needed and the date it is
       implemented.
   C. the middle lag, or the delay between the date a policy change is recommended and the
       date is it adopted.
   D. the inside lag, or the delay between the date a policy change is needed and the date it is
       implemented.
   E. the outside lag, or the delay between the date a policy change is recommended and the
       date is it adopted.

Short Answer Problems
(Answers and solutions are given at the end of the chapter.)

1. Accommodating Monetary Policy
This problem will aid you in reviewing the short-run and long-run effects of accommodating
monetary policy. Assume that the economy is initially in long-run equilibrium with actual
inflation equal to the Fed's target rate of inflation of 6 percent.

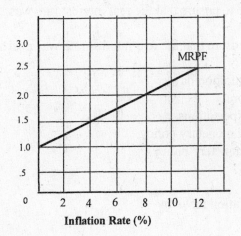

Inflation Rate (%)

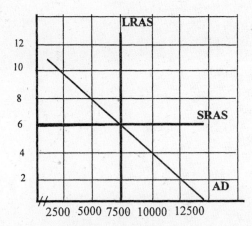

Aggregate Demand ($ bil.)

A. An increase in AD results in a new short-run equilibrium of $10,000 billion. Draw the new curve (parallel to the initial AD curve) and label the new equilibrium point A.

B. The increased in AD will result in a(n) _____ (recessionary/ expansionary) gap.

C. The output gap will cause inflation to _____ (rise/fall) and the SRAS curve will shift _____ (up/down). Draw the new SRAS curve and label it $SRAS_1$.

D. Assume the Fed implements an accommodating monetary policy. Indicate on the above graph the new long-run equilibrium by labeling the point B.

E. As a result of the accommodating monetary policy, point B indicates that the new equilibrium output is $_____, which is _____ (greater than / less than / equal to) the potential output.

F. Also, as a result of the accommodating monetary policy, point B indicates that the inflation rate is permanently _____ (equal to / higher / lower) than the Fed's initial target inflation rate.

2. Anti-inflationary Monetary Policy
This problem will aid you in reviewing the short-run and long-run effects of anti-inflationary monetary policy. Assume that the economy is initially in long-run equilibrium with actual inflation equal to the Fed's target rate of inflation of 6 percent.

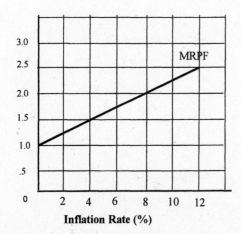

Inflation Rate (%)

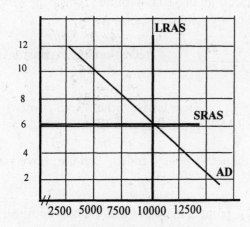

Aggregate Demand ($ bil.)

A. An increase in AD results in a new short-run equilibrium of $12,500 billion. Draw the new curve (parallel to the initial AD curve) and label the new equilibrium point A.

B. The increased in AD will result in a(n) _____ (recessionary/ expansionary) gap.

C. The output gap will cause inflationary pressures to _____ (rise/fall).

D. Assume the Fed does not want inflation to rise above its target. This implies that the Fed would need to _____ (raise / lower) its target real interest rate to _____%.

E. Maintaining its target inflation in response to the increase AD, further implies that the monetary policy reaction function (MRPF) curve will shift _____ (up / down), and the AD curve will shift to the _____ (left / right).

F. As a result of maintaining its target inflation, indicate on the above graph the new long-run equilibrium by labeling the point C.

G. Point C indicates that the new equilibrium output is $_____, which is _____ (greater than / less than / equal to) the potential output.

F. Also, as a result of the accommodating monetary policy, point B indicates that the inflation rate is permanently _____ (equal to / higher / lower) than the Fed's initial target inflation rate.

3. Adverse Inflation Shock

This problem will aid you in reviewing the short-run and long-run effects of an adverse inflation shock. Assume that the economy is initially in long-run equilibrium with actual inflation equal to the Fed's target rate of inflation of 6 percent.

Inflation Rate (%)

Aggregate Demand ($ bil.)

A. Assume there is an increase in the price of energy such that the current inflation rate rises to 8 percent. This would be reflected on the AS/AD graph by a(n) _____ (upward / downward) shift of the _____ (SRAS / LRAS / AD). Draw the new curve in the appropriate position and identify it with a subscript 1.

B. As a result of the adverse inflation shock, the economy moves to a short-run equilibrium at $_____ and a(n) _____ (expansionary / recessionary) gap is created. Label the short-run equilibrium point A.

C. If the Fed accommodates the inflation shock by raising its target inflation to 8%, the MRPF curve will shift _____ (up / down). Draw the new MRPF curve and label if $MRPF_1$.

D. In addition, the accommodating policy will result in a shift of the AD curve to the _____ (right / left). Draw the new AD curve and label AD_1.

E. On the graph above, indicate the new long-run equilibrium point, label it B.

F. At the new long-run equilibrium the output is _____(greater than / less than / equal to) the potential output, and the inflation rate is permanently _____ (equal to / higher / lower) than the Fed's initial target inflation rate.

G. If, on the other hand, the Fed does NOT change its target inflation rate, the AD and MPRF curves _____ (will / will not) shift. The short-run equilibrium the would be represented by point _____ and the economy would experience a(n) _____ (expansionary / recessionary) gap.

H. The output gap will gradually shift the _____ (SRAS / LRAS / AD) curve _____ (down /up) until a new long-run equilibrium was achieved (label this point C).

I. By maintaining its target inflation rate in response to an adverse inflation shock, the long-run equilibrium the output is _____(greater than / less than / equal to) the potential output, and the inflation rate is permanently _____ (equal to / higher / lower) than the Fed's initial target inflation rate.

IV. Becoming an Economic Naturalist: Case Study

In the textbook, Table 16.2 provides data on the CPI inflation and the core inflation rates for the U.S. during 2003-04. The data show that during 2003-04, despite substantial increases in the price of crude oil and the general inflation rate, the core inflation rate increased only slightly. This would suggest that the Fed was maintaining its target inflation rate in the face of an adverse inflation shock during that period. Has the Fed continued this monetary policy since 2004? Visit the web site of the Bureau of Labor Statistics at http://www.bls.gov/cpi/home.htm#data to examine the CPI and core inflation data and explain why you believe the Fed has or has not continued the policy of maintaining its target inflation rate since 2004.
Answer:

V. Self-Test Solutions

Key Terms
1. f
2. a
3. j
4. d
5. h
6. c
7. e
8. g
9. i
10. b

Multiple-Choice Questions
1. A
2. C
3. E
4. D
5. A
6. B
7. C
8. D
9. E
10. C
11. B
12. D
13. A
14. D
15. E
16. B
17. A
18. C
19. C
20. D

Short Answer Problems
1. A.

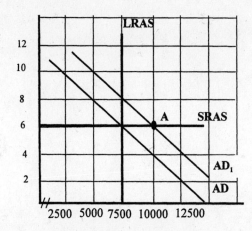

Aggregate Demand ($ bil.)

B. expansionary

C. rise; up

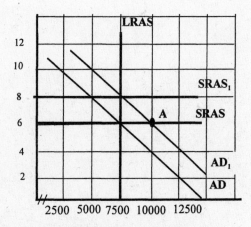

Aggregate Demand ($ bil.)

D.

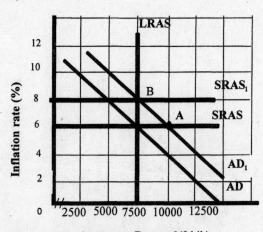

Aggregate Demand ($ bil.)

E. $7.500; equal to
F. higher

2. A.

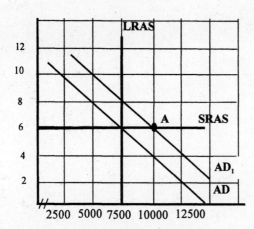

Aggregate Demand ($ bil.)

B. expansionary
C. rise
D. raise; 8%
E. up; left
F.

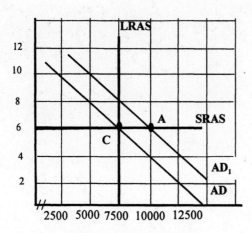

Aggregate Demand ($ bil.)

G. $7,500; equal to
F. equal to

3. A. upward; SRAS

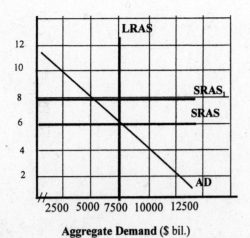

B. $5,000; recessionary

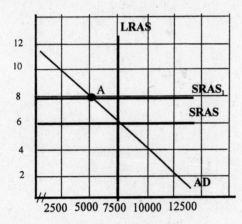

C. down

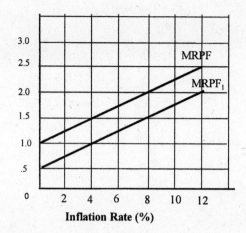

D. right;

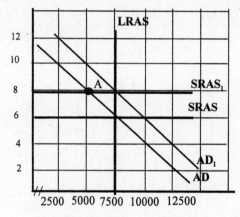

E.

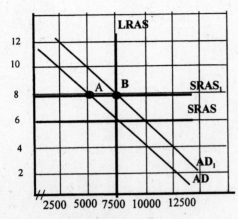

Aggregate Demand ($ bil.)

F. equal to; higher
G. will not; A; recessionary
H. SRAS; down
I. equal to; equal to

Chapter 17
International Trade

I. Pretest: What Do You Really Know?

Circle the letter that corresponds to the best answer. (Answers appear immediately after the final question).

1. The Principle of Comparative Advantage implies that each country
   A. should specialize in those tasks in which they do not have a comparative advantage.
   B. should specialize in those tasks in which they have a comparative advantage.
   C. should be self-sufficient.
   D. will be poorer if they trade with other countries.
   E. should specialize in those tasks in which they have an absolute advantage.

2. Autarky is a situation in which an economy
   A. has no diplomatic relations with other countries.
   B. has no direct access to water transportation.
   C. is economically self-sufficient.
   D. is not economically self-sufficient.
   E. does not use markets to allocate resources.

3. In a closed economy,
   A. consumption possibilities are identical to production possibilities.
   B. consumption possibilities are generally higher than production possibilities.
   C. consumption possibilities are generally lower than production possibilities.
   D. consumption possibilities are determined by the government.
   E. production possibilities are determined by the government.

4. If we compare a country before and after opening itself to trade, we generally find that
   A. total economic surplus is lower after opening to trade than before.
   B. total economic surplus is the same after opening to trade than before.
   C. total economic surplus is higher after opening to trade than before.
   D. producer surplus and consumer surplus are both higher after opening to trade than before.
   E. (C) and (D) are both true.

5. A closed economy is producing wheat at an equilibrium price that is lower than the world price. If it were to open itself to trade,
   A. the domestic price of wheat would rise and the country would import wheat.
   B. the domestic price of wheat would fall and the country would import wheat.
   C. the domestic price of wheat would be unaffected and the country would not import or export wheat.
   D. the domestic price of wheat would fall and the country would export wheat.
   E. the domestic price of wheat would rise and the country would export wheat.

6. An economy that opens itself to trade when the world price of a good is lower than the domestic price will
   A. gain consumer surplus, lose producer surplus and gain total economic surplus.
   B. lose consumer surplus, gain producer surplus and gain total economic surplus.
   C. lose consumer surplus, gain producer surplus and lose total economic surplus.
   D. gain consumer surplus, lose producer surplus and lose total economic surplus.
   E. experience no changes in consumer surplus, producer surplus or total economic surplus.

7. Protectionism is the idea that
   A. free trade must be protected against any restrictions.
   B. workers must be protected from safety hazards.
   C. free trade is injurious and should be restricted.
   D. consumption possibilities are greater than production possibilities and thus consumption possibilities protect production possibilities.
   E. child labor must be made illegal.

8. A tariff on imported sugar will
   A. raise the price received by domestic sellers.
   B. raise the price paid by domestic buyers.
   C. lower the amount of sugar that is imported
   D. cause (A), (B) and (C) all to occur.
   E. not have any effect on the price or the amount of sugar that is imported.

9. American textile producers may ask for quotas on imported textiles because
   A. consumer surplus has increased due to trade.
   B. producer surplus has decreased due to trade
   C. total economic surplus has increased due to trade.
   D. the price of textiles has risen.
   E. the amount of textiles that American producers can sell has increased.

10. Outsourcing refers to
   A. importing goods in which a country does not have a comparative advantage.
   B. exporting goods in which a country has a comparative advantage.
   C. encouraging high wage workers to emigrate.
   D. encouraging low wage workers from other countries to immigrate.
   E. moving jobs from high wage countries to low wage countries.

Solutions and Feedback to Pretest
The answers to the pretest are provided below along with the relevant Learning Objective from the Key Point Review. We strongly recommend that you take the time to review the appropriate material for each question you answered incorrectly.

Correct Answer	Learning Objective
1. B	1
2. C	2
3. A	2
4. C	3
5. E	3
6. A	3
7. C	4
8. D	4
9. B	4
10. E	5

II. Key Point Review
The Forest

This chapter focuses on international trade and discusses the reasons why countries trade and the effects of trade on a country and its citizens.

The central questions you need to be able to answer are:
- What is the primary basis for international trade?
- How does trade affect a country's consumption possibilities?
- What are the effects of international trade on consumer surplus, producer surplus and total economic surplus?
- How do trade restrictions such as tariffs and quotas affect consumer surplus, producer surplus and total economic surplus?
- What is outsourcing and what are its effects?

The Trees
Learning Objective 1: Explain why comparative advantage is the basis for trade.

The Principle of Comparative Advantage states that everyone does best when each person concentrates on the activities for which his or her opportunity cost is lowest. People should then trade with one another for those tasks in which they do not have a comparative advantage.

> **Hint: You should review Chapter 2 if you do not remember this concept.**

Learning Objective 2: Explain the difference between production possibilities and consumption possibilities. Define a closed economy and an open economy, and then show how an open economy has consumption possibilities that are greater than its production possibilities.

A country's **production possibilities** show the maximum combinations of goods that can be produced given the country's resources and productivity. A country's **consumption possibilities** show the maximum combinations of goods that can be consumed given the country's resources and productivity. When an economy is economically self-sufficient, a situation called **autarky**, its production possibilities and consumption possibilities are identical. The same is true for an economy that does not participate in international trade; this type of economy is known as a **closed economy**.

An **open economy** is an economy that participates in international trade. When an economy opens itself to trade, its citizens can specialize according to their comparative advantages and trade for those goods in which they do not have a comparative advantage. This means that they will be able to purchase goods at lower opportunity costs than before and thus their consumption possibilities will be larger than what they could produce on their own.

Learning Objective 3: Show how consumer surplus, producer surplus and total economic surplus are affected when a country opens itself to international trade. Identify the winners and losers when an economy opens itself to international trade.

The fact that trade expands a country's consumption possibilities suggests that total economic surplus expands when a country opens itself to trade. However, this analysis says nothing about whether it is consumers, producers or both who are receiving this increased surplus. A supply and demand analysis allows us to determine who collects the gains and who might bear the losses from trade.

There is a simple, 4-step rubric for determining the gains and losses from trade:

1. Draw a pair of supply and demand curves, find the equilibrium price and quantity, and then identify consumer surplus and producer surplus in the graph. (For example, see Figure 9.6(a) and Figure 9.7(a) in the text.) This is the **closed economy equilibrium**.
2. Locate the world price on this graph. The **world price** is the price at which a good is traded on international markets, and it will be either above or below the current equilibrium price. (For example, see, in the text, Figure 9.6(b) for a price that is below the closed economy equilibrium and Figure 9.7(b) for a price that is above the closed economy equilibrium.) This is the **open economy equilibrium**.
3. Identify consumer surplus and producer surplus for the open economy equilibrium. (For example, see, in the text, Figure 9.6(b) for a price that is below the closed economy equilibrium and Figure 9.7(b) for a price that is above the closed economy equilibrium.)
4. Compare consumer surplus in the closed and open economy equilibria to see whether it has increased or decreased. Do the same for producer surplus in the closed and

open economy equilibria. You now can say whether consumers or producers gain from trade.

In general, when an economy opens itself to trade, total economic surplus will increase. Further,
- domestic consumers win and domestic producers lose when the world price is below the closed economy equilibrium price.
- domestic producers win and domestic consumers lose when the world price is above the closed economy equilibrium price.

Hint: You should review Chapter 7 if you do not remember the concepts of consumer surplus, producer surplus and total economic surplus.

Learning Objective 4: Explain how the presence of winners and losers from trade creates pressure for protectionist policies such as tariffs and quotas. Identify how protectionism reduces economic efficiency.

No one wants to be made worse off, yet international trade can reduce either producer or consumer surplus while increasing total economic surplus. This leads to demands from the injured parties for **protectionist policies**, i.e. policies that restrict trade in order to reduce the loss in consumer or producer surplus caused by trade.

Two protectionist policies are tariffs and quotas. A **tariff** is a tax imposed on an imported good. This is typically used when the world price is below the closed economy equilibrium price; the tariff increases the price that domestic consumers pay for the good above the world price and reduces the amount of the good that is imported. This increases producer surplus relative the no-tariff situation, but it reduces consumer surplus and total economic surplus as well. There is thus a deadweight loss associated with a tariff. See, for example, Figure 9.8 in the text. A **quota** is a legal limit on the number or value of foreign goods that can be imported. This has the same effects on consumer surplus, producer surplus and total economic surplus as a tariff. See, for example, Figure 9.9 in the text.

Learning Objective 5: Define outsourcing and explain how it is related to comparative advantage and international trade.

Outsourcing is the act of replacing relatively expensive domestic workers with cheaper workers in overseas locations.

On the face of it, this idea seems very different from the rest of the chapter; outsourcing is about lowering the cost of factors of production while we have so far analyzed trade in goods and services, not factors of production. However, it turns out that outsourcing has exactly the same effect on consumer surplus and total economic surplus as opening an economy to trade when the world price is lower than the closed economy equilibrium price. Outsourcing lowers the cost of inputs and thus lowers the price buyers pay for the good and encourages them to purchase more of it; both of these factors increase consumer surplus and total economic surplus for this market.

A larger quantity of the good will be supplied and this may increase, decrease or leave unaffected producer surplus. For example, if jobs are outsourced by domestic companies, but the domestic companies continue to sell the good produced by overseas workers, they will reap the profits and thus increase their producer surplus.

Learning Objective 6 (Appendix): Analyze the effects of the world price, tariffs and quotas on domestic prices and quantities using equations for the supply and demand curves.

The Appendix to Chapter 3 showed how supply and demand curves can be expressed as linear equations and then solved to find the equilibrium price and equilibrium quantity. This is an extension of that skill; here, you need to be able to find the equilibrium price and equilibrium quantity and then show how these change when a lower or higher world price is available for the good and how this is affected by tariffs or quotas.

> **Hint: You should review the Appendix to Chapter 3 if you do not remember these concepts.**

III. Self-Test

Key Terms
Match the term in the right-hand column with the appropriate definition in the left-hand column by placing the letter of the term in the blank in front of its definition. (Answers are given at the end of the chapter.)

1. _____ A legal limit on the number or value of foreign goods that can be imported.

a. autarky

2. _____ An economy that trades with other countries.

3. _____ An economy that does not trade with the rest of the world.

b. closed economy

c. consumption possibilities

4. _____ The view that free trade is injurious and should be restricted.

d. open economy

5. _____ A tax imposed on an imported good.

6. _____ A situation in which a country is self-sufficient.

e. outsourcing

f. protectionism

7. _____ The combination of goods that a country's citizens might feasibly consume.

g. quota

8. _____ The price at which a good is traded on international markets.

h. tariff

9. _____ The act of replacing relatively expensive domestic workers with cheaper workers in overseas locations.

i. world price

Multiple-Choice Questions
Circle the letter that corresponds to the best answer. (Answers are given at the end of the chapter.)

1.   In general, a nation will enjoy a higher material standard of living by
      A.   becoming self-sufficient.
      B.   specializing according to absolute advantage and trading.
      C.   imposing tariffs and quotas.
      D.   specializing according to comparative advantage and trading.
      E.   producing only one good and trading for everything else.

2.   Suppose that the country of Benedictia is a closed economy. This means that Benedictia
      A.   is landlocked.
      B.   restricts immigration and emigration.
      C.   does not engage in international trade.
      D.   engages in international trade but only in some goods and services.
      E.   engages in international trade.

Use the following information for problems 3, 4, 5 and 6: Suppose that each worker in the United Kingdom (UK) is identical and can produce 72 computers or 180 tons of grain per year. There are 30 million workers in the UK.

3.   The production possibilities curve for the UK will be
      A.   a straight line with intercepts at 72 computers and 180 tons of grain.
      B.   a straight line with intercepts at 2160 computers and 5400 tons of grain.
      C.   a curve that is bowed out with intercepts at 72 computers and 180 tons of grain.
      D.   a curve that is bowed out with intercepts at 2160 computers and 5400 tons of grain.
      E.   a curve that is bowed in with intercepts at 2160 computers and 5400 tons of grain.

4.   The opportunity cost of computers in terms of grain is
      A.   2.5   C.   7.2   E.   180
      B.   0.4   D.   72

5.   Suppose that the world price per computer is twice as high the world price per ton of grain. The UK should
      A.   specialize in computers and trade computers for grain.
      B.   produce a some of both goods and trade for both goods.
      C.   specialize in grain and trade grain for computers.
      D.   not engage in international trade.
      E.   do something but I don't know what since there is not enough information provided.

6.   Suppose that the world price per computer is one-half of the world price per ton of grain.
     A.   specialize in computers and trade computers for grain.
     B.   produce a some of both goods and trade for both goods.
     C.   specialize in grain and trade grain for computers.
     D.   not engage in international trade.
     E.   do something but I don't know what since there is not enough information
          provided.

Use the graph below for problems 7, 8 and 9: the graph below represents a country's market for
DVD players without international trade.

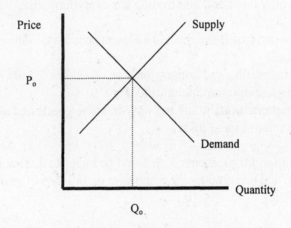

7.   Suppose that this country opens itself to international trade and that the world price of
     DVD players is lower than P_0. The price paid by domestic buyers will _____ and the price
     received by domestic producers will _____.
     A.   rise, rise
     B.   fall, fall
     C.   rise, fall
     D.   fall, rise
     E.   unaffected, unaffected

8.   Suppose that this country opens itself to international trade and that the world price of
     DVD players is lower than P_0. Buyers in this country will
     A.   purchase more DVD players and all DVD players will be imported.
     B.   purchase more DVD players, some of which will be imported.
     C.   purchase more DVD players, none of which will be imported.
     D.   purchase fewer DVD players and DVD players will be exported from this
          country.
     E.   purchase no more or fewer DVD players than they did before trade began.

9.   Suppose that this country opens itself to international trade and that the world price of
     DVD players is lower than P_0. This will cause a
     A.   gain in consumer surplus, a loss in producer surplus and a gain in total economic
          surplus.

B.   a loss in consumer surplus, a gain in producer surplus and a gain in total economic surplus.
C.   a loss in consumer surplus, a gain in producer surplus and a loss in total economic surplus.
D.   a gain in consumer surplus, a loss in producer surplus and a loss in total economic surplus.
E.   no change in consumer surplus, producer surplus or total economic surplus.

Use the graph below for problems 10, 11 and 12: the graph below represents a country's market for women's blouses without international trade.

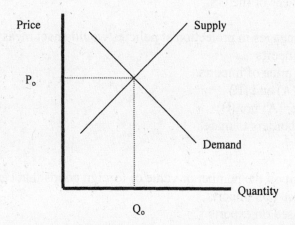

10.   Suppose that this country opens itself to international trade and that the world price of blouses is higher than P_0. The price paid by domestic buyers will ____ and the price received by domestic producers will ____.
A.   rise, rise
B.   fall, fall
C.   rise, fall
D.   fall, rise
E.   unaffected, unaffected

11.   Suppose that this country opens itself to international trade and that the world price of blouses is higher than P_0. Buyers in this country will
A.   purchase more blouses and all blouses will be imported.
B.   purchase more blouses, some of which will be imported.
C.   purchase more blouses, none of which will be imported.
D.   purchase fewer blouses and blouses will be exported from this country.
E.   purchase no more or fewer blouses than they did before trade began.

12.   Suppose that this country opens itself to international trade and that the world price of blouses is higher than P_0. This will cause a
A.   gain in consumer surplus, a loss in producer surplus and a gain in total economic surplus.
B.   a loss in consumer surplus, a gain in producer surplus and a gain in total economic

surplus.

C.   a loss in consumer surplus, a gain in producer surplus and a loss in total economic surplus.

D.   a gain in consumer surplus, a loss in producer surplus and a loss in total economic surplus.

E.   no change in consumer surplus, producer surplus or total economic surplus.

13.   If the US is a net importer of children's toys, free trade will only hurt
A.   domestic toy producers.   D.   domestic toy buyers.
B.   rich citizens of the US.   E.   foreign toy suppliers.
C.   poor citizens of the US.

14.   A country that engages in protectionist policies would enact measures to
A.   restrict imports
B.   raise the price of imports.
C.   do both (A) and (B)
D.   do neither (A) nor (B)
E.   open its borders to trade.

15.   A tariff is a
A.   legal limit on the number or value of foreign goods that can be imported.
B.   tax imposed on imports
C.   tax imposed on exports.
D.   tax imposed on domestic producers of a good.
E.   tax imposed on illegal immigrants.

16.   Suppose that a country is currently importing a good. Imposing a tariff on this good will
A.   Raise the price received by domestic sellers, lower the price paid by domestic buyers and increase total economic surplus.
B.   Lower the price received by domestic sellers, raise the price paid by domestic buyers and increase total economic surplus.
C.   Lower the price received by domestic sellers, raise the price paid by domestic buyers and decrease total economic surplus.
D.   Raise the price received by domestic sellers, lower the price paid by domestic buyers and decrease total economic surplus.
E.   Raise the price received by domestic sellers, raise the price paid by domestic buyers and decrease total economic surplus.

17.   A quota is a
A.   legal limit on the number or value of foreign goods that can be imported.
B.   tax imposed on imports
C.   tax imposed on exports.
D.   tax imposed on domestic producers of a good.
E.   tax imposed on illegal immigrants.

18.   Quotas and tariffs are similar in that both policies
       A.   generate revenue for the government.
       B.   increase the domestic price of the good on which the tariff or quota is imposed.
       C.   decrease the domestic price of the good on which the tariff or quota is imposed.
       D.   hurt domestic producers of the good and help domestic buyers of the good.
       E.   help domestic producers and domestic consumers of the good.

19.   Outsourcing is attractive to American companies because
       A.   High wage foreign workers can be replaced with low wage US workers.
       B.   High wage US workers can be replaced with low wage workers located abroad.
       C.   High wage US workers can be replaced with low wage immigrants.
       D.   Low price foreign goods can be kept out of the US.
       E.   consumer surplus is reduced.

20.   Jobs that are most likely to be outsourced are
       A.   those that can be managed with simple rules.
       B.   those that involve face-to-face contact.
       C.   those that cannot be carried out abroad.
       D.   covered by (A), (B) and (C)
       E.   not any jobs that are described by (A), (B) or (C).

Short Answer Problems
(Answers and solutions are given at the end of the chapter.)

1. Production possibilities and consumption possibilities
An economy has two workers, Paula and Ryan. For every day that they work, Paula can produce 4 computers or 16 shirts and Ryan can produce 6 computers or 12 shirts.
A.   Does the same person who has absolute advantage in the production of shirts also have comparative advantage in the production of shirts? Explain your reasoning.

_____

_____

_____

B.   How much of each good is produced in a single day if each worker fully specializes according to his or her comparative advantage? Shirts:_____
       Computers:_____
C.   Suppose that this economy can trade with another economy. Specifically, suppose that Paula and Ryan can buy or sell any amount of shirts at $33 per shirt and they can buy or sell any amount of computers at $100 per computer. Would this economy's consumption possibilities exceed its production possibilities if it engages in trade? Explain your reasoning.

_____

_____

_____

_____

2. Gains and losses from trade

Suppose that the graph below represents the market for iron ore in China. The closed economy equilibrium is at P_0 and Q_0.

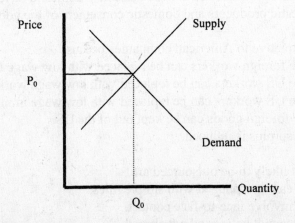

A.   Chinese iron mines are on the (demand/supply) _____ side of this market and Chinese steel producers are on the (demand/supply) _____ side of this market.
B.   Identify consumer surplus and producer surplus on the graph above.
C.   Suppose that the world price of iron ore is below the closed economy equilibrium price in China. Draw this on the graph above. The price paid by domestic buyers (rises/falls) _____ and the price received by domestic sellers (rises/falls) _____.
C.   Suppose that the Chinese market for iron ore is opened to international trade. Identify the new levels of consumer surplus and producer surplus on the graph above. What happens to the level of total economic surplus? Explain: _____
_____
_____
_____

4.   (Appendix problem) Working with the algebra of supply and demand in an open economy.

Suppose that domestic demand and supply curves for wheat in a small country are given by the following equations:

Demand: $Q = 5 - 0.2*P$ Supply: $Q = 1 + 0.8*P$

Quantities are measured in millions of bushels and prices are measured in dollars per bushel.
A.   Solve for the closed economy equilibrium price _____ and equilibrium quantity _____.
B.   Suppose that this country opens itself to international trade and that the world price of wheat is equal to 5. At this price, domestic buyers will purchase _____ bushels of wheat, domestic producers will sell _____ bushels of wheat and _____ bushels of wheat will be (exported/imported) _____.

IV. Becoming an Economic Naturalist: Case Study

The Central American Free Trade Agreement (CAFTA) was hotly debated in Congress during 2005. Two groups spent much time and effort lobbying for and against this treaty because it would reduce US quotas on imported raw sugar. (See, for example, "Sugar Still a Barrier to Securing Trade Pact," *New York Times,* June 29, 2005.) One group consisted of American sugar beet farmers and American sugar cane growers; the other group consisted of American sugar refiners who utilized primarily imported sugar cane. Which group do you think was in favor of CAFTA and which group opposed the treaty? Why? The article also states, "White House officials repeatedly tried to soften the opposition of sugar producers with side deals that would temporarily reduce the sting of the trade agreement." What types of "side deals" could "reduce the sting?"

Answer:

Self-Test Solutions

Key Terms

1. g	6. a
2. d	7. c
3. b	8. i
4. f	9. e
5. h	

Multiple-Choice Questions

1. D	6. A	11. D	16. E
2. C	7. B	12. B	17. A
3. B	8. B	13. A	18. B
4. A	9. A	14. C	19. B
5. C	10. A	15. B	20. A

Short Answer Problems

1. A. Yes, Ryan has comparative advantage and absolute advantage in computers and Paula has comparative and absolute advantage in shirts.
   B. 16; 6
   C. Yes. The world price is 3 computers per shirt; if Paula and Ryan produce 16 shirts and 6 computers they can trade away computers or shirts for larger quantities of either good than they could produce on their own.
2. A. supply; demand

B.   Figure 9.6 in the text shows these effects for the case of Costa Rican computers; the graphs are identical for the case of Chinese steel imports analyzed in this problem.

3.   A.   P = $4 per bushel, Q = 4.2 million bushels

       B.   Quantity supplied = 5 million bushels, quantity demanded = 4 million bushels; since quantity supplied exceeds quantity demand, exports = 1 million bushels.

Chapter 18
Exchange Rates and the Open Economy

I. Pretest: What Do You Really Know?
Circle the letter that corresponds to the best answer. (Answers appear immediately after the final question).

1. The nominal exchange rate is the
   A. market on which currencies of various nations are traded for one another.
   B. price of the average domestic good or service relative to the price of the average foreign good or service, when prices are expressed in terms of a common currency
   C. quantity of foreign currency assets held by a government for the purpose of purchasing the domestic currency in the foreign exchange market.
   D. rate at which two currencies can be traded for each other.
   E. rate at which a good in one country can be traded for the same good in another country.

2. The following table provides the nominal exchange rates for the U.S. dollar.

Country	Foreign currency/dollar	Dollar/foreign currency
Saudi Arabia (riyal)	6.167	.162
Brazil (real)	1.850	.541

   Based on these data, the nominal exchange rate equals _____ Brazilian reals per Saudi riyal or equivalently _____ Saudi riyals per Brazilian real.
   A. 1.053; .95
   B. .95; 1.053
   C. .30; 3.33
   D. 3.33; .30
   E. 6.490; .154

3. An exchange rate that varies according to the supply and demand for the currency in the foreign exchange market is called a(n) _____ exchange rate.
   A. overvalued
   B. undervalued
   C. fixed
   D. flexible
   E. real

4. The real exchange rate is the
    A. market on which currencies of various nations are traded for one another.
    B. price of the average domestic good or service relative to the price of the average foreign
       good or service, when prices are expressed in terms of a common currency
    C. quantity of foreign currency assets held by a government for the purpose of purchasing the
       domestic currency in the foreign exchange market.
    D. rate at which two currencies can be traded for each other.
    E. rate at which a good in one country can be traded for the same good in another country.

5. Net exports will tend to be high when the real exchange rate _____.
    A. is high
    B. is low
    C. equals the nominal exchange rate
    D. appreciates
    E. is strong

6. If a certain automotive part can be purchased in Mexico for 45 pesos or in the United States
    for $6.25 and if the nominal exchange rate is 9 pesos per U.S. dollar, then the real exchange
    rate for automotive part equals
    A. 1.25
    B. 51.20
    C. .125
    D. 0.8
    E. 8

7. The theory that nominal exchange rates are determined as necessary for the law of one price
    to hold is called
    A. the fixed-exchange-rate rule.
    B. the equilibrium principle.
    C. the law of supply and demand.
    D. purchasing power parity.
    E. international equality.

8. The price of gold is $300 per ounce in New York and 2,850 pesos per ounce in Mexico City.
    If the law of one price holds for gold, the nominal exchange rate is _____ pesos per U.S.
    dollar.
    A. .105
    B. 1.053
    C. 9.5
    D. 95.5
    E. 25

9. The purchasing power parity theory is not a good explanation of nominal exchange rate determination in the short run because
   A. there is no evidence that low inflation is association with less rapid nominal exchange rate depreciation.
   B. there is no evidence that high inflation is associated with more rapid nominal exchange rate depreciation.
   C. most goods and services are traded internationally and are standardized.
   D. many goods and services are nontraded and not all traded goods are standardized.
   E. most nominal exchange rates are fixed and foreign exchange markets do not bring the supply and demand for currencies into equilibrium.

10. The U.S. dollar exchange rate, e, where e is the nominal exchange rate expressed as Japanese yen per U.S. dollar, will appreciate when:
    A. real GDP in the U.S. increases.
    B. real GDP in Japan decreases.
    C. the U.S. Federal Reserve tightens monetary policy.
    D. U.S. consumers increase their preference for Japanese cars.
    E. the Bank of Japan tightens monetary policy.

Solutions and Feedback to Pretest

For each question you incorrectly answered, we strongly recommend taking the time to review the appropriate material before continuing. In the table below are listed for each question the pertinent Learning Objective from the following Key Point Review.

Correct Answer	Learning Objective
1. D	1
2. C	1
3. D	1
4. B	2
5. B	2
6. A	2
7. D	3
8. C	1
9. D	3
10. C	4

II. Key Point Review
The Forest

This chapter focuses on the role of exchange rates in open economies. The central questions you need to be able to answer are:
- What distinguishes the nominal exchange rate from the real exchange rate?
- How are flexible and fixed exchange rates exchange rates are determined?
- What are the relative merits of fixed and flexible exchange rates?

The Trees

Learning Objective 1: Define nominal exchange rate, appreciation, and depreciation
The economic benefits of trade between nations in goods, services, and assets are similar to the benefits of trade within a nation. There is, however, a difference between the two cases. Trade within a nation normally involves only a single currency, while trade between nations involves different currencies. Because international transactions generally require that one currency be traded for another currency, the relative values of different currencies are an important factor in international economic relations. The rate at which two currencies can be traded for each other is called the **nominal exchange rate**, or simply the exchange rate. Exchange rates can be of two broad types flexible or fixed exchange rates. A **flexible exchange rate** is not officially fixed, but varies according to the supply and demand for the currency in the **foreign exchange market** – the market in which currencies of various nations are traded for one another. Flexible exchange rates change over time. An increase in the value of one currency relative to other currencies is called **appreciation,** and a decrease in the value of that currency relative to other currencies is called **depreciation.** A **fixed exchange rate** is an exchange rate whose value is set by official government policy.

> **Note:** Exchange rates can be expressed as the amount of foreign currency needed to purchase one unit of domestic currency, or as the number of units of the domestic currency needed to purchase one unit of the foreign currency. These two ways of expressing the exchange rate are equivalent; each being the reciprocal of the other. Although the exchange rate can be expressed either way, to simply the discussion, the textbook authors have chosen to define the nominal exchange rate (e) as the number of units of foreign currency that domestic currency will buy.

Learning Objective 2: Define real exchange rates, and explain the economic importance of the real exchange rate
It is important to distinguish the nominal exchange rate from the real exchange rate. As indicated above, the nominal exchange rate tells us the price of the domestic currency in terms of a foreign currency. The **real exchange rate** tells us the price of the average domestic good or service in terms of the average foreign good or service, when prices are expressed in terms of a common currency. The real exchange rate is equal to the nominal exchange rate times the price of the average domestic good divided by the price of the average foreign good. Consequently, the nominal and real exchange rates tend to move in the same direction. The real exchange rate has important implications for a nation's trade. A high real exchange rate implies that domestic producers will have a hard time exporting to other countries, while foreign goods will sell well in the home country. Thus, when the real exchange rate is high, net exports will tend to be low. Conversely, if the real exchange rate is low, domestic producers will find it easier to export and foreign producers will have difficulty selling in the domestic market. Net exports, therefore, will be high when the real exchange rate is low. This cause-and-effect relationship suggests that a strong currency does not necessarily reflect a strong economy.

Learning Objective 3: Define the law of one price and purchasing power parity (PPP), and explain the PPP theory of exchange rate determination, its implications and shortcomings

What determines the value of flexible exchanges rates? The most basic theory of how nominal exchange rates are determined is called **purchasing power parity**, or PPP. To understand the PPP theory, one first has to understand the law of one price. The **law of one price** states that if transportation costs are relatively small, the price of an internationally traded commodity must be the same in all locations. If the law of one price were to hold for all goods and services, then the value of the exchange rate between two currencies would be determined by dividing the price of the average good in one country by the price of the average good in the other country. An implication of the PPP theory is that, in the long run, the currencies of countries that experience significant inflation will tend to depreciate. The rationale is sound because inflation implies that a nation's currency is losing purchasing power in the domestic market, while exchange-rate depreciation implies that the nation's currency is losing purchasing power in international markets.

Empirical studies have found that the PPP theory is useful for predicting changes in nominal exchange rates over the long run. The theory is less successful, however, in predicting short-run movements in exchange rates. One reason that the PPP works less well in the short run is that the law of one price works best for standardized commodities that are widely traded. Not all goods, however, are standardized commodities and not all goods are traded internationally. In general, the greater the share of traded and standardized goods and services in a nation's output, the more precisely the PPP theory will apply to the country's exchange rate.

> **Hint:** Recall also that the PPP theory rest on the assumption that transportation costs are relatively small. Depending upon the composition of an economy's output, transportation costs of its goods may be substantial and, thus, PPP theory may not be a good predictor of the country's exchange rate.

Learning Objective 4: Use supply-and-demand analysis to determine the short-run movements in flexible exchange rates

Supply and demand analysis is more useful for understanding the short-run movements of exchange rates. Anyone who holds a currency is a potential supplier of that currency, but, in practice, the principal suppliers of a currency to the foreign exchange market are that nation's households and firms. The demanders of a currency are, in practice, households and firms that want to purchase foreign assets or goods and services. The supply curve of a currency is upward sloping and the demand curve is downward sloping. The equilibrium value of a currency, also called the **fundamental value of the exchange rate**, is the exchange rate at which the quantity supplied equals the quantity demanded. Factors that cause shifts in the supply and demand for a currency will cause the equilibrium value of the currency to change. Some factors that cause an increase in the supply of the domestic currency are an increased preference for foreign goods, an increase in the domestic real GDP, and an increase in the real interest rate on foreign assets.

Factors that cause an increased demand for the domestic currency include an increased preference for domestic goods, an increase in real GDP abroad, and an increase in the real interest rate on domestic assets. Of the many factors affecting a country's exchange rate, among the most important is the monetary policy of a country's central bank. A tightening of a country's monetary policy increases domestic real interest rates, raising the demand for its currency and causing the currency to appreciate. Easing of monetary policy has the opposite effects. In an open economy with a flexible exchange rate, the exchange rate serves as another channel for monetary policy that reinforces the effects of real interest rates. Higher interest rates, for example, reduce domestic consumption and investment. They also cause appreciation of the currency and, as a result, imports rise and exports fall, reducing net exports. The decline in net exports, thus, reinforces the domestic effects of the tightened monetary policy. Monetary policy, therefore, is more effective in an open economy with flexible exchange rates.

Learning Objective 5: Define fixed exchange rates, devaluation and revaluation
Fixed exchange rates are a historically important alternative to flexible exchange rates. Fixed exchange rates also are still used in many countries, especially small and developing nations. A **fixed exchange rate** is an exchange rate whose value is set by official government policy (in practice, usually the by the finance ministry or treasury department, in cooperation with the country's central bank). Fixed exchange rates today are usually set in terms of a major currency (e.g., the dollar or yen), or relative to a "basket" of currencies, typically those of the country's trading partners. Historically, currency values were fixed in terms of gold or other precious metals. Once an exchange rate has been fixed, the government usually attempts to keep it unchanged for some time. Economic circumstances, however, can force the government to change the value of the exchange rate. A reduction in the official value of a currency is called **devaluation**; and increase in the official value is called a **revaluation**.

Learning Objective 6: Explain the fundamental value of the exchange rate and the implications of an overvalued or undervalued currency
Fixed exchange rates are not always consistent with the fundamental value of a currency (as determined by supply and demand). When the officially fixed value of an exchange rate is greater than its fundamental value, the exchange rate is **overvalued**, and when it is less that its fundamental value, it is **undervalued**. When the officially set value of an exchange rate is overvalued, the government has several alternatives for dealing with the inconsistency. It could devalue its currency, restrict international transactions, or become a demander of its currency. The most common approach is for the government to become a demander of its currency. To be able to purchase its own currency and maintain an overvalued exchange rate, a government (usually the central bank) must hold foreign-currency assets called **international reserves**, or simply reserves. Because a government must use part of its reserves to maintain an overvalued currency, over time its reserves will decline. The net decline in a country's stock of international reserves over a year is called its **balance-of-payments deficit**. Conversely, if a country experiences a net increase in its international reserves over a year, it has a **balance-of-payments surplus**. Although a government can maintain an overvalued exchange rate for some time by purchasing its own currency, there is a limit to this strategy because no government's reserves are unlimited. Eventually a government will run out of reserves, and the fixed exchange rate will collapse. A **speculative attack**, involving massive selling of domestic-currency assets by financial investors, can quickly end a government's attempt to maintain an overvalued currency. Such an attack is most likely to occur when financial investors fear that an overvalued currency will be devalued. A speculative attack, therefore, can be self-fulfilling.

Hint: Because the fundamental value of a currency is not readily known, whether a currency is overvalued is a matter of conjecture. Thus, a speculative attack may take place if currency traders *believe* a currency is overvalued. If enough traders *believe*, it can be a self-fulfilling prophecy. Thus, in part, governments must guard against any suggestion that its currency is overvalued to avoid the possibility of its becoming an accepted "fact" that can then be self-fulfilling.

As an alternative to trying to maintain an overvalued currency, a government can take actions to try to increase the fundamental value of its currency and eliminate the overvaluation problem. The most effective way to increase the fundamental value of a currency is through monetary policy. A tightening of monetary policy that raises real interest rates will increase the demand for a currency and, in turn, will raise its fundamental value. Although monetary policy can be used in this manner, it has some drawbacks. In particular, if monetary policy is used to set the fundamental value of the exchange rate equal to the official value, it is no longer available for stabilizing the domestic economy. The conflict between using monetary policy to set the fundamental value of a currency or using it to stabilize the domestic economy is most severe when the exchange rate is under a speculative attack.

Learning Objective 6: Compare fixed and flexible exchange rate systems
There are two important issues in comparing flexible and fixed exchange rates – the effects on monetary policy and the effects on trade and economic integration. A flexible exchange rate strengthens the impact of monetary policy on aggregate demand, when a fixed exchange rate prevents policymakers from using monetary policy to stabilize the domestic economy. Large economies should almost always employ flexible exchange rates because it seldom makes sense for them to give up the power to stabilize the domestic economy via monetary policy. For small economies, however, giving up this power may make sense when their history suggests an inability to use monetary policy to control domestic inflation. On the issue of trade and economic integration, supporters of fixed exchange rates have argued that an officially fixed exchange rate reduces or eliminates uncertainty about future exchange rates and, thus, provides incentives for firms to expand export business. The problem with this argument is that a fixed exchange rate is not guaranteed to remain fixed forever, especially if the currency comes under a speculative attack. Some countries, such as some of the European nations, have tried to solve the problem of uncertain exchange rates by adopting a common currency.

III. Self-Test

Key Terms
Match the term in the right-hand column with the appropriate definition in the left-hand column by placing the letter of the term in the blank in front of its' definition. (Answers are given at the end of the chapter.)

1. _____ The exchange rate that equates the quantities of the currency supplied and demanded in the foreign exchange market.

2. _____ An exchange rate that has an officially fixed value greater than its fundamental value.

3. _____ The price of the average domestic good or service relative to the price of the average foreign good or service, when prices are expressed in terms of a common currency.

4. _____ A massive selling of domestic currency assets by financial investors.

5. _____ A reduction in the official value of a currency (in a fixed-exchange-rate system).

6. _____ If transportation costs are relatively small, the price of an internationally traded commodity must be the same in all locations.

7. _____ An exchange rate whose value is not officially fixed but varies according to the supply and demand for the currency in the foreign exchange market.

8. _____ The rate at which two currencies can be traded for each other.

9. _____ Foreign currency assets held by a government for the purpose of purchasing the domestic currency in the foreign exchange market.

10. _____ An exchange rate whose value is set by official government policy.

11. _____ The net increase in a country's stock of international reserves over a year.

12. _____ An exchange rate that has an officially fixed value less than its fundamental value.

13. _____ An increase in the value of a currency relative to other currencies.

14. _____ The market on which currencies from various nations are traded for one another.

15. _____ An increase in the official value of a currency (in a fixed-exchange-rate system).

16. _____ The theory that nominal exchange rates are determined as necessary for the law of one price to hold.

17. _____ The net decline in a country's stock of international reserves over a year.

18. _____ A decrease in the value of a currency relative to other currencies.

a. appreciation

b. balance-of-payments deficit

c. balance-of-payments surplus

d. depreciation

e. devaluation

f. fixed exchange rate

g. flexible exchange rate

h. foreign-exchange market

i. fundamental value of the exchange rate

j. international reserves

k. law of one price

l. nominal exchange rate

m. overvalued exchange rate

n. purchasing power parity (PPP)

o. real exchange rate

p. revaluation

q. speculative attack

r. undervalued exchange rate

Multiple-Choice Questions
Circle the letter that corresponds to the best answer. (Answers are given at the end of the chapter.)

1. During summer 2005, the nominal exchange rate was one U.S. dollar to 10.6 Mexican pesos. The dollar per peso equivalent exchange rate equaled
    A. 10.6 dollars per peso.
    B. .106 dollars per peso.
    C. 9.4 dollars per peso.
    D. .094 dollars per peso.
    E. 106 dollars per peso.

2. A disposable camera cost $8 in the United States and 110 peso in Mexico during the summer of 2005. The exchange rate at that time was 10.6 pesos per dollar. The real exchange rate of the dollar (for disposable cameras) equaled
    A. 10.6.
    B. .77.
    C. 83.0.
    D. 84.8.
    E. .106.

3. During the 1980s, the United States had a balance-of-payments deficit with South Korea and Taiwan. The U.S. government complained that the governments of those two nations were manipulating their exchange rates to promote exports to the United States. Apparently, the White House believed that the
    A. currencies of South Korea and Taiwan were overvalued relative to the dollar.
    B. currencies of South Korea and Taiwan were undervalued relative to the dollar.
    C. South Korean currency was overvalued relative to the currency of Taiwan.
    D. South Korean currency was undervalued relative to the currency of Taiwan.
    E. dollar should be allowed to appreciate against the currencies of South Korea and Taiwan.

4. Between 1973 and 1999, annual inflation in developing nations that export mainly manufactured goods averaged 23 percent, while inflation averaged 59 percent in countries that mainly export raw materials. Other things equal, the PPP theory would predict that, in the long run, the currencies of the raw materials exporting countries should have
    A. been approximately stable relative to the currencies of countries exporting manufactured goods.
    B. appreciated relative to the currencies of countries exporting manufactured goods.
    C. depreciated relative to the currencies of countries exporting manufactured goods.
    D. had no predictable relationship to the currencies of countries exporting manufactured goods.
    E. been perfectly stable relative to the currencies of countries exporting manufactured goods because they maintained fixed exchange rates.

5. The PPP theory works better in the long run than it does in the short run because
   A. the law of one price only pertains to the long run.
   B. not all goods and services are traded internationally, and not all goods are heterogeneous commodities.
   C. all goods and services are traded internationally, and not all goods are heterogeneous commodities.
   D. not all goods and services are traded internationally, and not all goods are standardized commodities.
   E. all goods and services are traded internationally, and all goods are standardized commodities.

6. In the early 1980s, high interest rates in the United States attracted enormous amounts of capital into the United States to buy stocks, bonds, real estate, and other assets. All other things equal, supply-and-demand analysis of exchange rates would predict that the U.S. dollar would experience _____ relative to other currencies.
   A. depreciation
   B. appreciation
   C. devaluation
   D. revaluation
   E. purchasing price parity

7. During 2004 and 2005, the U.S. Federal Reserve Bank tightened its monetary policy and interest rates in the United States increased in order to reduce domestic consumption and investment spending. In the short-run, one would predicate a(n)
   A. depreciation of the dollar and an increase in net exports.
   B. depreciation of the dollar and a decrease in net exports.
   C. devaluation of the dollar and a decrease in net exports.
   D. appreciation of the dollar and an increase in net exports.
   E. appreciation of the dollar and a decrease in net exports.

8. The value of a fixed exchange rate in contemporary economies is
   A. determined by the supply and demand for a currency in the foreign exchange market.
   B. set by the government, usually in terms of gold or some other precious metal.
   C. set by the government, usually in terms of the currency (or basket of currencies) of the country's major trading partner(s).
   D. set by agreement of the central banks of the major trading countries of the world.
   E. determined by economic forces.

9. During the 1990s, the government of Malaysia fixed the exchange rate of the Baht to the dollar. During the spring of 1998, investors perceived that the Baht was overvalued and a speculative attack ensued. What alternatives did the Malaysian government have to deal with this problem?
   A. It could have revalued the Baht, limited international transactions, purchased Baht on the foreign exchange market, or tightened domestic monetary policy.
   B. It could have devalued the Baht, limited international transactions, purchased Baht on the foreign exchange market, or tightened domestic monetary policy.

C. It could have devalued the Baht, limited international transactions, sold Baht on the foreign exchange market, or tightened domestic monetary policy.

D. It could have revalued the Baht, limited international transactions, sold Baht on the foreign exchange market, or eased domestic monetary policy.

E. It could have revalued the Baht, limited international transactions, sold Baht on the foreign exchange market, or tightened domestic monetary policy.

10. During the 1930s, the United States was on the gold standard, creating a system of fixed exchange rates between the dollar and other currencies whose values were also set in terms of gold. As a result, monetary policy

A. could not be used to stabilize the U.S. economy during the Great Depression.

B. could be used to stabilize the U.S. economy during the Great Depression.

C. was immune to a speculative attack because devaluation was not possible.

D. was eased to counteract the banking panic and the bank failures during the Great Depression.

E. was used to decrease interest rates to counteract the economic decline brought on by the bank failures during the Great Depression.

11. When the real exchange rate of a country's currency is low, the home country will;

A. find it easier to import, while domestic producers will have difficulty exporting.

B. find it easier to export, while domestic residents will buy more imports.

C. find it harder to export, while domestic residents will buy fewer imports.

D. find it easier to export, while domestic residents will buy fewer imports.

E. find it harder to export, while domestic residents will buy more imports.

12. Between 1990 and 1999, inflation in the United States averaged 2-3% per year, while Mexico experienced double-digit average annual inflation rates. Since the Mexican government did not try to maintain a fixed exchange rate, the PPP theory would suggest that, in the long run, the Mexican peso would

A. appreciate against the dollar and Mexico's net exports to the United States decreased.

B. appreciate against the dollar and Mexico's net exports to the United States increased.

C. depreciate against the dollar and Mexico's net exports to the United States increased.

D. depreciate against the dollar and Mexico's net exports to the United States decreased.

E. remain stable relative to the dollar, with no change in Mexico's net exports to the United States.

13. The PPP theory would be most useful in predicting

A. short-run changes in the exchange rate for a country that mainly produces heavily traded, standardized goods.

B. long-run changes in the exchange rate for a country that mainly produces heavily traded, standardized goods.

C. short-run changes in the exchange rate for a country that mainly produces lightly traded, standardized goods.

D. long-run changes in the exchange rate for a country that mainly produces lightly traded, non-standardized goods.

E. short-run changes in the exchange rate for a country that mainly produces lightly traded, standardized goods.

14. The fundamental value of a country's exchange rate is
  A. constant over a prolonged period of time.
  B. determined by the supply of the country's currency in the foreign exchange market.
  C. determined by the demand for the country's currency in the foreign exchange market.
  D. determined by the supply of and demand for the country's currency in the domestic financial market.
  E. determined by the supply of and demand for the country's currency in the foreign exchange market.

15. During the latter half of the 1990s, real GDP in the United States grew faster than in most other industrial countries. All other things equal, supply-and-demand analysis of exchange rates would predict that, in the short run, the U.S. dollar would _____ relative to the currencies of the other industrialized countries.
  A. appreciate
  B. depreciate
  C. devaluate
  D. revaluate
  E. remain constant

16. If the central bank of England were to respond to a slowdown in the domestic economy by easing monetary policy, all other things equal, one would predict in the short run a(n)
  A. increase in the real interest rate, an increase in demand for the pound, and an appreciation in the pound.
  B. decrease in the real interest rate, an increase in demand for the pound, and an appreciation in the pound.
  C. decrease in the real interest rate, a decrease in demand for the pound, and a depreciation in the pound.
  D. increase in the real interest rate, a decrease in demand for the pound, and a depreciation in the pound.
  E. increase in the real interest rate, an increase in demand for the pound, and a depeciation in the pound.

17. If a country fixes the exchange rate for its currency relative to other currencies, and if the official exchange rate is overvalued relative to its fundamental value, then
  A. the most likely ultimate outcome is a depreciation of its currency.
  B. the most likely ultimate outcome is a devaluation of its currency.
  C. the most likely ultimate outcome is a revaluation of its currency.
  D. it will likely be able to indefinitely support its value by using its international reserves to buy its currency on the foreign exchange market.
  E. it can ease its monetary policy to increase the fundamental value of its currency and eliminate the overvalued status.

18. If exchange rates are flexible, a surplus in a nation's balance of payments would imply that the
    A. government will have to devalue the nation's currency.
    B. government will have to revalue the nation's currency.
    C. nation's exchange rate will remain unchanged.
    D. nation's exchange rate will appreciate.
    E. nation's exchange rate will depreciate.

19. Other things being equal, a recession in the United States combined with rapid economic growth in Japan would be expected to cause
    A. the dollar to appreciate against the yen.
    B. the dollar to depreciate against the yen.
    C. the yen to appreciate against the dollar.
    D. no predictable change in the dollar-yen exchange rate.
    E. Japan's demand curve for dollars to shift to the left.

20. In comparison to a fixed exchange rate system, a flexible exchange rate system
    A. weakens the impact of monetary policy on aggregate demand.
    B. strengthens the impact of monetary policy on aggregate demand.
    C. increases uncertainty about the future exchange rate.
    D. decreases uncertainty about the future exchange rate.
    E. is more likely to suffer from speculative attacks.

Short Answer Problems
(Answers and solutions are given at the end of the chapter.)

1. Nominal Exchange Rates
In this problem you can practice calculating the nominal exchange rates of currencies in terms of the amount of foreign currency needed to purchase one dollar and the number of dollars needed to purchase one unit of the foreign currency.

Nominal Exchange Rate for the U.S. Dollar (August 18, 2005)

Country	Foreign currency / dollar	Dollar / foreign currency
Britain (Pound)		1.08599
Canada (Dollar		0.824062
China (Yuan)		6.67466
Europe (Euro)	0.8148	
Japan (Yen)	109.84	
Mexico (Peso)	10.6345	

Source: *http://www.refcofx.com/currency-trading.html*

A. Based on the number of dollars needed to purchase one unit of the foreign currency, calculate the amount of foreign currency needed to purchase one dollar for the British pound, Canadian dollar, and the Chinese yuan in Column 2 of the above table.

B. Based on the amount of foreign currency needed to purchase one dollar, calculate the number of dollars needed to purchase one unit of the foreign currency for the European euro, Japanese yen, and Mexican peso in Column 3 of the above table.

C. During August 2005, in the Monterrey, Mexico, newspaper, *El Norte*, a popular American/ German make of automobile was advertised at the price of 152,100 pesos. During the same time, it was advertised in the *Austin American Statesman* newspaper for 18,995 dollars. Based on the above peso–dollar exchange rate and the advertised prices for the automobile, the real exchange rate (for the automobile) equaled _____ (round your answer to the nearest hundredth).

D. The real exchange rate for the automobile implies that the price of the U.S. automobile is (more/ less) _____ expensive than the Mexican automobile, putting the (U.S. / Mexican) _____ product at a disadvantage.

2. Supply and Demand Analysis of the Exchange Rate
Supply and demand analysis is applied to the determination of the exchange rate in this problem. You will determine the equilibrium exchange rate and analyze the effects of changes in various factors on the supply of or demand for dollars to determine the impact on the equilibrium exchange rate. Answer the questions below based on the following graph illustrating the supply and demand for dollars in the euro-dollar market.

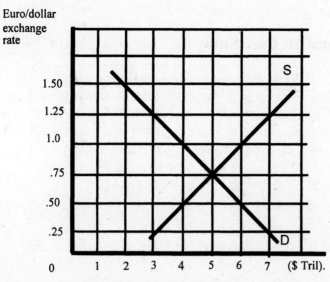

A. The equilibrium exchange rate of the dollar equals _____ euro(s) per dollar.
B. If European consumers' and businesses' preferences for American goods increases, the (supply/demand) _____ for dollars in the foreign exchange market will (increase/decrease) _____ and the euro/dollar exchange will (increase/decrease) _____.
C. If the U.S. GDP increases, the (supply/demand) _____ for dollars in the foreign exchange market will (increase/decrease) _____ and the euro/dollar exchange will (increase/decrease) _____.
D. An increase in the real interest rate on European assets will (increase/decrease) _____ the (supply/demand) _____ of (for) dollars in the foreign exchange market and the euro/dollar exchange will (increase/decrease) _____.
E. If the Fed tightens U.S. monetary policy, the (supply/demand) _____ for dollars in the foreign exchange market will (increase/decrease) _____ and the euro/dollar exchange will (increase/decrease) _____.

3. Fundamental Value of a Currency and the Balance of Payments Deficit

The demand and supply for Surican pesos in the foreign exchange market are given by the following equations (e is the Surican exchange rate measured in dollars per Surican peso).
Demand = 55,000 − 88,000 e
Supply = 25,000 + 32,000 e

A. The fundamental value of the Surican peso (e) equals _____ .
B. If the Surican government set the official exchange rate at .333 dollars per peso, the demand for Surican pesos would equal _____, and the supply of Surican pesos would be _____ .
C. The quantity supplied of Surican pesos would be (greater than/less than/equal to) _____ the quantity demanded for Surican pesos.
D. To maintain the fixed exchange rate, the Surican government would have to purchase _____ Surican pesos. Since the Surican peso is purchased at the official rate of 3 pesos to the dollar, the balance of payments deficit in dollars would equal $_____ .

IV. Becoming an Economic Naturalist: Case Study

In Economic Naturalist 18.1, the authors explain why a strong U.S. dollar does not necessarily imply a strong U.S. economy. For example, it compares the exchange rate of the U.S. dollar during 1973, when the dollar was worth more in terms of other major currencies and the economy was weak, and 2000 when the dollar was lower but the economy was stronger. Go to http://research.stlouisfed.org/fred/data/exchange. html to find the latest data on the U.S. dollar exchange rate and determine whether the dollar is stronger or weaker than it was in 2000. Discuss the implications of the change in the exchange on the current U.S. economy.

Answer:

V. Self-Test Solutions

Key Terms
1. i
2. m
3. o
4. q
5. e
6. k
7. g
8. l
9. j
10. f
11. c
12. r
13. a
14. h
15. p
16. n
17. b
18. d

Multiple-Choice Questions
1. D (=1/10.6)
2. B (=[10.6*8] / 110)
3. A
4. C
5. D
6. B
7. E
8. C
9. B

10. A
11. D
12. C
13. B
14. E
15. B
16. C
17. B
18. D
19. A
20. B

Short Answer Problems
1. A and B

Nominal Exchange Rate for the U.S. Dollar (August 18, 2005)

Country	Foreign currency / dollar	Dollar / foreign currency
Britain (Pound)	0.9208 (1/1.08599)	1.08599
Canada (Dollar	1.2135	0.824062
China (Yuan)	0.1498	6.67466
Europe (Euro)	0.8148	1.22729 (1/0.8148)
Japan (Yen)	109.84	0.009104
Mexico (Peso)	10.6345	0.094033

Source: *http://www.refcofx.com/currency-trading.html*
C. 1.33 (= [9.91 x 18,995]/ 152,100)
D. more; U.S.

2.
A. .75
B. demand; increase; increase
C. supply; increase; decrease
D. increase; supply; decrease
E. demand; increase; increase

3.
A. .25 ($55,000 - 88,000e = 25,000 + 32,000e$ or $30,000 = 120,000e$)
B. 25,696 (=55,000 - 88,000 x .333); 35,656 (=25,000 + 32,000 x .333)
C. greater than
D. 9,960 (=35,656 - 25,696)
E. $3,320 (=9,960 / 3)